The Suitcase Wife

inspired by a true story

by Tamara Michael

thesuitcasewife@gmail.com
suitcasewife@gmail.com

Author photo by Mike Williams

ISBN: 148492083X
ISBN-13: 9781484920831

TABLE OF CONTENTS

This book was inspired by a true story.

Sahara wanted to run away and explore exotic, off-the-beaten paths of the world. Considering Europe too predictable, Sahara booked a Himalayan trekking vacation in Nepal and returns changed, overflowing with memories, and with a relationship that would last for years.

Her adventures turn out differently than expected: meeting two unlikely traveling companions, hanging on for a harrowing elephant ride through the jungle, a surprise encounter with the Taliban, and the start of a special relationship. Sahara explores the world in a way that is unique and unlikely for most travelers.

Join Sahara as she packs a suitcase and leaves for her adventure as "The Suitcase Wife."

This book is dedicated to Bess who taught me how to travel, be adventurous and enjoy life, but never could turn me into a gourmet cook; and to fellow travelers Garry and Rich, who aren't gourmet cooks either but love life and good wine.

I feel grateful for the people who entered my life at precise moments to give support throughout this book-writing process:

Siobhan Olson who inspired me to tell the story.

Lloyd Rawson's and Tricia Geier's encouragement to stay with writing when thoughts of "what the heck am I doing" scurried through my mind.

Sandie and Linda, two secure women, for their understanding and friendship.

Thanks to everyone for your help with this adventure on paper; my travel adventures pale in comparison. Without your support, I wonder where the pages might have been stuffed away.

1

"Well, you'll have to go through Atlanta to get there."
I had heard that prelude to travel directions ever since moving to the South fifteen years ago. Sure enough, after flying in from North Carolina, there I sat at Atlanta's Hartsfield-Jackson Airport, waiting to meet my two traveling companions arriving from Pennsylvania. From Atlanta we would fly to Dubai, first stop before traveling along the ancient Silk Road trade route.

I tried to remember exactly how long it had been since my last travel adventure with Mark and Bill—exploring Mongolia and hugging goodbye in Beijing. Almost three years? I wondered whether we would still enjoy traveling together, but dismissed that silly thought, chuckling at the memory of some of our escapades. Surely our zest for new places, laughter, and fun wouldn't have changed. This time I had a big surprise for the guys: my transition to blonde from the brunette they had known for years. I couldn't wait to hear their comments, and Mark and Bill were never shy about voicing opinions.

The two men are brothers, Mark about four years older. Upon first meeting them, I wouldn't have guessed they were related. About the only physical trait they shared was a good-natured grin exposing beautiful teeth. The teeth were the first thing I noticed—probably because of my long orthodontic history. Mark was tall and slender, outgoing, talkative, and teasing. He had brown eyes and hair, the latter graying at the temples with a small bald patch behind. His quirky way of looking at the world and his quick wit kept fellow travelers amused on every trip.

The Suitcase Wife

Bill is more reserved, cautious, and straitlaced than his brother, and his balding area is also a bit wider under a slight comb over. Although shorter, he's more athletically built—and inclined—than Mark. Subjects that interest him are meticulously researched and readily shared, but his most memorable attribute is his piercing blue eyes. Of the three of us, he's the most photogenic.

Not only did the men share the same parents, but also both are married, have three children and are graduates of Lehigh University with engineering degrees followed by MBAs. They retired early after selling a company they had founded and managed together. Now both work as financial consultants. Best of all, they love to travel as much as I do. I know from experience that the brothers are congenial companions for exploring exotic or remote locations for three or four weeks. We have no need for five-star accommodations every night, and enjoy a similar appreciation for offbeat experiences. And it has never failed—adventure has always found us. I can barely wait for their arrival and our next chapter to begin.

"Sahara Smith, please see the gate agent."

Hearing my name called to come to the reservation desk, I wondered, "Now what?"

More seats, it appeared, were needed in the plane's coach section. I was upgraded to business class. I thanked the agent excitedly—my first upgrade and I didn't even have to pay extra for it! I'd sit up front drinking wine while Mark and Bill were crunched in coach, nursing their jealousy. To pass the time, I called friends back home in Winston-Salem crowing, "Guess who got lucky. I'm upgraded."

After Mark and Bill finally landed in Atlanta, the three of us hurried to the airline's lounge to catch up on several years over drinks and a snack. While chatting, I waited to hear comments about my change in hair color. The only response I ever got was two curious glances followed by two shrugs and a joint "Oh."

I wasn't able to resist blurting out my good fortune of being upgraded, knowing full well that if the tables were turned, Mark would be gloating. Instead he protested, "Thanks, Sahara. That's a fine welcome—you're abandoning us. After all these years—you're bailing out. Thanks, for the memory."

Reminiscing, laughing, and talking made time fly until a waiter warned us that our flight was boarding. We rushed to our gate, pulling out tickets and passports as we ran. Suddenly I noticed that the man's name on my boarding pass didn't match my passport. In the excitement of the upgrade, I had just assumed my boarding pass was correct. I tried explaining at the gate, but that man—whoever he was—was already seated in my business-class seat. Mark and Bill covered their amusement fairly well, but I just knew they were struggling to hold their laughter.

Maneuvering for us to sit together, Mark kindly asked a couple in my row if they would exchange seats so they could sit with their friend. The couple agreed, and Mark, Bill, and I settled in for our fourteen-hour flight to Dubai. When served a glass of wine, we toasted our reunion and drank to our coming adventures.

As soon as we arrived and entered the Dubai terminal, Mark charged through its corridors toward customs. He always wanted to be first in line and, by now, Bill and I were prepared to run to keep up with his long-legged stride. After passing quickly through customs and baggage claim, we stopped at an exchange to convert some dollars into dirhams, the currency of the United Arab Emirates, then moved on to the taxi stand.

The moment we stepped out of the terminal, sticky desert air enveloped us. Normally unaffected by heat, I felt drained of every drop of water in my body. At nine-thirty in the evening, the temperature was hovering around ninety-five degrees.

The Suitcase Wife

Faced with choosing in which of five long queues to wait for a taxi, Mark chided Bill for failing to treat us to a hired limo instead having to stand in the heat. After thirty-five steamy minutes, impatient for our line to slowly dwindle and exhausted from talking and drinking too much wine on the long flight, our turn finally came. I thought, "Nevertheless, it's good to be traveling with the guys again. It's been much too long, and I missed them."

Settled at last, in the taxi, Bill announced, "Here we are in Dubai, ready to travel the Silk Road."

Though the modern city bore little relation to the ancient network of trading routes connecting the Mediterranean to China, we had thought it would be a shame to be so close and miss this contemporary marvel of opulence.

First stop of our three-week vacation was the Burj Al Arab, a seven-star hotel constructed on an artificial island in the Persian Gulf. The twenty-eight story hotel was designed to resemble the wind-filled sail of an Arabian dhow. Before crossing the bridge to the island, the taxi driver stopped at the gatehouse so the guard could confirm that Mark, Bill, and I were on the hotel's guest list. When we arrived at Burj Al Arab's front door, employees swarmed from every direction to assist us. It didn't matter that our jeans-clad bodies weren't dressed as one might expect at a seven-star hotel, we were enfolded by luxury from the first moment.

In the lobby, a hostess in a traditional Arabic abaya invited us to sit on a soft leather sofa while she checked us in—no standing at a reception desk here! An attendant brought chilled towels to cool our hot faces after the taxi ordeal. A dish of large dates stuffed with candied orange slices on the coffee table offered sustenance. When the hostess excused herself for a moment, two Arab men lounging on a sofa opposite us nodded pleasantly. I, wearing no scarf over my hair and sporting glittery red polish on my toenails, whispered mischievously to Mark and Bill, "Wouldn't an ice-cold beer taste good right now?"

Just then, the hostess returned and announced, "We have upgraded you to a three-bedroom suite. Please follow me."

When Mark had made the reservation, he had specified a two-bedroom, 1,800 square-foot suite, thinking that one of us could sleep on its living-room couch—that's right, sleep on a couch in a seven-star hotel—but that's how we three think when traveling. Perhaps two men and a single woman with a different surname sharing a two-room suite in an Arab country was too much, or maybe more rooms were vacant off-season in Dubai; we didn't care about the reason and barely stifled the impulse to fist bump with a resounding—"yes."

On the way to our suite on the twenty-second floor, our heads swiveled from side to side to take in the architectural splendor of the hotel. Fountains sprayed dancing multi-height water arcs between the two sets of escalators from the lobby to the next level. There a vast atrium, the world's highest at 590 feet, featured tall columns and pointed arches decorated with blue and aqua Arabic geometric designs, highlighted by plenty of 22-carat gold leaf. They encircled its central fountain and pool. We crossed the atrium to the elevators and went up to our floor, where we were welcomed by Ramsey at the butlers' reception desk. He joined the hostess to lead us to our suite, open the door, and wave us in with a bow.

The three of us barely suppressed gasps of amazement at the spacious elegance facing us, but Ramsey showed no hint of amusement at our reaction. The two-story suite was entered through a beige marble-columned foyer with a polished marble floor and a sweeping spiral staircase to the left. A clock was projected onto one of its walls, not a real clock, but it kept time!

Ramsey, one of the butlers on call twenty-four hours a day, gave us an introductory tour, after which Mark and I, eager to share our good fortune with friends and family, asked him about online access for our laptops. Within minutes of his placing a call, the IT manager arrived, and Mark and I were online. Bill, who didn't travel with a laptop, used the computer in the suite's office area. Absolutely nothing was too much trouble.

As soon as we were alone, we ran around the suite, exploring each room like small children. Giddy from lack of sleep, excitement, and disbelief at our good luck, the three of us finally said goodnight and retreated to our separate bedroom suites. Burj Al Arab's world-famous brunch awaited us tomorrow.

2

Half awake, I momentarily believed I could never leave my luxurious bed in the Burj Al Arab. Eventually pulling on shorts and a T-shirt, I called up the stairs to wake up Mark and Bill—I'd already forgotten last night's instructions about using the intercom system. Walking through the parlor, living room, bar area, and dining room, I finally reached a kitchen as large as my living room back home. I had no intention of cooking but remembered spotting a coffee/espresso maker last night.

Bill and Mark soon swooped down to join me for coffee and fresh fruit. Then we began to explore the suite in earnest. Once we opened the remote-controlled shades and draperies covering floor-to-ceiling windows on two sides of the suite, the blue-water Persian Gulf sparkled below in brilliant sunlight. We had a bird's eye view of The Palm, a grouping of artificial islands shaped like a palm tree, and saw that along the Jumeirah coastal line were beaches for resorts like the Burj Al Arab as well as architecturally spectacular business centers.

Our bedrooms each had a separate dressing room and a bathroom with gold-plated fixtures and sconces, a raised Jacuzzi, marble floors, and shelves brimming with full-size Hermes cosmetic products. Bill and I had insisted that Mark take the largest bedroom suite since he had made the reservation—and it had its own exercise room.

Downstairs, beyond the columned foyer with tall glass sculptures in its corners, was the parlor, but Mark, Bill, and I decided we would spend more time in the adjacent living room which was less formal in appearance. Fresh flowers decorated the blue marbled bar, and the dining room with two mirrored walls featured eight chairs covered in blue-silk fabric at the long table. Mark stepped off the dimensions of the suite, figuring roughly that it ranged between seven and eight thousand square feet—a far cry from the eighteen hundred we had originally reserved.

Hunger was not to be a problem. Three crystal compotes full of fruit, several boxes of nuts, stuffed dates, candy and a bottle of red wine waited to satisfy any snacking needs. A comfy chaise lounge tempted Bill to lie back and pluck grapes from the compote. I peeled one with my teeth making believe I was preparing it for a god. "Sorry, guys, you don't qualify," I said, plopping it into my mouth.

We suddenly realized time was fast passing and rushed to our blue and gold-flecked bathrooms to prepare for brunch. One of my friends, Harry, who lived and worked in Dubai, was joining us, eager to see the hotel's interior luxury.

Although several years older, Harry hadn't gained weight, and his cornflower blue eyes still sparkled. His hair however was wispier than I remembered. We took the panoramic elevator from the lobby to the twenty-seventh floor where the restaurant was located 660 feet above sea level. Then we walked the length of the restaurant to enjoy the fabulous view of the two manmade island developments, The Palm and The World, a cluster of islands shaped to resemble continents.

Tables upon tables in the serving area were laden with food to enrapture an epicure—lobsters, sushi, scallops, and shrimp prepared in many ways. Caviar, to my delight, was offered in six varieties. Mark soon found his favorite: pan-seared fois gras with pumpkin and raspberry sauce. Wok and pasta stations, an oyster bar, dim sum, and a myriad other choices boggled the mind. The dessert buffet wouldn't have lived up to its reputation without two tables devoted to chocolate. Even gourmands were remarking, "Chocolate soup? I've never heard of that before."

After finishing our outrageously good desserts, Bill declared that he had to try the chocolate soup. He smiled beatifically after the first spoonful and ate it all, while we watched in disbelief. "Ah-h-h," he said, "the *soup de grâce*."

I said, "Where does he put all that food?"

Our chairs, already eased backwards to accommodate our indulgence, were finally pushed back in earnest so as to waddle to the elevator. "How could I have eaten so much?" was often repeated, but by the time the elevator button was pushed, we had justified it as an once-in-a-lifetime experience.

Next was a tour of the hotel. First we showed Harry our suite, then decided to check out the hotel's Al Mahara underwater restaurant. From the lobby, we descended about three stories in an elevator/virtual submarine to enter it. The room's dominant feature was a huge seawater aquarium made of acrylic glass seven inches thick. Sharks circled, while colorful fish of all kinds and other marine life went about their normal businesses. Diners sat at tables next to the tank to partake of life underwater.

We decided our favorite attraction was the hotel fountain's shooting waters in the atrium. One stream of water, the Volcano, was said to shoot up 105 feet, but we never saw it erupt.

We made plans to meet Harry for lunch in two days—hard though it was to think about food after our recent gourmet extravaganza. Bill, Mark, and I returned to our suite, and collapsed on living-room couches like beached whales. No sooner had we stretched out, when the door buzzer sounded.

Bill opened the door to the butler in his tuxedo and ever-present smile, holding a tray with white linen napkins, silver forks and knives and *more food*—not just one cherry torte, but two cherry tortes on gold-trimmed glass plates. Any other time, it would have been a welcomed treat, but now? When the butler departed, Mark groaned, "I need some Alka-Seltzer. I can't even look at food anymore!"

"We need some exercise," remarked Bill, probably the most fit of the three of us; although Mark and I watched our weight, Bill took his physical training seriously. Getting into, or as I more aptly described, "stuffing into" our swimsuits was the next order of business. I "covered up" with shorts and white blouse over my suit, and we headed to the beach.

Jumping into a complimentary golf cart, the driver took us back across the bridge to an adjacent sand beach. From there, we could look back and appreciate the beautiful architectural profile of the Burj, topped by a cantilevered helipad. Bill remembered reading that the helipad was once transformed into a grass tennis court for a match, and, reportedly, Tiger Woods had hit a few golf balls around it, too.

We posed for beach photos, then ran to jump into the gulf. The ninety-degree-plus water temperature was not very refreshing as we paddled around, but at least, we could claim to have gone swimming in the Persian Gulf, also known as the Arabian Gulf. I hate getting sand in my things, especially my towel, so when Mark suggested going to Wild Wadi Water Park to get out of the sun for a while, I was ready to go.

Burj Al Arab provided free access to the water park, and its entrance was a short jitney ride from the hotel. Mark, Bill, and I all felt that our trip so far was less adventurous than was usual for us and hoped the water park would add some excitement. As soon as we entered, we looked at each other in dismay; it was jammed. Of course, it was Holy Day, a time to spend with family. We saw women and girls in the water, dressed not in swimsuits but in full-length dresses of light-weight fabric—no bikinis at this pool. The wading pool was gigantic and full of people. Deciding not to fight the crowds, the three of us returned to the Burj.

Instead of the front door, the jitney dropped us off at the hotel's side door, making us feel a bit inappropriately dressed. As soon as we stopped, however, we spied an outdoor pool behind the hotel and headed there straight away. The pool was smallish, but overlooked the Persian Gulf. Best of all, its water was cooled and much more appealing than the hot Gulf water. "A chilled pool," I marveled. "Expense is nothing at the Burj when catering to their guests."

The next morning, with time at the Burj dwindling, we donned swimsuits for another attempt at Wild Wadi Water Park, which opened an hour prior to public admission to accommodate hotel guests. Mark, leading the way as usual, suggested that we go on the big slide, pointing toward Jumeirah Sceirah, the tallest water slide outside of North America. Bill was all for it, but balking, I said, "Are you nuts? I'm not going up there. You go ahead, I'll wait and watch."

I'm not afraid of much, but snakes and water slides are on the list. The guys took time to flap their elbows and cluck like chickens, but I shooed them off. They didn't even scream coming down; it wasn't in them to do something so "girly." We three headed to a tube ride with eleven more modest slides. After grabbing a tube, water blasted us up and down, around curves, and through tunnels along the course of the rollicking ride. "This is much more to my taste," I laughed.

With the public opening hour fast approaching, we chose next a huge wave pool filled with refrigerated water for a final cool down. Several young girls in very modest lime-green and pink swim outfits also frolicked there as the calm, cool water transformed itself into ocean waves.

Mark, Bill, and I got back to the hotel with barely time to pack, but all those precious Hermes products went off the shelves and into our suitcases, as did slippers, flip-flops, and a canvas bag emblazoned with the Burj emblem. In an effort not to damage the American traveler's reputation, I asked the hostess before we left if the toiletry items were meant to be taken. She was told us that they were "our gift to our guests."

3

We took a taxi downtown. Our next hotel paled in comparison to the Burj, but it wasn't $1,300 a day, either. Even though we had agreed to spend only two nights at the Burj, Bill remarked that we should have stayed a couple more nights. That surprised both Mark and me, since Bill, above all, knew the value of a dollar. Actually all of us did; that's why, after the splurge at the Burj, Mark had used points for one room downtown we could all stay in—two queen beds and a rollaway. The sleeping assignments were obvious, and the price was right.

While waiting for our room, I scanned the lobby and saw mostly business suits and traditional dress—a much more mundane atmosphere than we had just left. Mark paced impatiently, stopping only to book us on a desert "dune bashing" safari tour for the afternoon. He always maintained our lengthy "must-see" list and tried to keep us on schedule. As soon as our room was ready, we deposited luggage and quickly headed back down to meet Nevil, the tour leader, and climb in his Toyota SUV 4 X 4 for the desert ride. A tall, slender woman with dark brown hair and eyes had already claimed the front seat. Kathy was a software-company representative from the United States and seemed young—certainly younger than I.

Our route to the desert dunes passed a lot of new construction, then miles and miles of desolate sand. Bill and Mark wondered aloud, "How is this place going to look in a few years? How many tall buildings will be built? How many homes, water wells, and pools will be in this desert?"

Nevil stopped at a meeting area to wait for SUVs filled with adventure seekers from other hotels. As we stretched our legs and chatted idly, Nevil suddenly offered to buy me an ice cream. I politely declined, but he persisted in questioning me. I was polite and cordial but not forthcoming, instinctively feeling it better to maintain distance—so what if he was tall, dark, and rather handsome? All I signed up for was to go four-wheeling; I was already traveling with two fun, intelligent, and attractive men.

As other vehicles began to arrive, Nevil made a final check of the Toyota's tires to be sure they were full of air for the sand adventure. We strapped ourselves into our seats and off we went, the last vehicle in the caravan. All at once, the SUVs began to race across the dunes raising clouds of sand. Everyone grabbed for anything stable as we slid down the side of one dune and sped up another, never knowing whether we'd make a hairpin turn or meet another vehicle head on. Yells and screams accompanied every crazy turn the SUV made, Nevil demonstrated his driving skill, talking all the while to Kathy in the front seat beside him—explaining the intricacy of his maneuvers, making moves on her, or maybe just practicing his English.

Before the dust had settled, the caravan proceeded to Sharjah, one of the seven United Arab Emirates or states, for camel rides, lamb barbecue, and some belly dancing. Mark, Bill, and I had ridden enough camels on past trips to forgo that part, but memories of a camel ride in the Mongolian desert rushed back to me—and Bill couldn't keep quiet. "Sahara, remember when your camel wouldn't cooperate and you got off and walked, pulling him along. That was a funny sight— the camel herders thought so too!"

Kathy, however, had never had a camel experience and wanted to try it and have a photo to prove it. "Okay, Kathy, get on your camel and I'll take your photo," I said, thinking to myself, "Better you than I."

We headed down the hill for grilled lamb with sides of roasted potatoes, drumsticks, hummus, and tabouli. The food was quite tasty, if touristy. The next event, belly-dancing, called for audience participation and Mark and I were chosen to be in the show. Both of us harbored a latent trait of showmanship and weren't shy about performing. If truth were known, we loved it.

When the party ended, we started back to Dubai. At the desert's edge, Nevil stopped at a store to deflate the tires to normal pressure, and we all got out to stretch our legs. Suddenly I heard Mark yelp with pleasure. He had discovered the coveted Magnum ice cream bars on sale there, not cheap, but so delicious. Wherever we travel, we're always on the look-out for Magnum bars. When least expected, the treats appear.

Kathy, it turned out, was staying at our hotel, so we included her in plans to explore the city. Harry had arranged a visit to the floor of the Dubai Financial Market, to which most tourists don't have access. A security check was required, but, surprisingly, photography was allowed. Activity on the stock exchange floor the next morning was slow. Harry pointed out several Dubai companies on the ticker, and I noted the men's attire. Some were dressed in traditional Arab garb: the *dishdasha*, a long, pristine white tunic that set off their darker skin and a *gutra*, red-and-white checked head scarf held in place by an *agal*, a black circular cord. Others favored slacks or jeans with dress shirts as they stood around kiosk video screens or talking in groups on the floor. In the absence of trading action, we took a few photos and decided to leave. All five of us squeezed into a taxi and drove past a skyline of skyscrapers and active cranes, "that never seemed to end," as Bill commented.

Harry said, "Dubai's building growth at the moment has cornered the market on 25 percent of the world's cranes."

Marveling at the new construction, we were especially impressed by the Burj Dubai, a building that would be, upon completion, the tallest in the world. Harry said no one knew exactly how tall that would be, as the builders were keeping it a secret.

"What are those stunning triangular buildings, Harry?"

"Those aluminum and glass skyscrapers are the Jumeriah Emirates Towers—one's an office complex and the other a hotel."

New construction didn't seem to end until we reached the Mall of the Emirates, home of an improbable indoor ski slope. With outdoor temperature topping a hundred degrees, air conditioning hit us hard as we entered. Harry had chosen for lunch a restaurant with a window table overlooking the Ski Dubai slope. It wasn't as long or as steep as most outdoor runs—except that we were sitting before a large window in a mall restaurant in Dubai watching people ski. Even children on tubes slid down the slope, ending up near our window.

Harry had to rush back to work, so the goodbyes were brief. Kathy, Bill, Mark, and I went straight to the indoor slope. Mark and Bill skied often. I demurred, ranking it about even with camel riding. Presumably Kathy skied, since she grew up in Colorado.

"But no skiing for us," Bill reminded, citing our decision not to take chances on jeopardizing the rest of the trip.

We rented boots, parkas, and leggings. By the time we suited up, we were thankful for the extra layers. Mark whipped out a hat and gloves that he had packed. "Well, don't you just think of everything?" I said, "And just couldn't be bothered to suggest that Bill and I bring them, too? Thanks, pal. No wonder your luggage is so heavy!"

The entrance to the Snow Park led into a cavern where we took turns posing for photos in front of a huge dragon sculpted in ice. The dragon, its wings glowing iridescently, towered over us. Mark posed smugly in his warm beanie and gloves. Bill had his baseball cap, but I could only make my fingers into a tight fist to keep them warm—without much success.

Close up, the indoor ski slope was enormous to the point of incredibility, but its snow was icy, not fluffy. To see the entire sprawling area, we climbed stairs to a viewing plat-form. Chairlifts ran to the slope's top, and artificial evergreens dotted the landscape—everywhere except in the ski run. In lieu of skiing, Bill and Mark spotted a toboggan chute that looked fun.

Grabbing small, red plastic toboggans and climbing a short stairway to the head of the chute was easy. Harder was sitting in the right place so that one could lie back flat, legs slightly bent and feet together, with the entire body atop the toboggan for the fast ride down. Soon we were banking on curves to increase our speed. Bill asked me to take a photo, "an action shot," as he was arriving at the bottom. That led to more rides and photos. We decided to leave when we got tired of waiting in line with the increasing number of real children arriving after school. Before we reached the exit, however, a snowball battle developed. Having gloves, Mark easily won by patting together actual balls. Snowballs from our ungloved hands were hardly respectable.

Our next destination was the Chillout, Dubai's ice lounge where seventeen U.S. dollars entitled us to a fruit drink and warm clothing to withstand the frigid temperature of the lounge. Each of us was handed a parka, boots, and dispos-able knit gloves. Mark, of course, pulled on his own gloves. An attendant directed us to another room called the buffer zone where our bodies acclimated to the temperature changes for a few minutes. Another door opened; inside the ice lounge it was 21°F. A hostess escorted us to an ice table with ice seats covered with sheepskins.

Waiting for our "mocktails," the cold soon penetrated our jeans, and we walked around to see the room's ice sculptures. One wall duplicated the Dubai skyline with its towering build-ings and architectural wonders. On the opposite wall was the bar sculpted entirely of ice, with shelves displaying ice martini glasses, stacked ice tumblers, and an ice decanter. The walls were covered with tiles of ice, and a freestanding sculpture of a camel and a palm tree stood near the exit. Kathy thought it was too cold to enjoy working there.

"Work? You're the only one who works," Mark said. "We don't do that anymore, remember?"

We drank our "mocktails" without having the ice glass stick to our lips, snapped a few pictures and left, heeding the recommendation to stay only forty minutes. Outside the heat felt even hotter. The final attraction was Dubai's Gold Souq or market. Kathy wanted a purse for her niece; I wanted to see the gold jewelry and watches; and Mark was always ready to negotiate a bargain. Bill was along for the company.

The first and frequently repeated words we heard as we wandered the Gold Souq were "I will give you a good bargain."

An enterprising young man dressed in jeans overheard Kathy mention a purse and immediately said, "Follow me, I get you good price for good purse."

Thinking there was safety in numbers, we followed him a twisting, turning way through the souq until he made a sharp turn and headed down an alley, looking back to make sure we were still coming. When we passed a garbage dump larger than a souq stall, Mark whispered, "Where is this guy taking us?"

We looked at each other and shrugged, but still we followed. Bill asked me if I could remember the way out.

"I think so, or I have a general idea at least."

The young man stopped at a nondescript building, led us up three flights of steps, and knocked on a door. Arabic words were exchanged and several locks clicked open. A hand beckoned us in. By now, all four of us were seriously thinking, "What have we gotten ourselves into?"

Shelves of purses lined the walls from floor to ceiling, and glass cases displayed watches. Kathy looked at the purses but couldn't find one she liked. The prices weren't a great bargain either. We brave souls thanked the men and left. On the street we paused to get our bearings, and Mark asked, "Who remembers the way back?"

Fortunately, everyone did. The smell of the garbage heap told us we were near the real souq. Later, we learned that shops like that were illegal, but by then we could laugh about being misled. That night we took Kathy to dinner to wish her safe journey, then retreated to our room to pack for our early morning flight to Islamabad. Concerned about luggage weight, we planned to check in together so that if one suitcase was overweight, we could shift items to a lighter one.

A black stretch limousine arrived promptly at five o'clock to pick us up. We were barely functioning and the air was steaming already. A chipper driver stowed the luggage and opened a door for Mark, Bill, and me to slide in. On the backseat were cold washcloths, bottles of cold water, and chocolates. That early in the morning, the ride to Abu Dhabi airport only took one hour instead of two.

I was dressed conservatively in long khaki pants, a long-sleeved shirt, and low hiking shoes that replaced my usual sequined flip-flops. A long white scarf could cover my hair, if necessary. I didn't want to be disrespectful in Islamabad and embarrass the guys. Checking our luggage, there was no weight problem, even with the Hermes stash. We went to the gate for our flight to Pakistan. When the plane took off, I closed my eyes and let my mind drift back to how I had met my two fabulous traveling companions and become the "suitcase wife."

4

Nine years earlier, living in Alabama and unfulfilled by my work, I felt I was facing a stop sign in my life and didn't know what to do about it. Resign and look for another job? I had worked more than twenty-five years for a government agency and didn't want to throw away all my benefits. Sell my house and move to another state? I longed to get away but knew that running from dissatisfactions without addressing the causes would solve nothing.

I was ambitious. I had wanted to pursue an education and move out of the family home, not necessarily in that order; since my family relationships were "arm's length," at best. Growing up, my mother and I seldom agreed on any topic, much less, on how life was to be lived. My father's behavior ranged from explosive tirade to silent withdrawal. From my earliest years, intimate relationships were almost nonexistent. In truth, I learned how to manage a business operation better than how to maintain close friendships.

Marrying young and soon having a son, I had felt my life being poured into the mold of suburban housewife and mom. Looking back, I realized that my son Peter had been the best influence to enter my life. The anchor of responsibility he brought countered my tendency to rebel or "go wild." I had learned to accept limits on my dreams, but not to stop dreaming.

Years later, after divorcing, my life and career rocketed into opportunities I had never thought possible. I had my share of adventures in transferring to new work locations in Pennsylvania, followed by promotions to New Jersey, Louisiana, and Alabama. Each move taught Peter and me more adaptability, learning to make new friends and appreciate the variety in our great country.

My professional successes and the friends I made had enriched my life, but they had never erased my feeling of being an observer out of step with the mainstream. Since childhood, when I had nearly drowned in a swimming pool, I had experienced déjà-vu; though, of course, I had had no name then for the feeling of living on two levels. The image of me looking down at myself lying just below the surface of the water, long hair floating around me, remained indelible. I had always felt the world held much to experience, and now I wanted to get on with it. My inner turmoil, it seemed, had suddenly rushed to the surface for release. But how?

A family therapist I had heard about might be a start. I made an appointment, even though it went against the grain to admit that I needed help. The therapist's kind, yet challenging, sessions raised issues I had chosen to ignore and rekindled my aspirations. As the months passed, I had looked inward, read mind-expanding books, attended workshops on aspects of the spiritual world, and studied Reiki or energy healing with a shaman—all the while remaining mostly silent about my explorations. I was regaining interest in the world and all its possibilities—especially in seeing more of it.

By January, I had plowed through my hectic holiday work schedule with determination, and in the new year found my optimism returning. But I had had no time to investigate trips or even to look at a travel brochure and video that a friend had given me. When Presidents' Day provided a three-day weekend in February, I was tired of moving the package every time I dusted the coffee table and promised myself a quick look before tossing it. The "watch/throw video" was about to be checked off my must-do list.

Sitting cross-legged in front of the VCR, I had watched Buddhist monks in Nepal fill the screen. Quite unexpectedly I began to sob. Tears poured down my cheeks. At that precise moment, I knew, without a doubt, that I must take this trip. I immediately called for the particulars, but the travel agency was closed for the holiday.

"Just as well," I thought, since my main weekend task was income taxes and probably no space was left, anyhow, on trips that started in just two months.

On Tuesday morning, I again telephoned the agency about the trip to Nepal with the Tengboche Monastery post trip. One itinerary was to depart too early in April for me; another had too few people interested in the post trip to offer it. However, one was to leave two days after the income-tax deadline on April 15, and it could accommodate another traveler.

By that afternoon, I was sitting in the accountant's office with my tax receipts in hand and high hopes that I wouldn't owe the Internal Revenue Service too much more money. A huge tax bill might end any chance of a trip, let alone all the way to Nepal. Dan, my accountant, promised to figure my taxes promptly after I mentioned the trip riding on the tax outcome. In fact, he called the next day with the bad news.

"Sahara, you do owe some money, but everyone in this office thinks you should go anyway. How many chances will you have for a trip like this?"

By then, I had already decided I was going, even if it meant taking out a loan. Something inside was insisting that I take this trip. I called my friend Steve to see if he could join me on the adventure, but after reviewing his calendar of pre-arranged business trips and mandatory meetings, he had to decline. My luck was better. My boss approved the four-week vacation, and I booked the trip for one, thinking that would be more adventurous anyway.

When my ambitious plan became more widely known, comments ran the gamut. My minister expressed enthusiasm, "You will be changed and won't come back the same person as before. One of my friends had a similar trip—he returned changed. What a great spiritual experience you will have."

The Suitcase Wife

Others seemed to feel differently, looking puzzled as if I had gone off the deep end. A male friend in northern Alabama even asked if I were going through a mid-life crisis. I tried to respond, saying that I did feel an inner excitement, not particularly religious in purpose, but leading me toward discovery.

Perhaps one day my friend would experience a similar feeling, but for now, he remained confused. I wondered how I could actually explain or describe this overflow of anticipation to others who had no frame of reference. I couldn't comprehend it myself. I had trusted my intuition and found courage to act on it.

When I told my staff about the trip, a young woman confided, "You are so cool. I'm not trying to butter you up, but I do wish I could be more like you. I would love to travel, but there's no one to go with me."

I advised the employee not to give up on what she really wanted to do, to take a few steps at a time to gain confidence. "Going alone is no big deal, plus it's fun; you meet more people when you're by yourself and forced to interact with others instead of just the friend traveling with you."

Then my employee confessed that her only friend was a negative person who didn't want to do much of anything. I found myself speaking from the heart, "Look at the situation and get rid of all the negative things in your life to allow room for the positive to enter. Let me tell you, negativity is a drain on your life, physically and mentally. Go out and experience life—you can never guess what might happen."

When my attention turned to actual preparation for the trip, pieces began to fall in place like a puzzle. The travel agent had advised me to start training every day, since the trip was rated "challenging"—meaning physically demanding and requiring conditioning. Living on the beach in Gulf Shores, Alabama, didn't offer much opportunity for high elevation training.

"Climb bleachers in a football stadium," the agent had suggested, "with two telephone books in your backpack."

"Two Gulf Shores or two Los Angeles phone books?" I'd asked.

Silence on the other end of the line—apparently the agent hadn't appreciated levity. I thought to myself, "Forget stadium bleachers; we don't even have a stadium in Gulf Shores—I'll climb condo steps."

From the many high-rise condominiums stretching along the beach, I picked the tallest and phoned the manager to ask permission to train in their stairwell after work. I had even offered to sign a liability waiver in case I had an accident hiking up and down stairs. One of the joys of living in a small town manifested in the manager's answer, "That won't be necessary, Sahara. Don't worry about it. We trust you."

Endurance training would have to wait for weekends. With February, March, and April becoming milder, hiking for hours could be relaxing as well as build stamina. By coincidence, a tape arrived on aerobic breathing and exercises to increase lung capacity. I had ordered it for general health improvement without knowing I'd soon be in an elevation which demanded just that. I could practice breathing during the week when it was impossible to train physically for the recommended three to four hours a day.

My immediate next step was to find the necessary items of clothing and equipment. Never having trekked before, this was definitely confusing: What's a Packtowl? Non-leather or leather hiking boots? Binoculars 8x21 or 10x21? Big deal, what's the difference? Where do I even buy all this stuff?

On my first shopping expedition, backpacks hanging on hooks lined a store's wall. Which one would serve me the best? Different weights of long underwear added to my confusion. From childhood, I only knew the white waffle-weave kind that bagged at the knees. Years of living in the South hadn't required long johns or hiking socks ranging from warm to warmest.

I finally decided to purchase all-leather hiking boots. Two days later, the final list of packing recommendations arrived in my mailbox suggesting "lightweight nylon boots." My "all-leathers" would just have to do.

Not only did I need to figure out what to buy for three and a half weeks of travel, but also what would fit into a duffel bag measuring fourteen by thirty inches with a thirty-three pound maximum weight limit. I finally decided to rent a sleeping bag in Nepal rather than schlepping one from the States, thus making more room in my duffel bag.

Having never overcome my dislike of injections, I was chagrined to find that inoculations were the most important item on my must-do list. Recommended vaccinations included polio, cholera, diphtheria, tetanus, hepatitis A and B memomune vaccine, and typhoid. I had had to view them all not as needles but as insurance policies: the temporary discomfort of obtaining them meant peace of mind in Nepal.

Filling prescriptions, purchasing a Nepal tour book, finding a compact medical kit and other supplies consumed my free time. Trying to find long johns and a down sleeping bag in Alabama in March raised the eyebrows of more than one salesperson until I explained the trip. The irony of college spring breakers in bikinis covering Alabama's white sand beaches while I shopped for winter clothes brought a smile. Clothing catalogs were featuring summer collections while their selections of winter clothing were almost nonexistent. Fortunately, patient mail-order salespeople gave me invaluable guidance and assistance.

Even coincidental events began to occur.

At a neighborhood party, I was introduced to a man who had lived in Nepal for years. He suggested that I take a small dose of aspirin every day during the ascent to Tengboche Monastery. It should help with adjusting to altitude. Leaving the party, I shook my head in disbelief, "What are the odds I would meet a person here in Alabama who had lived in Nepal?"

The church bulletin announced the sign-up for children's church camp, costing $125, and I customarily sponsored a child in the congregation. The next day's stack of mail had included an envelope appearing to contain a check. Since I wasn't expecting any checks, I opened it first and was surprised to find a check for $125.55. I couldn't believe it was the amount needed. While paying to sponsor a camper, I told the church secretary about the unusual coincidence.

Later I reflected, "Why am I still surprised when events like these occur? I should know that the Universe works in its own way. But it's still amazing!"

My physical training continued with a three-day regimen of climbing up the condo's fifteen-story stairwell and back down without stopping, carrying a fully loaded backpack. I always checked in with the condo's receptionists to give an approximate finishing time, so they could call for help if anything happened. My stamina increased until I could easily complete six climbs up and down in fifty minutes, but I still wondered if it would be enough at high altitude.

On the weekends, I walked for three hours every Saturday and Sunday to build endurance. These hikes were relaxing— just nature and me. A wildlife refuge trail twisted through a natural thicket, past a little lagoon and lake, and over sand dunes descending to the sugar-white sand beaches of the Gulf of Mexico. Sights like that of newly hatched snakes and sounds of circling birds overjoyed me.

Picture a woman wearing hiking boots, shorts, T-shirt, and a loaded backpack striding briskly along the beach. The number of stares and try-not-to-notice glances I collected convinced me that those people were thinking "crazy lady." The inquisitive looks only increased as the weather grew warmer. Once I was unable to resist asking a particularly interested elderly couple, "Are you curious? May I help you?"

The Suitcase Wife

The woman replied seriously, "Why, yes. We thought you must be a nature lover, too. We brought hiking boots for our vacation here and wondered where we could hike."

Chastened, I gave them directions.

Toward the end of March, one Saturday dawned cold and windy. Undaunted by the unusual beach conditions, I layered my clothes for easy removal if I got too warm. My new convertible pants, windbreaker, and black gloves provided a preview of their ability to perform, and they worked—I should stay warm in the Himalayas.

Condo stairwell climbing increased to five times a week as the day of departure neared. My dedication to fitness in preparation for this imminent physical endeavor exceeded anything I had ever done. I had actually begun to look forward to the endurance preparation; it provided concentration and solitude.

All of my conditioning, however, didn't prepare me for a surprise the Sunday morning before departure. After early church services, I began my weekend hike. Warm weather, blue skies, green water, and white sand had contributed to a perfect day for enjoying nature and hiking. After about two and a half hours, I veered off the beach for the thirty-five minute walk back to the parking lot on a trail heading over the sand dunes. I reached the top of the dunes and turned around for one final glimpse of the Gulf of Mexico before my trip. Deeply touched, I lingered for a moment, then continued on to the parking lot.

I started walking with head down to keep my hat on in facing the warm land breeze. Suddenly I heard a metallic sound behind me and blanched, thinking I had dropped my car keys in the sand. I looked down, then remembered that they were hooked inside my backpack. I wondered briefly what could it have been, then shrugged my shoulders and turned back to the trail. Taking a step forward, I didn't believe what I was seeing—a couple making love, their legs sticking out into the trail and most of their bodies hidden by a small dune. White capris with lime green polka dots lay bunched at the edge of the trail. Stunned, I rubbed my eyes, "I'm really not seeing what I think I'm seeing?"

I coughed discreetly, but no response. The lovers were transported. Leaving the trail, I walked over the dunes around them, then circled back to the path. My guardian angels must have warned me with the metallic sound not to step on them.

The next day, I told my friend Bobby, a local realtor, about the trail incident. After he stopped laughing, he asked if I had recognized them. I laughed, too, and answered, "Not from that angle!"

Seeing the humor in the unexpected makes life more interesting. I only hoped my guardian angel would accompany me to Nepal.

5

The night before departure, I packed everything but a few items to add in the morning and went to bed. My sleep was deep, and a dream vividly portraying a mandala appeared not once but twice: the second time, its brilliance increased and pushed me even deeper into sleep. Upon waking, I remembered the dream and flipped through Frederich Lenz's book, *Surfing the Himalayas,* until I found a picture of a mandala, one similar to that in my dream. After reminding myself to watch for this mandala design on the journey, I was off to the airport.

As I checked in, a nearby Delta reservationist overheard me asking to check my luggage all the way to Kathmandu. The woman in dark-blue uniform said, "Excuse me for eavesdropping, but I heard you mention Kathmandu. I just returned from Nepal and loved every minute of the trip. I even felt safe walking alone in Kathmandu and was never bothered by anyone. My favorite place was Tiger Temple Lodge in the jungle."

"That's on my itinerary too. I can hardly believe I'm going, and now I can't wait until I'm there."

"Are you going with friends?"

"No, I'm not. I'll be meeting people in the travel group, but I'm by myself," I answered.

"Have fun, but I know you will. Good luck and safe travels," the reservationist wished me.

While changing planes in Atlanta for my flight to Los Angeles, I met a couple, identified by their luggage tags, who would be traveling with the same tour group. Our excitement was contagious and we all embraced, agreeing that people from the South always want to hug. We couldn't wait to get to Nepal.

The Suitcase Wife

During the flight I continued reading *Surfing the Himalayas* about the premise of "emptying your mind" and "just going with the flow." With book in hand, I drifted off to sleep and saw a golden electrical bolt head directly towards me. I felt it hit my lip, startling me and pushing my body back into the seat. I woke up. The plane had suddenly hit turbulence.

Arriving safely in Los Angeles, I found my son Peter's friend waiting to greet me. He had come from his home in Newport Beach for a leisurely dinner together and catching up. I lost track of time causing me to make a mad dash to the International Terminal barely making it to the Thai Airways gate in time. Berating myself, I thought, "Wouldn't it be ironic if I missed my flight after all this preparation?"

My fellow travelers had already gathered in the gate area and introduced themselves. I met Betsy, my roommate-to-be for the next three weeks.

"I did numerology based on our birthdates, and it appears we'll have no problem being compatible on this trip," I said.

The look I saw on Betsy's face clearly said, "Oh, No! What planet did she drop in from? I have to put up with her for three weeks? Spare me!"

I thought about how would I describe Betsy: "Older and much quieter that I am; that's probably a plus: neither of us will be fighting for airtime to talk. I don't think she's had an easy life either. I could be mistaken, but I don't think so. Betsy seemed easygoing, but until you travel with someone for a few days, it's really a crap shoot. I'll definitely get to know her better after rooming with her."

Betsy was about five and a half feet tall, had short blonde curls in contrast to my long dark hair pulled back into a ponytail. Both of us were excited about this trip and the post trip trek to Tengboche Monastery.

Upon meeting two brothers from the Philadelphia area, Mark and Bill, I mentioned that I had lived in Pennsylvania at one time.

"Where did you live?" they asked in unison.

"Allentown."

"My brother and I went to college in Bethlehem."

"So did I! Where did you go?" I responded.

"Lehigh University."

"You won't believe this. I went to Moravian College."

Lehigh University and Moravian College's south campus were directly across the Lehigh River from one another. These two men and I were students at the same time, but we hadn't known each other. I immediately thought, "All the coincidences are still occurring. How is this going to play out?"

Having arrived late, all the aisle seats, which I preferred, were taken. "Oh, great!" I thought, "Now, I'll be crammed in the middle or in a window seat all the way to Bangkok."

The reservationist kindly offered, "I'm assigning you a window seat with no one in the middle seat for more room. That's the best I can do for you."

I reminded myself, "Don't complain. You arrived late, so be thankful. It could be worse; you could be stuck in that middle seat."

"Okay, I'll take it. Thank you so much for your help," I told the reservationist.

I boarded the plane and proceeded to my seat. Much to my surprise, a small elderly Cambodian woman occupied the window seat in my row. I leaned over and whispered, "Excuse me, you are in the wrong seat."

The woman looked up at me, shook her head and shrugged her shoulders, apparently not understanding English. She finally handed me her boarding pass showing her actual seat to be on the aisle. Happily, I motioned for her to stay in the window seat, and I'd take the aisle.

The Suitcase Wife

Both the elderly woman and I had gotten what we wanted. "Now how cool is that," I thought, "The coincidences are still holding. Who knows in what form they'll appear."

The flight's stopover in Osaka, Japan, for crews to clean the aircraft and refuel, provided an opportunity for me to talk with my new roommate and the two brothers. I decided that Mark was more gregarious than Bill, because he had hurried to walk with me to the waiting area with questions about my years in Pennsylvania—I'd also heard him during the night, conversing with any available traveler.

When Bill caught up with us, we chatted like old friends. Betsy joined us and pitched right into the conversation. I soon found that she seemed openminded and adventurous. Best of all, she had no intention of sitting in a hotel room. Betsy was as eager to explore the sights and sounds of Kathmandu and Bangkok as I. Relaying the Delta agent's assurance of women's safety in Kathmandu, I mentioned to Betsy my plan to hire a car and driver in Bangkok during our return trip. We both wanted to see the city without any traffic concerns. By the time we reboarded the plane in Osaka, the two of us were confident we'd be good companions.

When we landed in Bangkok to change planes to Kathmandu, we found an apparent mix up. A room at the airport hotel was no longer available for freshening up after the long overnight flight, although it had been included in the tour. Everyone was griping, but no one wanted to pay extra. I immediately decided I wasn't going to sit around and complain; I rented a day room in the terminal to shower, change clothes, and lie down to rest before the flight to Kathmandu.

Feeling restored, I later meandered to the Kathmandu gate to rejoin my fellow passengers. Suddenly I recognized someone I knew at the gate. Blinking my eyes, thinking that it couldn't possibly be Gregg Braden, I remembered that he had advertised a spiritual trip to Tibet trekking to various monasteries promoting world peace. Pointing at Gregg, "I know that guy, and I can't believe I would run into him," I told those around me.

Their doubtful looks said, "Oh sure, she meets someone she knows in Bangkok, who's also flying to Kathmandu, right?"

Rising from my seat, I walked toward Gregg. After a hug and hellos, Gregg asked if I were here with a spiritual group.

I answered, "No, I'm not. They don't know it yet, but they'll be more spiritual after I am done with them in three weeks."

Gregg laughed, knowing of my reputation for having a "smart" mouth—which occasionally got me into trouble. We had met earlier when friends from Alabama and I attended his seminar on spiritual development. Oddly, one of the friends had told me to tell Gregg hello if we ran into each other. When I delivered the message, he laughed again, "Boy, did she ever manifest this meeting."

Gregg introduced me to his wife and his knowledgeable trip leader, Jeff. He briefly described their trekking itinerary. We spoke of the Dalai Lama's urging his people to return to Tibet and preserve their culture from further destruction. I told Gregg I had recently read his book *Walking Between the Worlds*.

When I returned to my group, several people asked about my acquaintance.

"I told you I knew him," I reminded them and proceeded to explain about spiritual paths and say that I was also on a path of spiritual exploration. A "that's-nice" look swept over several faces, but the customary eye rolling was politely omitted.

Although the flight to Kathmandu was uneventful, I loved the beautiful color of the flight attendants' silk dresses and the matching airsickness bags. Deciding that I wanted a custom-made silk suit in the same lavender shade for my son's upcoming wedding, I thought it would be no problem to purchase in Kathmandu or Bangkok. "That's if our schedule allows me to go shopping."

6

Arriving five hours later in Kathmandu, I obtained a Nepal visa and retrieved my duffel bag from the luggage carousel. Slinging it over my shoulder, I walked to meet our guide, Gopan. He was wearing dark-tinted glasses and showing a gorgeous smile of straight, pearly white teeth against dusky skin. About five feet six and slightly overweight, Gopan had short-cropped black hair. Perhaps his complexion made his teeth appear so white; I made a mental note to check them out later. He said, "I want you to gather outside the terminal to the left and wait for everyone else."

When I passed through the outside doors, a wave of familiarity washed over me, as if I were returning home after being away. I didn't feel like a stranger in a foreign country halfway around the world. Even the people I saw seemed familiar.

Gopan oversaw the loading of luggage on the bus, as we waited patiently, absorbing the new atmosphere. A collection of discordant sounds and sights grabbed my attention. Across multiple traffic lanes in front of the terminal, a sea of signs advertised hotels. A man jiggled each sign and yelled at the travelers to capture their attention and business. I assumed they were paid for every person they lured to a hotel. *Stay at the Yak and Yeti Hotel.* "That hotel sounds like fun," I thought.

The reality of staying in a third-world country didn't register with me until we left the airport for the hotel. As the bus approached the exit gate, I saw a man in a small booth. When official business was completed, he removed a concrete block from a rope holding down a pole that had blocked passage. The pole lifted, and the bus traveled under it. It was then that

The Suitcase Wife

I realized the process was not automated. It was the first of many hand-controlled procedures we'd experience over the next three weeks.

Navigating the streets through Kathmandu to our hotel unfolded another new experience for me. On unpaved streets, cows, sacred in the Hindu religion, lounged amidst traffic, unbothered by swerving vehicles and undaunted by the sounds of horns, horns, and more horns. The animals lay there until late afternoon when their inner clocks signaled time to return home for the evening.

Closer into the city, traffic navigated the intersections without the luxury of traffic lights. A momentary break in the chaos allowed the bus to continue through an intersection. Few words were exchanged between the bus driver and his string-bean thin assistant, who draped his arm out the window and banged on the side of the bus to signal the driver when it was safe to pass. The driver responded by blowing the horn, warning the vehicle he was overtaking. The air was filled with a feeling of vibrancy, or perhaps, a feeling bordering on madness.

Looking out my window, I observed workers with shovels and pickaxes digging trenches and holes, while others stood and watched. Huge marijuana plants with their feathery-leafed stems flourished by the roadways. Small shops butted up against each other with open fronts offering no protection against the dust collecting on the wares. Dust settled everywhere.

The driver veered off the main road, heading down narrower streets, past the Buddhist temple Swayambhunath, better known as the Monkey Temple. Then it passed a private school with uniformed children leaving for the day, and squeezed past more vehicles to enter the Hotel Vajra's parking lot. What a welcomed sight it was. We would have two nights here before heading out again. Just thirty-four hours ago, I had left my home in Alabama and arrived here exhausted and exhilarated at the same time.

The weary travelers entered the Hotel Vajra's courtyard and walked up wide brick steps to the lawn, landscaped with lush green plants, shade trees, and colorful flowers in terra cotta pots. Scattered white lawn chairs offered respite while Betsy and I waited for room assignments and instructions for the next few days. I, lost in my own world, examined the exquisite workmanship of intricately carved wood decorating the windows, the eaves, and the doors. Peacefulness pervaded the courtyard, so remote from the wildness of the streets.

Gopan said, "For those travelers going on the post trip, please give me your passports and an additional photo. I must have them to get your Himalayan trekking permits."

I hesitantly relinquished mine, hearing my aunt's voice reverberate in my ears, "Remember, never allow your passport out of your control. Hang on to it at all times. It would very difficult to replace if you lost it."

I had always admired Aunt Luci, my father's sister. A former model and college English professor, she had never married, rejecting all proposals in order to retain her freedom. Luci, statuesque, dark-haired, well-traveled, and well-read, had her life cut short by a tragic accident. I had been devastated. We had had great visits and trips together and were looking forward to more before she died. Luci had traveled to Northern Africa and Europe alone for nine months in 1950 and kept a diary of her experiences meeting scores of characters. Deep down, I had always wanted the exciting life Luci had carved out for herself.

Gopan handed out room keys and said, "The welcome dinner will be served at six o'clock in the dining room. For now, you have a free afternoon."

As Betsy and I walked up to our second-floor room, I took note of a sign for the Sunset Bar, which pointed to the rooftop, and thought that definitely worth visiting. Our room overlooked the courtyard. Its high ceilings and spaciousness welcomed us, after sitting in cramped airplane seats. As soon as our bags were delivered, we headed to explore the rooftop bar. Stepping over the threshold, I gasped at what I was seeing—container after container planted with brilliantly colored flowers. Reds, pinks, yellows intermingled with green plants. The white tables and chairs sparkled in the sun, contrasting to the red brick terrace they rested upon. "Let's have a beer to celebrate," I suggested.

My pulse quickened as we decided where to sit. Looking over the brick wall, I saw Buddhist prayer flags strung from the heights of buildings across streets to tops of facing buildings. The strings of blue, green, red, yellow, and white flags fluttered in the wind. Farther away, I spied Swayambhunath on top of a hill; its whitewashed dome and gleaming gold spire glistening against the clear blue skies with not a cloud in sight. I must go there, I thought to myself.

Eventually Mark and Bill joined Betsy and me at our table. We chatted aimlessly, getting better acquainted. The brothers enjoyed traveling, but their wives had opted to stay at home this time, preferring not to brave the primitive conditions described in the trip brochure. I asked the others if they had been on this kind of trip before; all of them had. I admitted that it was my first trekking trip, and I had no idea what to expect. "But, I'm in good shape. I play golf and at one time played tournament racquetball until my back operation. Too much information?"

The conversation led here and there finally going back to meeting Gregg in the Bangkok airport. I explained that Gregg and I shared a belief in the power of thinking about something and it's becoming reality. I recounted the recent incident of the aisle seat as a manifestation of possibility.

I could see in the eyes of Mark and Bill and Betsy that they were not understanding what I was saying. Nevertheless, I definitely felt a vibrational energy on the rooftop so strong that I was slightly dizzy and saw color splashes before my eyes. "Just hang on and discover where this is taking you," I thought, as we went back to our rooms to prepare for dinner.

I loved the smorgasbord of vegetarian choices and followed Gopan's suggestion that everyone eat well and head to bed early. Though exhausted, the good night's sleep I hoped for was not to be. Cats yowled all night long in the courtyard beneath the window. Some were in heat; others were just fighting.

At four o'clock in the morning, roosters had joined the cat cacophony, followed by cooing doves and chirping birds. The smell of wood fires burning touched my nostrils. Kathmandu was waking up and so was I. I couldn't imagine a better way to start the day, except minus the cats. Quickly dressing, I hurried to the rooftop to watch the sun rise. Absorbing the city's growing sights and sounds, I grew thirsty and went downstairs to get a pot of tea.

While waiting at the restaurant counter, I struck up a conversation with a local artist, a slender young man wearing black-framed glasses, sitting alone. "My name is Kanti," he said in perfect English, "Where are you from?"

My answer concluded with a similar query. "I have come home," he said. "I am a painter of pictures. My training was originally in finance, and I studied in your country in the states of Indiana and Michigan. I liked living there, but I missed Kathmandu. At first, I didn't know what to do here. Now I have a small art gallery in the hotel."

He invited me to attend a theatrical production, called *The White Tiger*, to be performed in his gallery during the next three weekends. I promised to visit his gallery, but said I couldn't come to the play because we would be trekking. I left with my pot of hot tea and returned to the still chilly rooftop to watch the early sun tint Kathmandu with delicate pinks and oranges.

Smoke curled from chimneys; men and women trudged to work; Buddhist monks emerged on rooftop terraces for prayer sessions. Little by little, I saw Kathmandu start a new day. At six o'clock, music called down from the Buddhist temple on the hill to signal the beginning of prayers there. Within forty-five minutes, the sight of the sun sparkling on Swayambhunath's golden spire was stunning. I finished my tea and my journal of the past few days, then went back to the room.

Betsy, who had managed a short nap after the cats' howling had ended, was almost dressed for breakfast and couldn't wait to say, "In *Kat*hmandu, what else would you expect?"

"Ouch, that's so bad, it's good," I complimented her.

Betsy, with her sense of adventure and humor, was proving to be a good match. I had hoped for a good roommate and there she was.

7

Traveling opportunities had always brought new ideas, and already this trip was no exception. The first sightseeing excursion took us to Buddhist temples, Boudhanath and Bhaktapur—a short bus ride from the hotel. On the way, we passed a funeral procession with the deceased wrapped in golden fabric, lying on a stretcher made of two green bamboo stalks and ropes and draped with red, pink, and yellow flower garlands. Another aspect of this country's intense use of color, I thought.

As we walked between buildings to the entrance of Boudhanath stupa, the eyes of Buddha painted on its tower stared down at us. These eyes, on the tower's four sides, were always observing what everyone was doing, even the Buddhist monks and their followers praying and spinning prayer wheels. Boudhanath was the largest stupa in Nepal—the third largest in the world.

Gopan began to describe the symbolism attached to the temple's different sections. "Its four-tiered base represents earth and the white dome on top of it symbolizes water. Notice the tower adorned with the eyes of Buddha atop the dome. The first tower section represents fire; the next section, air; and the final section, the ethers. Also look closely at the symbol between the eyes; it is used as our number 'one' and symbolizes that all life is one."

He enlightened us about Buddha and his teachings of seeking truth, light, and knowledge. I could identify with everything he was saying. After the short lecture, Bill came over to ask if I understood all that.

I responded, "Understand? I'm trying to live it."

"I know you are," he said.

Bill and I found Mark just a few paces away in a T-shirt shop. When we joined him, he was engaged in a price negotiation. At length, we walked away with embroidered T-shirts stating "Top of the World – Nepal." Mark's purchases and the many to follow, had already earned a repeated refrain from our fellow travelers: "What has he bought now?"

When rejoining the group, who were walking around one of the stupa tiers, we noticed several men above us on the dome replacing old, faded prayer flags. Suddenly, drops of water splashed on us and, looking up, we saw not a cloud in the sky.

"What was that?"

"It can't be rain!"

Up on the dome, we saw that the men were sloshing yellow saffron water from large containers onto the stupa's dome as a blessing to Buddha. Those small men had climbed up a ladder propped against the dome, with water containers on either end of a long pole balanced over their shoulders. Mark commented that so much strength and balance weren't evident in men so short and thin. Bill decided that since the saffron water had sprinkled us, we were blessed. I thought we should accept all the blessings we could get.

Within two days of meeting the Pennsylvanians, I couldn't believe how much I enjoyed traveling with Bill and Mark. They were fun, adventurous, smart, courteous, kind, and robust. I was sorry not to meet their wives, who didn't like adventure trips, but looked forward to traveling with the men for the next three weeks and enjoying our developing friendship and shared sense of humor.

After another of Mark's bargaining sessions and some photo taking, we boarded the bus to Bhaktapur, a ninth-century fortified city with a square surrounded by magnificent architecture. Walking from building to building, we posed for photos in front of each. For me, it was the first of my twenty-eight rolls of film. Gopan, jokingly remarked, "I never had a group take so many pictures."

Bill, Mark, and I politely listened to the tour lecture, until we got to the Fifty-Five Window Palace with its Golden Gate leading to the palace's inner courtyards. The gleam of the gold surrounding the gate mirrored the gleam in Mark's eyes when he spotted a military guard with a Ghurka knife belted around his waist. The mustached, green-uniformed guard at the gate wore a brown hat with its strap barely touching his chin. Mark, undaunted by the uniform, decided that he really needed that knife.

As the group strolled through narrow courtyards to the Hindu temple's entrance, Mark whispered to me to stay behind with him. He said, "I want to buy that knife, and I need someone to take a photo."

I agreed, and Mark approached the guard. After a flurry of offers and counteroffers, the guard accepted a sum of fifteen dollars. Negotiations included a photograph of Mark and the guard exchanging money for the weapon, as proof of the transaction.

I thought, "This is fun, and a fabulous twist on normal sightseeing of looking, asking some questions, and moving on to another sight to repeat the routine. Did I say the word 'routine'? Not for me anymore!"

This kind of unusual situation was right up my alley. I wanted a Ghurka knife, too, but the guard had already sold his to Mark. He walked back to the entrance, and Mark and I saw him close the entrance door to the Golden Gate and open a smaller door. We watched him remove another knife from a large mound of Ghurka knives, fasten it on his white belt, and return to wait for the next gullible tourist. That would be me, but I didn't care. What a story it made, complete with a knife and a photo of me purchasing a knife from the guard. This racket was just another scheme to make a living—the economic theory of demand governed by the supply of knives.

Again, I thought that I really liked hanging around with Mark and Bill. Mark was a bit crazy, but not in a bad way.

As the group left the temple, an eleven-year-old boy followed us, asking each one what state we lived in; then he named the capital of that state. He even knew that Washington, DC, was the capital of the United States. Remembering how difficult it had been to memorize the state capitals in school, everyone was impressed by the youngster's ability. "Maybe," Mark ventured, "it was the tips that encouraged him—it's called entrepreneurship. All the same, it's midday; why isn't he in school?"

The group meandered across the square and down a side street toward a market where shops specializing in *thankas* caught my attention. Gopan asked if I knew what they were, and I shook my head, not having a clue. He explained that the Tibetan rectangular paintings on silk depicting mandalas, deities, and the Wheel of Life represented Buddhist teachings. *Thankas* are usually very colorful and detailed paintings. I examined several, but my eye always came back to a black and gold one rather than the brightly painted ones. With negotiating assistance from Gopan, I purchased the intricately painted mandala. He assured me that I had gotten the very best price.

More rounds of bargaining at another T-shirt shop yielded more souvenirs before the group finally boarded the bus back to Kathmandu for lunch at a small restaurant in the Thamel area, known as a tourist ghetto. It was a congestion of hotels, restaurants, shops, bars, and intersecting roads, but the pleasant, sunny weather persuaded our tour group to walk back to the Hotel Vajra after lunch. The dirt streets overflowed with people and vehicles; electrical lines crisscrossed overhead; dust-layered storefronts opened to the street; and vendors hawking tourist treasures attacked our senses. We saw women dressed in brightly colored garments of orange, red, blue, and green. Children, some with the most mournful looks on their faces, begged for money. Gopan nervously warned,

"We do not want to become a nation of beggars. Please do not give them any money or anything else."

Noises and horns of all types blared. Vehicles clogged the streets, ranging from three-wheeled pedal cabs to small four-passenger taxis to Chinese tractors with three wheels. A crushing number of pedestrians added to the complete chaos as we walked toward the hotel. At the confluence of six streets, I stopped to gawk at the stream of humanity and vehicles dodging each other to travel their chosen paths. I remarked to Mark and Bill that Kathmandu beat every city I'd seen in terms of congestion, but curiously, I didn't notice any offensive odors—which couldn't be said of some crowded cities in the United States.

Just then, the skies blackened with threat of a downpour, and most of our group hurried back to the hotel, while Betsy, Bill, Mark, and I continued walking toward Dunbar Square. When we spied a sign reading "E-MAIL and Telephone Calls – Second Floor," the four of us entered to inquire about the cost and take shelter. For the equivalent of fifty cents, I was able to email several friends, announcing my safe arrival and sending a hello from Kathmandu.

When we all finished our messages and phone calls, rain was falling in sheets, and the electricity had started to falter. Deciding to try for a taxi rather than walk through mud puddles, we went downstairs, and, just outside the door, a taxi was parked. After a harrowing ride through vehicles and street construction, Hotel Vajra was a welcome sight. Betsy later said, "We didn't even get wet. Maybe there is something to this manifestation stuff. It sure worked for that taxi!"

At the hotel, the others retreated to their rooms, I encountered Kanti in the lobby and accepted his invitation to see his art gallery. He proudly showed me around the space, explaining *The White Tiger* play's storyline, and telling me more about himself. An hour passed, we hugged goodbye with promises to see each other before I left Nepal.

The Suitcase Wife

Having a free evening with no dinner scheduled, Bill, Mark, Betsy, and I decided to go to a Thai restaurant. The taxi driver misunderstood—perhaps on purpose—and drove us to a Nepali restaurant instead. After removing our shoes at the entrance, a waiter directed us to the second floor for entertainment. We sat cross-legged on floor pillows and watched Nepali folk dancing performed by women in native costumes, then had dinner downstairs. The politeness and friendliness of the Nepalese added to the start of this almost unbelievable vacation.

8

After packing for our Annapurna trek scheduled for the next morning, I had trouble falling asleep and woke up four hours later at three o'clock. I tried meditating, but every pore was still open absorbing the atmosphere of Kathmandu and I couldn't relax. At five o'clock, with sleep eluding me, I quietly left the room and went up to the rooftop.

Kathmandu was shrouded in fog—it was breathtaking. I thought that it was like the IMAX movie *Everest* when a helicopter flew over foggy Kathmandu. I had wanted to feel this mysterious blue-gray fog ever since seeing that movie.

After breakfast, we boarded the bus for our first trekking experience. The harrowing ride to the airport proved normal for the Nepalese, but for us, it was like the game of "chicken" that children played by riding bicycles at each other, only to veer off at the last moment before crashing. Our bus decided to pass another bus on the four-lane road. That wasn't too sensational until a white sport utility vehicle started to pass both buses at the same instant. Three abreast, we headed down the highway into two lanes of oncoming traffic. Who would give way? Finally, the SUV backed off, allowing the oncoming traffic to flow unimpeded. As soon as possible, the SUV again attempted to pass, this time successfully. Mark and Bill yelled simultaneously, "Can you believe this?" "This is wild!"

At the airport, having no problem with luggage weight, we waited and waited for the Lumbini Airways plane. The wait calmed me. This was our first indication of Nepali time—things happen when they happen. Sure enough, the plane finally arrived. The group boarded, our duffels were loaded, and the plane took off for Pokhara and the Annapurna range of the Himalayas. During the flight, I visually surrounded the plane, the group, and the flight crew with white light and angels to give everyone an added layer of protection for a safe journey. When the plane landed and we were walking to the terminal, Bill approached me saying, "I wasn't afraid we'd crash, because you were on the plane and I knew nothing was going to happen to you."

"Well, I did try to surround the plane with white light and angels, just in case," I admitted.

That didn't surprise Bill, and he continued, "I'll make sure I sit near you from now on. Your angels won't let anything happen to you or to me."

At the Pokhara Lodge, we relaxed on the lawn until Gopan, standing on the opposite side of the lawn from Betsy and me, made the room assignments. As he began, I leaned over to Betsy and whispered, "Our room number is going to be seven."

Gopan continued down the list of assignments, finally reaching Betsy and me. He said, "Betsy and Sahara, your room number is seven."

I laughed. I had known it, but stating it and having it confirmed was a different matter. Betsy announced to the whole group, "I have to tell you, she did say that seven would be our room number."

Room assignments completed, we met our porters for an introduction to trekking. The well-groomed porters resembled one another in having black hair and being thin and short with strong upper bodies. All of them wore orange shirts with dark green pants. Gopan told Betsy and me that our porter's name was Kharna. I told my new friends, "That's close enough to Kharma, for me."

Mark and Bill's porter was named Nandala—very similar to mandala, as I pointed out. Everyone groaned and laughed at the same time.

"Perhaps, some in the group will open their minds to new ideas by the end of the trip," I thought.

A bus transported us to the center of Pokhara and the Hungry Eye restaurant, which offered a variety of dishes for lunch. I selected the spicy, hot vegetable curry and hoped I wouldn't regret it. Leaving the Hungry Eye, a noticeable absence of the traffic congestion and the constant noise of Kathmandu relaxed me. It was quiet here. Mark, Bill, and I decided to walk down to Phewa Lake, the second largest in Nepal. I marveled to myself at how quickly the three of us had become friends and wanted to spend time together. I speculated that because we were the youngest ones on the trip, maybe we had more in common.

After paying a boatman eager for customers, we were rowed around the lake in his small boat to see a temple on a small island and the first of the area's many stepped terraces we would see used for farming. The boatman knew a few words of English, just enough for Mark, Bill, and me to catch the drift of his efforts. He pointed out Machhapuchhre, better known as Fishtail Mountain, its name coming from two Nepali words: *machha* meaning fish and *puchhre* meaning tail. Machhapuchhre was considered sacred, and the locals allowed no climbing on the mountain. It was a beautiful sight with its majestic snow-covered slopes and sharp summit, which no one had ever reached, respecting the wishes of the Nepalese.

After the restful boat ride and stroll toward the Pokhara Lodge, another e-mail sign caught our attention. We entered the store and sent more messages home—this time with a "reply to author" stating we would return in one week to pick up any messages. I emailed Patsy, a friend whom I thought would reply. Bill, Mark, and I decided on the spot to email our way through Nepal, because it was such a contradiction. We could email, a technological advancement, but at the same time, observe the clerk meticulously record the amount of money given him in a ledger book.

We walked on to the Pokhara Lodge in a light rain, arriving in time to relax briefly before our six o'clock briefing, where we were all given a hat and stick for trekking. I announced that I wasn't eager for another meal at the Hungry Eye and wanted sleep more than dinner. Exhaustion from all the excitement had finally set in. Aching and chilled, I crawled under a blanket and fell sound asleep until six o'clock the following morning. Awakened by the sound of birds chirping instead of cats howling, I had finally gotten the deep sleep I needed.

Following breakfast, our porters tied a white scarf around each of our necks signifying good luck and a safe journey. Mark, Bill, and I agreed, chattering: "Let's go. I'm ready to do some trekking. We're finally going. Can you believe it?"

We walked down the lane to a bus with our duffels tied on its roof and soon started to the trailhead in the Annapurna range. On the road, we encountered a group of pack animals sauntering casually down the middle. Animals have the right-of-way, so the bus waited until they eventually moved to the side.

Up a mountain road, the bus stopped again, this time for an accident ahead on a curve. A bus and a red SUV had crashed head on, backing up traffic above and below the point of contact and delaying us for an hour. Fortunately, no injuries had occurred. My head scanned back and forth, taking in all the activity. Hundreds of people milled about chatting, using the bushes as a bathroom, taking photos, or sitting uncomfortably in crowded buses. Police eventually arrived to redirect traffic, and our bus continued on its way.

At the trailhead, the duffels were handed down to our porters. Slinging my backpack up on my shoulders, I crossed the road. I hoped that my first step on the trailhead would be not only the first step of trekking, but the beginning of many enjoyable scenes, experiences, and people. Taking time to savor meant more to me than rushing. Gopan had understood what I meant when I told him, "The end is not that important, I want to experience the journey there. That's what counts to me."

The trek began by climbing eighteen concrete steps. I commented to Mark and Bill, "Concrete steps? I thought we were going trekking."

The steps soon turned into dirt and stone paths. The paths led us past oxen pulling plows with men standing upon them to push the blades deeper and churn the ground in the terraced fields. The occasional flick of a switch on the oxen's backs urged them from row to row through the fields. The simplicity of farming methods recalled to me days I had never seen, centuries ago. My ancestors in Pennsylvania had farmed; after moving from the Poconos to escape hostile Indians, they had bought property farther south in Pennsylvania to farm and start a butcher business.

We trekkers went up and down hills, seeing more beautifully sculptured terraces carved into the mountainsides, the only possible way to farm on the steep slopes. Passing through small villages, sheaves of wheat leaned against the stone walls of buildings with roofs of thatch and slate. Women sat on their haunches, picking through the wheat grains to remove any foreign matter. Everything was done manually with no mechanization in sight. I kept pinching myself, still not believing I was trekking in Nepal.

Friendly children followed us along the trail. The real reason for their curiosity was speculation about what might be in our backpacks. Some asked for money, sweets, or pens for school to which everyone, as we had been instructed, politely answered, "No, I'm sorry, I don't have anything."

Gopan, considering the varied endurance levels of the trekkers, stopped for frequent water breaks and shopping at villages, which yielded more souvenirs and an uptick in the local economy. At one rest stop, the porters had placed the bags on top of a stone wall while we drank water. My porter pantomimed, "Do you want to try to carry your bags the way I do it?"

Experiencing life as a porter was right up my alley. Kharna carried two duffel bags weighing at least sixty pounds total and used his forehead, not his back, to carry the load. The duffel bags were strapped together with a headband attached. Slipping the headband over my forehead and leaning my body forward to counterbalance the load, I held the band in place with my hands to avoid being yanked backwards by the weight. My head hurt, and I confessed, "I can't even imagine carrying this load up and down these slippery rock trails and doing it wearing flip-flops. Porters aren't even tall."

The porters were slightly built, but their agility and strength, especially in their necks, astounded everyone. The trekkers had a real appreciation for their skills. We knew it wasn't an easy job and compensation was bound to be small. I told Mark and Bill what it was like to try to carry the duffel bags.

"Thank goodness this isn't my time to be a porter; perhaps I was one in a past lifetime, but not this one."

"I thought you might at least try to levitate," Bill said sarcastically.

"I'm saving that for the Himalayas, as the *pièce de résistance!*" I shot back.

As we trekked into the "Bee Village," Gopan asked, "Do you see those things hanging on the side of the buildings? Do you have any idea what they might be?"

No one did. He explained that the villagers made beehives from hollowed out logs. They drilled holes through the sides and made round wooden disks to plug each end. Then they attached them to the side of their homes.

I was looking at all the beehives and not paying attention. I slipped and almost fell on the rocky downhill path.

Gopan, offering to carry my backpack, told me, "Next time, let me know when you're going to fall."

"No problem," I told him, "I can do that."

As the rain steadily increased, the stones grew increasingly slippery. I asked Gopan, "Are there any more stone steps to navigate?"

"Yes!"

Just kidding, I said, "Get ready, I might be falling."

Those words were barely out of my mouth when my feet slipped. I caught myself, probably not with the most graceful of moves, but I didn't fall.

Gopan suggested that I step sideways down the rocky paths so as not to fall again. "Don't step with your toes facing forward."

I had known better than to make such a dumb remark about being ready to fall: "I need to change my thinking patterns to avoid making bad ideas come true."

As we trekked through damp areas in the forest, up and down the trail, leeches attacked us appearing from out of nowhere. Little one-inch leeches, clinging to rocks, stretched into two-inch leeches, wildly waving themselves back and forth and straining to attach their bodies to any human passing by. Gopan warned, "Quickly! Quickly! Move! There are many leeches, please walk fast!"

Several trekkers didn't listen. At a rest stop, they removed their boots and found leeches gnawing on their feet. The leeches had squirmed their way into the boots. I proudly announced, "No leech made it into my leather boots to suck my blood."

With the rest stop over, I quickly walked ahead of everyone to find a secluded place in the woods for a bathroom break. Picking a spot free of leeches wasn't difficult. However, the leeches quickly picked up my human scent. I looked down, seeing upright leeches lashing themselves around hoping to attach themselves to something, specifically me. I rushed to finish and avoid any chance of leeches crawling inside my pants or boots. My body shivered at the thought.

A short distance away, we saw the day's final destination, the Sanctuary Lodge. Crossing a suspension bridge over the Modi River loomed ahead; a wooden-planked suspension bridge, with open sides, suspended by cables over the chasm. My heart raced harder. I feared heights, but refused to let anyone else know it. Allowing the person in front of me to reach the other side, I swallowed, took a deep breath, and rushed as fast as I dared across the bridge, holding on the side cables as I walked the entire length. I celebrated to myself that I had done it: "That wasn't so bad. It didn't sway *too* much."

Little did I know, but the next few weeks would offer more suspension bridges to cross, some not nearly so sturdy as this one. With the first bridge crossing behind us, we hiked a short distance, turning left into the Sanctuary Lodge compound. An ex-Ghurka soldier greeted us and pointed to the path toward the dining-area porch.

Local men had constructed the lodge, but ex-Ghurka soldiers managed it. They had gained a reputation as fierce fighters while serving in the British army. In the lodge, each of eight bedrooms had a private bathroom complete with a flush toilet and hot water and electricity.

My eyes swept over the landscaping of red and white flowerbeds and "Sanctuary Lodge" spelled out with smooth, white-painted river stones on the lawn. Porch chairs positioned outside our rooms, welcomed Betsy's and my tired bodies. "I'm taking off my boots and checking for leeches before I grab a book," I told Betsy.

Feeling relaxed after an hour, I headed to the main dining room for the afternoon Happy Hour. My stomach and intestines churned and growled. "Oh no," I thought, "Please don't let this be the beginning of an intestinal problem. I can't afford to be sick on the trail. I'd better be cautious in what I eat."

Around the table in the lodge, enjoying beverages, the group rehashed the day's activities. I said that I could have happily trekked for another two hours, that my days of conditioning had paid off.

"Sure you could have hiked on—Gopan was carrying your backpack. How did you manage that?" Bill asked.

"He offered, so I accepted. No big deal."

During dinner, I mentioned that I wasn't feeling well, and a flood of suggestions about foods to avoid poured my way. Thinking that, at the least, a few days of Pepto-Bismol stretched before me, I headed back to the room. Sitting on the porch outside, I contemplated the beautiful scenery, peace, and serenity that surrounded me. Despite feeling physically troubled, I was comforted by this connection to nature and the universe, represented by the stars just beginning to glow dimly.

Sanctuary Lodge was solar-powered and turned off its electricity in the early evening, making reading possible only by flashlight. After an active day, I dozed off quickly, only to awaken at two o'clock in the morning to the loud roar of the nearby stream. I thought, "If it isn't cats crying or birds chirping in the middle of the night, it's now rushing water."

Lying in bed, my intestines rumbled with irritation. I decided to direct healing energy into my abdominal area. Rubbing my hands together until they became warm, I laid them on my abdomen, feeling some relief.

At five-thirty, no longer able to lie in bed, I dressed and strolled down to a large rock overlooking the river for a morning meditation outdoors. Acknowledgment that I was a part of nature and not separated at all was confirmed by the voice of the river and by the rising sun. As that realization overcame me, tears slid down my cheeks. On the way back to the lodge, I looked up and saw magnificent Sacred Mountain emerging before me, its awesome beauty breathtaking. The dawn-tinged sky was a perfect backdrop and contrast to the towering mountain's white snow-covered peaks.

9

Day two of the trek, we climbed steep steps to narrow foot-wide trails and trudged through loose earth up the hills. My breathing became labored, but I attributed it to the more difficult physical activity. After constantly rising, the trail leveled off, and I had my first long-range view of the morning. Unfortunately what I saw was another suspension bridge looming in the distance. This time, however, I felt a bit more confident, so I enjoyed the day's first relatively level walk. By the time we had reached the bridge, I was thinking, "I've got the hang of this, no problem."

I closely followed two porters across the bridge, not taking into account that the more people crossing at the same time, the more the swaying increased. The bridge's floor boards were old and loose and caused my trekking stick to poke into the crevices instead of falling on a board's flat surface. Somehow I kept my balance, even looking over the side to realize that the river gorge was deeper than yesterday's. I made it across the river, gaining more confidence and made a mental note, "Next time, I'll remember to wait until others cross first before I start."

When his group had all crossed to the other side, Gopan announced that from here on we would encounter many mule and yak trains loaded with supplies for the remote villages. He said that the trains *always* have the right-of-way and cautioned everyone to move out of the way fast, because sometimes there was very little time to react. When yak bells clanked through the crisp air, Gopan's group remembered his directions and quickly moved to hug the side of the mountain and allow the fast-moving animals to pass. Yaks stopped for nothing and for no one.

Betsy, Mark, Bill, and I were walking together as we trekked higher and higher. We came to a house with a large stone terrace overlooking the valley and the sacred Fishtail Mountain, stopping to photograph the beautiful view and have a water break on the terrace. When the entire group had arrived we were invited inside the home to see how a Nepali family lived.

A mother, holding a small child in her lap sat near the entrance as we filed in. I noticed several small kittens cuddled up together on a towel in a bedroom. The kitchen was small with a tamped-down earthen floor, and small grates were positioned over a wood cooking-fire on the floor. With no countertops or cabinets with a sink, the women had to squat to cook meals and wash dishes. I said to Mark, "I thought I had it bad, but these poor women's knees and backs must be killing them by the time a meal is over."

As we left, Mark videotaped the women and children, who broke into giggles when they saw themselves on the video replay. Thanking the women for their hospitality, Gopan's group trekked back to Sanctuary Lodge. When the trail cut through cornfields, I noticed broken, foot-high corn stalks and asked Gopan what had happened. He explained that corn, their main source of food, was damaged by a recent hailstorm. Farmers were concerned that not enough was left for winter. Having just been in a family's home, I could feel their concern for a less bountiful harvest when they relied so heavily on their crops for survival.

The combination of too much water and a small bladder soon sent me heading into the woods again. I told Gopan I would catch up and asked him to take my backpack. Cautiously entering the brush by the side of the trail, I was pleased to find no leeches but I brushed against a stinging nettle plant. It felt like thousands and thousands of needles pricking my skin, and they would burn for hours. I caught up to the group and retrieved my backpack just in time to see Mark in action.

Never able to pass up an opportunity to bargain, Mark had spotted a knife, strapped to the waist of a farmer plowing his terraced field. He asked Gopan to help him with the language to acquire his next treasure. Climbing over rocks, they crossed the farmer's field and started negotiating a price. The farmer finally settled for five U.S. dollars, and both he and Mark were happy. Wonder if they, too, have an old saying about one man's junk is another's treasure? The entire transaction was videoed by someone in the group, and our majority opinion was that the farmer was already laughing, "Can you imagine, an American just paid me five U.S. dollars for that old knife?"

After a light vegetarian lunch at Sanctuary Lodge, we set off for another trek, more like a hike, to Birethanti, a small village nearby. A dog from the lodge followed us on the trail. Suddenly a village dog attacked with teeth bared. Growling and lunging at each other, the dogs were difficult to separate. Village women threw rocks at the lodge dog. We hurried on when the fight came to an end as quickly as it had started. Because of the delay, a plan to visit children in school was aborted. Most had left for the day, and only a few boys were playing volleyball on a terraced area. They played quietly—no showboating, no yelling or screaming, another example of graciousness and politeness to each other.

Following Gopan, the group continued through Birethanti and up another path to a waterfall. Mark, Bill, and I climbed down a steep embankment to a seemingly crystal-clear pool at the waterfall's base. I reached my cupped hands into the cool water and splashed refreshing water over my face. Immediately I saw brown foam formed by the waterfall collecting on the water's edge. I'd once been told that brown foam meant polluted water, full of bacteria. Whether my information was correct or not, I yelled to the group, "Don't touch the water—it's polluted."

The Suitcase Wife

When we three climbed back up the hill, I wiped my face and hands with an antiseptic cloth. Then Bill mentioned that he would swear he'd seen a body or something down there wedged between two rocks with more stones on top of it. He thought he'd seen the heel of a foot and was positive about the bad odor. With binoculars, Mark, Bill, and I tried to focus on the area, but nothing was clear. Finally two guides walked down the hill to get a better view. When they returned, they said that it was just a monkey. Mark, Bill, and I looked skeptically at each other; Mark said quietly, "We've not seen any monkeys nearby, nor have we been told we were in monkey territory."

"That wasn't any monkey," Bill said, as we resumed walking.

The group came upon two porters, each carrying a four-tiered wire cage packed with chickens. Seen from the rear, the cages covered most of the porters' bodies, showing only their legs from their knees to their sandaled feet.

When we met small children on the trail, most of them would place their palms together, raise them to their chests, and say *namaste*. They nodded their heads, their equivalent of a friendly hello.

We saw two small children who were enjoying a simple game; their squeals of laughter brought joy to my heart. Each pitched a bottle cap toward a line drawn on a concrete step. Whoever got closest to the line won, and hit his fist on top of the other boy's fist. The game's simplicity and the boy's ingenuity to create fun from practically nothing reminded me of a time in my life when there wasn't money for fancy toys. After a brief stop in a local art gallery, we returned to Sanctuary Lodge for dinner and another early light's out at nine o'clock.

I awoke at a quarter to two in the morning, seeming unable to get off my American time and get in Nepal's time zone. I wondered how much longer this would last. I took a short nap, only to rise at five-thirty and walk down to the river.

This time when I sat meditating on the rock, I felt as if I were a bubble in the stream—full of joy, life, and always changing. The river's roar surrounded me.

Coming out of my reverie, I watched three young boys standing in the river pulling in their fishnets. When they walked past me, the boys said hello in English. Pointing to the string of fish, I asked, "How many fish did you catch?"

When they showed their seven fish, I noticed their eyes glancing towards the Sony Walkman on the rock behind me. One boy, with excitement in his voice, said, "Walkman?"

I nodded.

"How much?"

I hesitantly answered, "Three thousand rupees."

His eyes widened in amazement. My meditation tape was the only one I had, but the boys didn't care; the opportunity to listen to a Sony Walkman delighted them. One of the boys understood English quite well, and remembering that I had purchased a Nepali music tape in Pokhara, I ran back to the room to fetch it for them to hear. Everybody was fascinated, the boys by the Sony Walkman and me by the consideration the boys showed one another. Each allowed the other to listen without rushing—no poking, yelling, or grabbing at the earphones. Such patience and fairness amazed me once again.

One of the Ghurka soldier guards came down to the river to check out the situation. He asked me if I were all right. I replied, "I'm fine, I was just talking to the boys about fishing."

10

After eating breakfast and packing our laundered trail clothing, the group met for the two-and-a-half-hour walk back to the tour bus. Several people, including Mark, were feeling ill. Arrangements were made to take them back to Pokhara after leaving the rest of us at the trailhead for Dhampus. Goodbyes were said to the ill ones, and we began the strenuous uphill climb through what I christened the Land of the Leeches—which, by the way, attacked again.

At the first water break, porters pulled out bags of cotton balls soaked in salt water to rub the slithering leeches off our boots before they squirmed into the shoes' crevices and through mesh insets. Apparently leeches disliked salt and loosened their tenacious grip. Fortunately, my "all-leathers" were splendid again; the leeches couldn't crawl in. As added insurance, I carried a small branch as I walked to flick them away. I confessed to Bill that leeches gave me the willies.

He said, "Sahara, just treat them as a part of trekking and ignore them."

"I wish," raced through my mind.

As before, when the leeches smelled humans, they gyrated vigorously, hoping to attach to anyone who came near. I had had enough. At the next break, I decided to get in front of the group and let the trekkers behind deal with the leeches activated by my scent. The fast climb was difficult, but it paled in comparison to the leeches. I had seen Nepali women gathering forest greens, casually reach down to pick leeches off their sandaled feet as they chatted. To them, it was life; to me, it was disgusting.

The Suitcase Wife

I—and a porter who had secretly followed me as protection—finally reached a flat section overlooking a valley. While we waited for the others, I scanned the valley: miles and miles of terraced green fields and small white buildings scattered here and there. Overcast skies softened illumination of the scene, but the view was still spectacular. It was easy to see why supplies had to be transported by mule or yak. The rugged terrain discouraged laying railroad tracks or building highways.

As the rest of the group arrived, everyone took off their boots and socks to check for leeches. Good news: no one had an extra passenger. Trekkers sat down on a bright blue tarpaulin for a simple picnic lunch of hard-boiled eggs, coleslaw, pizza slices, bananas, and the usual bottled water. Warm and exhausted from the uphill climb, several people lay on their backs holding up blue, red, and yellow umbrellas for shade. I asked Betsy, "Doesn't a vision of Mary Poppins pop into your mind with all these umbrellas?"

"Sort of," Betsy said, trying to be nice.

Energized by food, the trekkers took only half an hour to reach Basanta Lodge in Dhampus, about 5,400 feet above sea level. Near the end of the trail, we saw several bulls and cows grazing in adjacent fields. Gopan warned us to keep a safe distance from the animals, but his words were scarcely said when the closest bull decided to butt Pete, a retired white-haired doctor from Oregon, who had failed to move fast and far enough from the field's edge. The blow, from anything but a bull, would have been more like a nudge. Fortunately, there was no injury except to Pete's ego. He had appeared to be a calm man, but his anger flared so quickly he had to be restrained from hitting the bull with his stick. Privately I thought, "There's another side to this man I never want to experience again. His wife is probably happy she decided to stay home alone for three weeks."

Arrival at the Basanta Lodge ended another trekking day, but several walked past the lodge to see the view. A long table and chairs had been set out for dinner on a gently sloping rear lawn bounded by a two-foot stone wall. However, the view was obscured by clouds, and within minutes rain began falling. The outdoor dinner was forced inside.

By this time, my stomach and intestines were in turmoil, and pink Pepto-Bismol tablets were a constant presence. I'd been careful to drink bottled water, but it suddenly dawned on me that I'd consumed dairy products—yogurt, cheese, milk— that I avoided at home because they made my stomach cramp. I could only think that excitement overcame my caution. What else could have made me think I could eat dairy in Nepal?

Following a light dinner, I dressed warmly and sat out on the back lawn with Bill and Pete until ten thirty, watching the stars above the Annapurna mountain range. In such complete darkness, the stars seemed to jump out of the sky. I said that I had never seen stars look so large and so close and wished that Mark could see them, too. Bill agreed and wondered how he was doing. I thought that Bill seemed lost without his brother, but said nothing. The quietness was invaded only by the sound of crickets. I felt peacefulness moving through my whole body. I remembered all the night sounds since arriving in Nepal—cats in Kathmandu, birds chirping in Pokhara, the river's roar at Sanctuary Lodge, and now the crickets of Dhampus. Only two sounds were conspicuously absent—cars and horns.

Like clockwork, I woke up at quarter till two again, and my usual tactics to ease myself back into sleep were ineffective. Feeling I might miss something and my body filled with energy, I crawled out of bed at five o'clock to watch the sunrise on the Annapurna mountain range. With a chill in the air, the shimmering light turned the mountain peaks pink against the white snow. Clouds intermittently covered the peaks, including Machhapuchhre.

As the sun rose higher, Bill wandered out to join me, while I sipped electrolyte fluid to replace some of the nutrients I had lost. "This stuff tastes terrible, but I can only hope it helps me later."

After breakfast, we packed and started down to the bus, waiting at another trailhead. Initially the cool mountain temperature required long underwear, at least for me, who hated feeling cold. As the sun warmed and the elevation dropped, I heated up, but there wasn't a place in sight to remove my long johns. I told Betsy I should have toughed it out this morning. Betsy just nodded.

Along the trail, a dog attached himself to me. During lunch, Bill remarked that my four-legged friend had walked with me the entire way. I told him that I seemed to attract animals, and followed with a story:

> Several years ago, when I hiked the Grand Canyon Bright Angel Trail, a mountain goat bounded from the brush, stopped in the middle of the trail waiting for me to come closer. Keeping about ten feet ahead of me, we walked until we came to a switchback. Then he would leap up the side of the switchback and wait for me in the middle of the trail until I came around the bend. Proceeding to the next switchback, he would look back to make sure I was still following. The goat and I continued in this manner through four switchbacks, before he left me. Other hikers mentioned that he seemed to be my pet.

I enjoyed telling the story, but thought, "They'll all think I'm crazy now, for sure."

The trekkers, strung out along the trail, approached a village, and several small children rushed out to stare at us. They seemed especially attracted to Paige, the shy, sweet wife of a North Carolina accountant. The children tugged at her red jacket tied around her waist, then, as she was quite petite, tugged on her. Paige, emphatically said "No, No, No," shaking her finger at them. Suddenly one of the little boys ran ahead of her, stopped, pulled his pants down, and mooned her. Everyone was amazed and laughed wondering where he had learned that stunt in Nepal. Paige was still stunned— straitlaced, conservative Paige, of all people the little boy could have chosen to moon, was funny in itself. She was still bemused when Gopan's group boarded the bus to return to Pokhara for lunch at the Hungry Eye.

I asked Bill if that was the only restaurant in town. Bill figured that maybe it was, but anyway he had planned to hurry back to the lodge to see how Mark was doing. I told him I would stop by later. Walking back to the Pokhara Lodge alone, I stopped in several stores for handmade paper and postcards, and strolled past makeshift shops with corrugated metal roofs topped by large rocks to hold them down in strong winds. I saw men sitting under trees, vigorously treadling their ancient sewing machines to stitch T-shirts and shorts for tourists. Stopping at the e-mail office produced no results, no replies.

When I arrived at the lodge, I went first to check on Mark. He looked fairly good but said he still didn't feel great and didn't think he'd be able to go trekking up to Tengboche Monastery.

"Don't say that, you've got to go with us! You don't have a choice. You had *better* get better. Tonight, just get all the rest you can," I gently scolded.

With a welcome free afternoon, I sat on the lawn reading, but when dinner meant going back to the Hungry Eye, I mentioned to Gopan that I couldn't eat there again. "All I really want are some crisp McDonald's french fries."

Later I thought, "Like he knew what I was talking about when I asked for McDonald's french fries! No wonder he looked at me so strangely."

11

I slept until three thirty the next morning, feeling triumphant at last and meditating until a reasonable time to crawl from the bed. Before breakfast, Betsy and I checked on Mark who still felt bad. I remembered the echinacea I had brought, after debating whether or not I would need it. Now I figured that Mark had been the reason it went into the suitcase. He swallowed the medicine, while I reminded him again that he must get well to go on the Tengboche Monastery extension. All the way to breakfast he assured Betsy and me that he was trying.

We left Pokhara Lodge, with more white scarves around our necks to insure a safe journey. It was a two-hour bus ride to our starting point for paddling down the Modi River. At first, we saw boys in long pants, long-sleeved white shirts, and red-and-white-striped ties and girls in dark skirts and white shirts with backpacks slung across their shoulders, waiting for a school bus.

Shortly before arriving at the river, the bus driver stopped and Gopan advised, "We're stopping for a potty break—either go now or hold it for the next two hours while we float down the river."

I looked around, saying to Betsy, "I don't see any restrooms—only the great outdoors. This must be no time for modesty."

Gopan instructed us, "Women to the left side with bushes and rocks. Men to the right."

It was amazing how inhibitions were swept aside. Back on the bus, we traveled a short distance, before continuing down a deeply rutted incline just wide enough to maneuver. All the passengers severely listed to the right. At the river's edge, guides gave us paddling lessons and instructions as to what to do if anyone fell out of the raft. We were issued blue helmets, yellow paddles, and faded orange lifejackets. I said to Bill, "I hope I can remember all this, especially if I fall into the river. You'll help me out if I go overboard?"

"Sure, no problem, Sahara; but don't worry, you won't be falling in. The water doesn't look too rough," Bill reassured me.

Mark, Bill, Betsy, two other travelers and I climbed into a blue rubber raft. Mark insisted that Bill and I sit in front, since the guide had requested stronger paddlers to sit there. "Okay? Does that work for everyone?" Mark asked.

All agreed that Bill and I would be the front paddlers. Mark said, "I'm going to sit in the back, because I'm still not feeling up to snuff."

By Mark's opting out of the main action, we knew he was sick. After our waterproof duffel bags were tied down in the middle of the raft and three paddlers were seated on each side with one foot in a stirrup for paddling support, our guide pushed off. He hopped in and led some paddling practice in the calmer waters of the Modi River. When he screamed, "paddle," Bill and I were to dig into the water and paddle hard, especially through rapids. We went down the Modi River a short way, until it flowed into the Seti River, which we would travel to the end of the trip. As we moved slowly through the placid water, I became quiet to let the river claim me and calm flow through my body.

Mark called up to Bill, "With me back here out of commission, can you please video the sights? And don't forget, pan slowly or people will get sick watching it."

"Sure, any other instructions?" Bill answered.

The raft floated past water buffalo cooling themselves in the river. As Bill scanned them with the camcorder, Betsy's head got in the way. Joking, I said, "Can you tell which is which?"

Everyone booed or hissed, and Mark said, "Sahara, *that* wasn't very nice, just wait."

From the reactions, I knew that memories would be long, and paybacks would come later in the trip; the only uncertainty was *when*.

Floating through the countryside, no electric wires spoiled photos; only terraced farms dating back centuries and thatch-roofed buildings were evident. The river extended its bounty to fishermen throwing large triangular nets and cast nets. Children frolicked in the water and yelled and waved to the passing rafters. A stony beach provided a rest area for a box lunch from—where else—the Hungry Eye restaurant. I said to my raft mates, "I hope this is the last time I eat Hungry Eye food. It might be the best tasting and safest food in Pokhara, but I'm tired of it."

Refreshed, we pushed off down the river again, going through a valley and Class 2 rapids before arriving at the riverside camp that would be our home for two nights. We had expected nothing more than sleeping bags, but this was the best—yellow tents erected on a concrete floor with a thatch-roofed pavilion over each tent. Inside were clean linens and pillows on the cots, a pitcher of boiled water on the table between, and even rugs on the floor. Zippered netting over the tent's entrance allowed ventilation and a view of the outdoors.

"This is my idea of roughing it, especially in the middle of nowhere," I exclaimed. "Pretty cool."

On the tiny porch, two cushioned rattan chairs invited sitting, reading, or watching the river rush by. Toilets and showers, complete with hot and cold water, were in a building close to our tent.

"These little luxuries sure surprised me," said Betsy, "I never expected this, did you, Sahara?"

"Hardly, and I'm so glad I'm not going to sleep on the ground. Can you imagine some of our fellow travelers sleeping on the ground? It would never happen," I replied.

We had barely inspected our tent, when afternoon tea was served outside at the round stone conversation pit in the middle of the compound. Afterwards I checked on Mark who still wasn't feeling well. He told me he didn't think he'd be well enough to go on the Tengboche extension, and I asked if I could try some energy work on him. When he agreed, I placed my hands above his body feeling the energy travel through my body, down my arms, into my hands, and into Mark's body. Although the outside temperature wasn't hot, I soon became wet with perspiration running down my body and face, dripping off my chin. When I finished, my hands were still extremely warm and pulsing.

"I don't have a clue as to whether it worked," Mark reflected. "A wave of something went across my abdomen, and, when I closed my eyes, waves of swirling colors passed by."

"I truly want you to join the group for the Himalayan trek. It wouldn't be the same without you. You've *got* to go. Bill will really miss you and worry, if you don't."

Dinner was announced, and we headed down the stone path, bordered with flowers and plants, to the dining room. A dreadful thought popped into my mind that maybe the Hungry Eye did the catering for this river camp. Much to my delight, an in-house staff had prepared an excellent meal. I even got what I had wished for last night—crispy french fries were served as an appetizer. They weren't in a yellow and red McDonald's holder, but they were delicious and just what my stomach wanted.

Sleeping soundly until four thirty the next morning, I tiptoed out of the tent and climbed the ladder to a tree house overlooking the river to meditate. When I came down, I strolled to the beach where a young boy, throwing a cast net, gradually worked his way up the river to where I was standing. He pulled the tiny silver fish out of his net each time, tucking them into a small woven basket tied with a cord around his waist. The quietness of the morning, interrupted only by the slap of the cast net against the water, the birds, and the crickets chirping in the background enveloped me.

Slowly everyone awoke in camp, and an attendant came to serve tea in each tent. Betsy and I heard him approach with his standard greeting: Good morning, how are you today? I walked out of the tent for tea listening to my Sony Walkman which he noticed. Asking, if he could listen, I explained that I hadn't brought any music cassettes. He seemed disappointed. In this remote spot apparently no radio stations were available for listening either.

After breakfast, everyone except Mark followed several guides to Saranghat, a small village. Although we all wanted Mark to take it easy and get well, we missed his bargaining enthusiasm. Passing terraced rice paddies plugged with tender shoots, the guides explained the irrigation system that allowed water at the top field to flow down into the lower levels. The sight of bright green, multi-layered fields with sparkling clear water cascading down the hillside through each paddy was mesmerizing.

We hiked through cornfields, careful not to trample the farmers' future food supply, climbing up hills, through streams, over logs crossing gullies. At one point, a fence blocked our passage. Someone had cut notches into two logs at intervals as high as a step and leaned them against both sides of the fence. Carefully each hiker climbed sideways up, over, and down the fence. Farther down the path, a young boy, waving his arms, shouted for us to stop. He pointed to an agitated hive of black bumblebees whose stings were very dangerous. The hikers waited patiently until the bees retreated into their hive, then quickly and quietly slipped by.

The village, as soon as we arrived, affected us all with a feeling of being caught in a time warp. It was immediately apparent that this wasn't a shopping stop. Resting on a bench and looking around the village, I thought that probably very little had changed in the past hundred years, except maybe some of the clothing styles and dishes made of metal. Women still used a centuries-old rice huller. Gopan pointed to a corncrib on stilts several feet off the ground from which an eagle's wing fluttered in the breeze and asked if anyone knew what that eagle's wing was used for. Someone guessed that it scared away birds from eating the corn.

"Yes, that's right. What else?" Gopan continued. No one answered.

"It's also used to scare off evil spirits."

Walking through the village, I noticed several substantial stone buildings and asked Gopan why there was such a great difference between them and the other homes. He explained that those sons were serving in the British army and sent their pay back home, so their families could afford to build better houses.

A woman passed carrying such a huge amount of greenery on her head that she could barely be seen herself. Gopan asked if anyone could guess her name. Without waiting for a reply, he answered his own question, eliciting a chorus of groans: "She's the tree lady."

Small girls approached the strangers with obvious curiosity. One of them, in a lace-trimmed purple and red dress, with turquoise and pink bows in her ponytail, openly stared. She was so natural and ingenuous, willing to have her picture taken but unwilling to smile unless something truly amused her. Gopan had already instructed the travelers: "When you photograph individuals, please respect their privacy and first ask if they would like to have their photo taken."

We went down a hill to a school for children five to ten years old. The schoolteacher escorted the curious travelers into an empty classroom where he answered questions about education and his school. Then we crossed the schoolyard to a cluster of stone buildings with slate roofs. A few of the classrooms had windows without glass. Quiet children in one classroom were working intently. In another, four little girls were singing Nepalese folk songs, and we crowded the small doorway to listen. Finding no space left to stand, I circled around to the open window to peek in and listen. When the little girls spied me at the window, they began to giggle. I smiled happily, thinking what a delight it was to hear their laughter.

More squeals of surprised laughter rang out when Paige's husband Ralph took teeth out of his mouth and pretended to swallow them. The children were wide-eyed and spellbound trying to figure out whether he had really eaten his teeth. When supposedly he coughed the teeth back out, the amazement grew. Ralph held up them up for the children to see, then surreptitiously replaced his bridge. The little children laughed and clapped so hard, Ralph repeated his trick. Even the adults were amused by his silliness. No wonder that the children were befuddled; it was unlikely that many people here would have that kind of "bridge."

Saying goodbye to the students, we headed back to the river camp on the same trail. I felt good walking, and Gopan, another guide, and I started to pick up the pace and hike harder and faster. There was no plan or agreement to do so; it just happened. I needed the strenuous workout, and surprisingly, I kept up with their practiced strides until a short distance from the camp. My body was dehydrating; I said, "Let's stop for water, I need a break."

I drank from my water bottle while Gopan and the other guide drank from the nearby stream. Happy to feel good again, there was no way I would drink stream water and risk recurrence of my stomach complaints. We soon continued our race back to camp, and arrived half an hour ahead of the others. Later, I told Bill that I definitely needed that fast-paced exercise to stay in shape for the Himalaya trek.

I showered and dressed, then stopped in to check on how Mark was feeling. Finding him a bit better, I asked if he wanted another energy session. He agreed but needed a few minutes to finish postcards to his wife and children. While waiting, I meditated, and an unmistakable message came to me: "Drink water to flush out the system, not fruit juice. Would you wash your body in fruit juice?" I shared the message with Mark before starting. My hands turned red hot as the energy poured through them; at one point, it felt like molten lava flowed from my hands. When the energy gradually subsided, I knew the session was over. Mark told me that he had seen white light but couldn't hold it very long. "I still don't think I'm going to be well enough for the Tengboche trek, but I do know that I'm feeling better."

"No! Think positively—you *will* be going. I suggest that you visualize the flight to Lukla in the Himalayas, putting on your hiking boots, and trekking up the mountain trails—and having the stamina and strength to do it."

Actually I was thrilled that he had seen white light, which made me think he was healing. I wondered how Mark really felt about my energy sessions and meditation messages. He was too kind a person to laugh at my beliefs, but then he could refuse them, couldn't he?

In the early evening of our final night on the river, I sat with my fellow travelers in the stone-circled area. During these late afternoon happy hours, we chatted about the day's events and speculated on what tomorrow would bring. Several of the group said that they had all agreed to ask me to conjure up a Bengal tiger when we got to the jungle the next day. Taken aback, I laughed, "First off, I'd call that *to manifest* and not *to conjure.*"

When I saw that some of them were serious, I said, "Secondly, I can't do it all by myself; you're all going to have to help. Here's how: go to bed tonight and think about the Bengal tiger, about wanting to see it; then send that thought out to the universe."

I watched total disbelief spread over most of their faces and could almost hear their thoughts: "Oh, sure, lady—and what planet did you say you were from?"

Nevertheless, if I had had to guess, I'd venture to say almost all of them would do exactly what I had suggested. I knew for sure that I would.

"Will it work?" I wondered.

12

I woke up early as usual and headed to the river. At home I would have lain in bed and waited for the alarm to get me up for work, but here it was different—relaxed and not a care in the world. Who wouldn't love this life? Getting away from my normal routine was exactly what I had needed.

Heading back from the river in time for breakfast, I noticed a small wooden trough with a carved head of a Bengal tiger at one end, water spouting from its mouth. I wondered if that were an omen and pointed it out to Mark, Betsy, and Bill when they joined me. "Here's your Bengal tiger, folks. We did a great job of manifesting, didn't we?" I said.

We ran into Pete at breakfast, and he appeared confused. Concerned, I asked if I could help. He gazed back at me and very seriously asked me what day it was. Realizing that one sometimes loses track of time when traveling in a foreign land, I told him what day it was. Then he confessed that he knew the days at home by what his wife made for breakfast: Monday, oatmeal; Tuesday, fruit and yogurt; Wednesday, pancakes; Thursday, soft-boiled egg and toast; Friday, cereal with fruit; Saturday, waffles; and Sunday, eggs and bacon.

"No wonder you're confused," I said, "not a single breakfast on our trip has matched your schedule."

I wondered how one lived on such a set schedule, but figured if it worked for them, that was all that mattered. "Losing track of time is one of my goals," I decided, but, I don't think it's Pete's intent."

After breakfast, everyone changed into bathing suits and went to the riverbank. The porters had secured our waterproof duffel bags on rafts awaiting us for the trip along the

The Suitcase Wife

Seti River. During recent rainstorms at the camp, the rafts had been pulled out of the water for safety, but the sky was clear that morning. Bill became excited when he saw the water flowing swiftly from the storms and asked Betsy and me if we were ready for a wild ride. With the rise in water level, the day's rafting promised to be lively. I shared Bill's enthusiasm; Betsy, not at all. We were told that this would be the final river run before the start of the monsoon season. The river guide steered the raft into the current as Bill and I gave each other a high five to signal our readiness for a day of hard paddling.

We paddled intermittently at the guide's signal and went through some fairly mild Class 2 rapids safely. A waterproof barrel strapped to the raft up front between Bill and me kept cameras dry in rough waters, and the two of us were responsible for collecting and stowing cameras away—in addition to our serious paddling duties. Bill said, "We have to get this routine down by judging how far away the rapids are and how much time we need to get the cameras passed up and sealed in the barrel before we have to start paddling hard."

For the most part, our timing was good—except for one occasion. We got the cameras into the barrel, but had trouble replacing the metal sealing rim. In the struggle to close the barrel, my foot slipped out of the raft stirrup. Just then, the guide yelled at Bill and me to paddle. The raft was heading into serious rapids. I started to paddle as hard as I could without the stirrup.

The raft was rocking from side to side, buffeted by the rapids. The guide shouted louder, "Paddle! Paddle!"

The raft heaved to the side. I felt my body slip toward the water. In a split second I tried to remember the instructions about what to do if anyone fell in the river. Quickly I stopped paddling and, flinging one arm over the barrel, held on until the raft righted itself for an instant. I saw two choices: stop paddling and hang on or fall overboard. I hugged the barrel and rode out the rapids.

When we reached calmer water, my paddling partner taunted, "Isn't it time you stopped loafing and started paddling?"

I shot back, "Thanks for reminding me, Bill. I almost fell out of the damn raft."

Bill wasn't completely unscathed from the episode either; he had cut his finger trying to secure the barrel's metal rim and worried about infection. Soon, the rapids behind us, we relaxed and laughed at various silly comments. Drifting down the Seti, we saw children swimming, water buffalo drinking at its banks and men fishing with a triangular type of net used for hundreds of years.

Since Mark, Bill, and I had at one time lived close to where George Washington had crossed the Delaware River, Mark tried to recreate the scene for the rafters by kneeling in the raft, his helmet substituting for a tricorne, and urging, "Stroke. Stroke," while everyone else paddled, and he looked serious.

"Mark, in case you haven't noticed, we're paddling, not sculling," I teased. "In Philadelphia we do that on the Schuylkill River, not the Delaware."

When we came to more rapids, children on the bank watched and hollered, as we paddled through the turbulent water. Even grown Nepalese men and women, on occasional suspension bridges high above the water, stopped to wave and shout. I was reminded of my childhood living near the Northeast extension of the Pennsylvania Turnpike, when my friends and I would stop on the overpass and wave to the cars passing below, always hoping the occupants would notice and wave back. The real prize was when a trucker would blast his truck's air horn. Similarly the Nepalese children enjoyed our responsive waves and shouts. These were probably distractions in their mundane lives, as they had been for me in Pennsylvania.

Shortly before the rafting portion of the trip ended, my fellow travelers reminded me that they soon would expect me to manifest the Bengal tiger. I tried to ignore them, feeling uncomfortably pressured.

The rafts finally reached our destination, a beach scattered with large boulders. Gopan instructed us to pick a boulder, get changed behind it, and meet him at a building atop a small hill. I scanned the beach for an appropriate boulder. All the so-called "bathhouses" were out in the open with nothing in sight but a road and the building up the hill. I, not wanting to sit in a wet bathing suit for two and a half hours, felt this was no time for modesty. "I'm changing," I told Betsy, "and ignoring any catcalls from vehicles up on the road. No big deal."

By the time we were changed, the porters had toted all the duffel bags up the stony hill and hoisted them atop the bus roof for tying down. The next leg of our adventure was the ride to Royal Chitwan National Park to see the elusive Bengal tiger—maybe. Soon we saw monkeys scampering on the beach by the river, the first sighting of monkeys since leaving Kathmandu. The elevation here was lower than when we hiked in the Annapurna range near Pokhara.

The bus traveled on toll roads through small villages. At tollbooths, a fellow jumped off our bus to pay the appropriate fees, said to be allocated to financing road improvements. One particular tollbooth listed the fees in red letters on a white board—fifteen categories covered passage of any vehicle or animal. A bus, truck, or lorry commanded fifteen rupees, while a big tractor only cost ten and a small bus, five. The toll for Nepalese rickshaws was five rupees, but the costs to foreigners rose dramatically. Large foreign trucks required payment of seventy-five rupees, and their autos or taxis paid twenty-five rupees, five times as much as natives paid. Reading down the board, I found that each mule cost two rupees; a goat or pig, five rupees; a child, one rupee. The rate for a buffalo was an outrageous twenty-five rupees. I thought it not too different from the States, where we charge tolls, too.

Looking out the bus window a bit farther down the road, we saw the toll rupees at work. Local men were making road improvements by paving stretches of road without any means of mechanization. My father and brothers had had a paving business, so my interest in the Nepalese process was piqued. Men dumped a large tray of heated tar into a large tray of stones, mixing everything together before spreading it over the roadway with shovels.

We stopped in Narayangadh, a melee of sounds and sights, for a rest stop—as if a person could "rest" in that hubbub. Animals asleep in the streets were dodged by buses crammed with people inside and out, clinging to the roof for dear life. Bicycles with red, blue, green, and yellow containers piled higher than their riders slowly glided down the street. A three-wheeled cab with a torn canvas awning, pedaled by a young man in a white shirt and dusty, black trousers with the legs rolled up, moved slowly by seeking a passenger. Motorcycles, bicycles, automobiles, and elaborately painted trucks, brightly decorated with gold and silver tinsel, added to the carnival atmosphere in the streets. Erratically dodging each other, they all kicked up the dust and honked constant warnings of efforts to pass.

I noticed that pedestrians looked many times in all directions before crossing the street. My ears, eyes, and nose were bombarded. Mark, Bill, Betsy, and I sat at a sidewalk shop for a while just to watch the traffic circus. Lining the streets were small stores, dusty havens for conversation with friends, not unlike the dust-covered Kathmandu stores.

"I guess one learns to live with dust, but can you imagine the people's lungs? They must be coated with pollutants," I commented.

Mark, the master explorer of commercial establishments, discovered that the shop had a beverage cooler, and we all ordered an ice-cold bottle of soda. Having been without benefit of electricity for the past few days, the sparkling drink quenched our thirst and washed away all the dust.

"Oh, does this taste good! It's almost too cold, don't you think?" I purred.

"It tastes good to me, and I don't care how much it costs!" agreed Mark.

At this point, we would have gladly paid two dollars for anything cold, but the sodas had cost the handsome sum of ten cents each.

"That was the price when I was a kid," exclaimed Bill.

Soon we boarded the bus for our final destination of the day. Leaving Narayangadh, the guide pointed out a Tuborg beer factory and a paper mill hugging the river.

"The amount of pollution discharged into the river must be horrendous," said Mark quietly, shaking his head.

A broken-down vehicle, with a man lying under it to repair the problem, soon blocked the middle of the roadway; but the bus was able to maneuver around it, and we were on our way to the jungle, but first we had a river to cross.

13

At the Narayani River, the tour group transferred from the bus to our next mode of transportation—long boats powered only by a long pole, a paddle, and the current of the river. Our oarsman poled us upstream along the bank, where at a predetermined point, he paddled across the river, until catching the current that pulled us across the river to the opposite bank, which was flat and stone strewn. Three rough-hewn yellow painted planks, nailed to two limbs stuck in the ground served as the sign welcoming us to Temple Tiger Lodge. "Isn't that cute, it even has tiger paw prints painted on it," I pointed out to Betsy.

Before climbing into waiting open-backed jeeps, lodge attendants gave each of us a wet cloth to wipe our hot, dusty faces, and a red dot was placed on our foreheads to signify a blessing.

Mark leaned over, saying to me, "How about if, in addition to the blessing, they make the Bengal tiger appear?"

I laughed, nodding my head. Following a fruit drink, the guide swept his arm to the right toward two small structures, constructed of tall reeds lashed together. What else could they be, but bathrooms? A sign directed women to one enclosure and men to the other.

I said to Betsy, "Actually, a bush would work just as well."

Climbing into and standing in the rear of an open jeep, Betsy, Mark, Bill, and I traveled over a dusty, rutted road behind other jeeps churning up billows of dust, heading to Temple Tiger Lodge. Although the dark green jeeps had padded seats in the back, no one sat down; we all wanted to experience the wild ride. Bill said, "No seat could offer cushioning from all these bumps anyway."

Although our jeep kept to a distance to avoid dust, it still filtered into our nostrils. Sunglasses kept most of it from blowing into our eyes. Grabbing the jeep's roll bars, my mind drifted to movies like *Indiana Jones*. Even thoughts of *Jurassic Park* entered my head as we entered tall elephant grass and jungle vegetation.

I remarked to Mark, Betsy, and Bill, "This trip still far exceeds my wildest expectations. Every event tops the one before."

The jeeps finally reached the lodge, riders covered in fine mocha-colored dust. Walking to the main dining area for room assignments and instructions about the elephant safari, Mark observed that they gave us those wet wash-cloths at the wrong end of the jeep ride, and he sure could use one now.

Bill pointed out that we had taken five different modes of transportation today: raft, bus, long boat, jeep, legs, and soon would be taking the sixth—an elephant."

Betsy and I strolled to our assigned bungalow on stilts, overlooking the jungle. Unpacking, we remembered to hang our wet swimsuits on a clothesline but strewed everything else around the room in disorganization totally unlike our nor-mally neat room. What a day it had been. Needing to collect myself, I asked Betsy if she minded if I meditated.

"No problem, I'm leaving to write some postcards anyway. See you in twenty minutes for the elephant safari!"

Barely into the meditation, I suddenly experienced three horizontal streaks of golden lightning cross in front of my closed eyes. A vision appeared approximately one foot away and slightly to the right side of my head. This vision or pic-ture was like a single frame of movie that had been stopped. I had never experienced anything like this before. In the vision, a field of thin brown sticks, like reeds or grass, surrounded an oasis of green in the middle, with a row of trees in the background. I tried to understand the scene's message, mentally asking what was I supposed to know.

The vision remained, but provided no more meaning or reason for being. When I tried inserting myself into the scene itself to gather more information, the vision disappeared. I felt unsettled; it was my first experience with a vision, and it left me confused.

I quickly changed into my jungle green shirt and khaki pants, following instructions to dress in muted colors, rather than white or red, for better camouflage in the jungle. Walking to the elephant stand to board the elephants, I was unusually quiet; the vision had affected me deeply.

Mark suggested that the four of us go on the same elephant. We climbed a ladder to board a large Indian elephant, decorated with designs on its ears, forehead, and trunk. A wooden platform with posts at the corners and a railing around the top provided seating space. We hoped that it was securely anchored on the elephant. Several blankets cushioned the surface. Mark and Bill, being gentlemen, offered Betsy and me the front corners while they took the rear. We each straddled a post and dangled our legs over the side, resting on the elephant's prickly hair. I could feel it through my pants. As we patiently waited for the group to board, the four of us took photos as usual, but an odd feeling persisted in my body and mind.

Two other American tourists, traveling on their own, joined the afternoon safari. As our elephant lumbered away from the staging area, I accustomed myself to the rocking motion of its gait, clumsy yet deliberate, as it descended into the elephant grass and jungle. Looking around, I couldn't help but notice that two of my fellow travelers were wearing a white shirt and a red shirt.

"What part of the instructions didn't those two guys understand?" I asked Mark riding behind me, "Were they even listening? Now they're sticking out like a flame in a dark room."

Gopan had cautioned their group earlier not to venture alone or on foot into the jungle. He said that tourists who had refused to heed the warning haven't lived to tell the story. We spotted a wild boar, then a rhinoceros. The experienced elephant drivers surrounded a group of four rhinos, including a baby, for the riders to see and take photos. What beautiful creatures they were with their armored plates, large innocent eyes, and single horn.

"After seeing this terrain," Bill said, "we'll stay on the elephants and take no chances."

Our English-speaking driver commanded his elephant to begin moving through the grasses. Suddenly he rose from his slouching position on the elephant's shoulders to full height. The elephant began vibrating with a low-pitched sound, almost purr-like, but deep. We heard an elephant trumpet farther away from us. Everyone and everything was on high alert. Elephants went from excited to frenzied, as did their drivers; anticipation gripped the passengers. The driver turned and said softly, "Tiger nearby."

At the sound of an elephant's trumpet in the distance, our driver took a long iron rod and smashed it in the middle of the elephant's skull. The elephant took off in the direction of the trumpeting. No longer plodding, the elephant now ran with its legs on each side pumping in unison. The four of us grabbing the platform's rail were jostled back and forth and up and down, as it raced through the jungle at a feverish rate.

Swiftly moving through the grasses and brush, we came to a clearing. I gasped, "I can't believe what I'm seeing!"

The exact same scene I had seen during my meditation appeared before me. I felt a burst of energy and understood: "This is the place where we will see the Bengal tiger."

Taking a true leap of faith, I leaned back to Mark, whispering, "If we are going to see the Bengal tiger, it's going to be right here. I've seen it in a vision."

The words were barely out of my mouth when a Bengal tiger crossed our path, its golden orange color magnificent. I sobbed aloud, then stifled my moans, remembering our instructions to be quiet on safari because sounds travel in the jungle. Mark missed seeing the tiger despite my warning, because he was filming in another direction; but he told his brother and Betsy that Sahara had said we would see it right there.

A few seconds later, another Bengal tiger crossed our path, and another chase was on. Our driver aggressively pushed the elephant through the brush and trees, in pursuit of the elusive tigers. Racing through the jungle, our driver tried pushing aside low-hanging tree branches with a bamboo pole to keep them from hitting his passengers. I noticed the futility of attempting to protect us and drive the elephant simultaneously, and said: "Forget about the branches, we'll take care of them. Just go after the tigers!"

That's all he needed to hear. With branches flying, snagging clothes and hats, we had the ride of our lives, but the Bengal tiger was once again elusive. As we slowed down, I noticed the perspiration pouring off the driver's face, I ripped the purple bandana off my neck and offered it to him. He gladly accepted. Waving his hand toward a distant spot, he said, "The tiger is gone, far away, we won't see it again."

The driver's excitement seeing the Bengal tiger had matched our own. Sadly Mark missed the second tiger sighting as well—videotaping in the wrong direction again. After the frenzied ride, our elephant needed rest and water. We leisurely returned to the lodge, allowing it to stop occasionally for water—the least we could do after the incredible chase. We observed more animals in the wild: barking deer, white-tailed deer, different types of birds, but no monkeys.

"The next thing I want to see is monkeys swinging in the trees," I told the driver who smiled kindly at me. Bill remarked that seeing a Bengal tiger in the wild, not once, but twice would have satisfied most people.

"Don't get me wrong. I'm ecstatic, elated, overjoyed at seeing the tigers, but I do want to see some monkeys."

Monkeys were still on my must-see list. I concentrated on monkeys frolicking in trees and put the thought out into the universe. If it had worked for a tiger, surely, it would work for a monkey, I calculated.

As we headed back, the driver, listening to our conversation, attempted to find monkeys. Eventually he gave me the bad news: "No monkeys."

We gazed at a gorgeous sunset, the sun's orange glow emanating across the evening sky and trees silhouetted in its brilliance.

Near the end of the afternoon safari, only a short distance from the elephant stand, our driver suddenly stopped to point up into the trees. What was there? Monkeys jumping and swinging from limb to limb. I saw my monkeys. This time my fellow travelers weren't surprised.

Bill remarked, "Whatever Sahara wants, Sahara gets."

Stiff-muscled, we slowly climbed off the elephant's back, thanked, and tipped our driver. Walking to the dining area with Gopan, he nonchalantly mentioned, "I understand you saw the Bengal tiger."

I quickly replied, "Yes, it was really cool."

"Do you know how rare it is to see the Bengal tiger?"

Somewhat smugly, I answered, "Yes, I do."

"No, you do not *understand* how rare," Gopan insisted. "If you see the Bengal tiger, you will see it during the morning safari. It has rarely been seen on an afternoon safari."

I proceeded to relate every detail of the safari to Gopan, beginning with my vision during mediation. Gopan didn't reply—he just shook his head, while another guide who sat nearby listening, looked at me in wide-eyed disbelief.

As other tourists drifted into the dining area, they began asking each other where they were from. When I answered with Alabama, Gopan put a hand on my shoulder and said, "No, Kathmandu."

I had some final thoughts, "Well, how about that? We did see the Bengal tiger, but I know that our entire group manifested that experience by everyone's energy and desire being concentrated on one thing. Our hope became a reality."

14

Food served at dinner offered a selection of spicy dishes, but by now my digestive system had calmed down enough to handle spicy food. After dinner Betsy and I retreated to our bungalow, and I finished my journal writing by flashlight when the sun set. The lodge management allowed no candles since cabins constructed of wood with a thatched roof would go in a flash if they ever caught fire. The staff provided lanterns for use until occupants were ready to go to sleep, at which time they were to be placed outside on the small porch. Paper-thin walls allowed sound to travel like in the jungle. Conversations—or anything—could be heard in neighboring bungalows; it was no place for telling secrets, or especially, for gossiping about others in the group. One small room in the back of the bungalow had a toilet and showerhead with a drain in the floor. The jungle's damp air refused to dry clothes.

At five o'clock the next morning, staffers awoke everyone, knocking on doors and bringing tea. Betsy, Mark, Bill, and I met one half hour later for the morning elephant safari.

"This won't be nearly as exciting as yesterday afternoon's safari," I remarked to Betsy, "but, watching the sunrise while sitting on the back of an elephant will be unique. I don't feel we'll see a tiger this morning."

Another group of tourists heard two rhinos fighting and saw one rhino running away with a bloody back. There weren't any Bengal tigers to be seen, however; but we did spy some fresh tiger paw prints in the mud. I considered that it would be greedy to expect a repeat of yesterday's excitement.

Following breakfast at seven thirty, the next stop was a nature cruise. The four of us shared a jeep with the two independent tourists, Charlie and Skip, from the previous day's elephant safari. I knew they had to be adventurous since we met them in the middle of a jungle. Both were slim and in good physical shape. When Charlie offered his hand to help me into the jeep, I didn't need to look up to thank him; we were even in height. I noticed his straight teeth before his blue eyes and styled gray hair. Skip, the more reserved of the two—whose occasional smile revealed less-than-perfect teeth—had deep-set brown eyes, hidden by a pair of aviator sunglasses. We learned that the men were executive directors of large nonprofit organizations in the United States.

Standing in the back of the jeep as we traveled over dust-clogged lanes back to the river, I casually mentioned to Charlie, my interest in metaphysics and spirituality. I had become more comfortable speaking about my own journey. After I told the story of my vision followed by the Bengal tiger's appearance, Charlie commented, "You may be a shaman. A friend of mine back home is one. I suggest that you read *The Way of the Shaman* by Michael Harner."

"Well, I'll be," I thought. "One never knows who will cross paths and what common interests will arise. Discovering shared beliefs is a happy surprise."

The jeep stopped, bringing me back into the present to photograph mother monkeys clutching their young in one arm as they climbed up to higher limbs. Peacocks with long plumes flew up ahead of us, and barking deer scampered into the brush.

When we reached the river, we boarded longboats for a trip down the Narayani. After seeing egrets and crocodiles, a tidbit of information from the guide caught my attention: no dolphins were seen in the river now.

"That's because there must be pollution," I whispered to Betsy, "We're always happy to see dolphins in the waters in

Alabama, because it means the water isn't polluted and they can survive."

The guide continued to explain that the paper mill up the river in Narayangadh had polluted the water, and the dolphins left. I hoped that the government would initiate pollution control and preserve Nepal's exceptional beauty and natural resources.

After lunch back at Temple Tiger Lodge, I told Betsy that I was going to catch a nap before the elephant talk.

An hour later, pulling on my boots, I headed to the elephants' living area where they were readied for the safaris and nursed back to health when ill. Their drivers lived there, too.

The lecture by Karan, a skinny, short, dark-skinned guide, was packed with elephant statistics and information and followed by Q & A, both lasting for an hour and a half. Everyone, thinking it would never end, restlessly shifted in our seats. At one point a driver demonstrated how he mounted his elephant. The elephant unfurled his trunk, then lifted it as the driver walked up the trunk onto the top of its head.

"Hey Mark, do you think you could do that?" I teased.

"I think I might need to lose a few more pounds to get as skinny as that driver and not put a strain on the poor elephant."

Karan asked who could guess how many times the sum of the elephant's foot circumference equaled the elephant's height from the ground to its shoulders.

Guesses ranged from four, to six, eight, or ten. Karan shook his head after each response.

I offered, "One?"

Another shake of his head. Karan informed us that the correct answer was two times.

Looking at the elephant's foot and his massive size, one would hardly think it would only be twice the circumference.

"Now, that is great trivia information," I told Bill and Mark, "I can't wait for the next cocktail party."

After discussing the elephant's eating habits, Karan asked if anyone wanted to feed the elephant.

Of course, everyone did. We were tired of sitting! As I extended my bundle of grass toward the elephant, I noticed Mark, Betsy, and Bill whispering to one another, smiling. As Betsy took the photo of me, they all yelled, "Which one is the elephant?"

The three burst into laughter. Their memories were long, just like an elephant's. "You're right, I guess I deserve it after the water buffalo wisecrack. I knew that would come back to haunt me," I admitted.

All I could do was laugh and be a good sport; I had asked for it.

I told Betsy that I was skipping dinner, but not because I was sick. There was just too much food every day. I was beginning to feel like one of the elephants.

After sleeping fitfully for a short period of time, I heard a loud bird caw all night long, robbing me of a good night's sleep. When a lodge employee brought the morning tea at five o'clock, I 'greeted' him at the door before he had a chance to knock. I had already meditated before the group gathered at five thirty for the final morning's elephant safari. Several, including Bill and Mark, chose to stay in bed. I, however, didn't want to miss a thing.

A wild boar fled up the hill as we approached. Monkeys, deer, a baby rhino with its mother, and a huge male rhino were some of the wildlife. The beauty of lumbering atop an elephant through the swamp and jungle stimulated my senses. As the elephant ploughed through deep waters, I felt it might sink so far as to submerge with us on his back. The loud sucking sound of his legs pulling out of the mud indicated depth. It sounded like a deep slurp.

At breakfast, the talk around the table turned to photographing the rhinos, provoking a smart-aleck remark, "Which one was the rhino and which one was Sahara?" Everyone started laughing, and someone mentioned that I had started it. I laughed, too, admitting that I had. I also recognized that now everyone was in on the act, not just Bill, Betsy, and Mark.

The fellow Americans Charlie and Skip left Temple Tiger Lodge early to board a plane in Narayangadh back to Kathmandu rather than risk bodily injury by hiring a driver to motor them back. After seeing a girl killed on the road and two accidents on their drive to Temple Tiger Lodge, they believed their chances for survival increased by flying. We said our goodbyes, wishing them safe travels.

Two hours later, our group, reversing transportation modes from our arrival two days ago, went to the Narayangadh airport to fly rather than raft out of the jungle. En route, the broken down truck remained exactly where we had seen it on our way to Temple Tiger Lodge. Obviously the driver hadn't repaired it. Passing through town, its crazy sights and sounds shocked my senses more than ever after the jungle's peacefulness and relaxing quietness.

Arriving at the airport, whom did we see but Charlie and Skip. Although scheduled to leave earlier, their plane had been diverted from Kathmandu to Lukla to help get trekkers out of the Himalayas. A dense fog socking in Lukla had caused such a buildup of departing trekkers that a sudden break in weather caused any available plane to be diverted to ease the glut of stranded passengers. Mark, Bill, Betsy, and I wondered if this were a hint of things to come.

Two young schoolboys of Narayangadh practiced their English by making conversation with travelers waiting for planes. They were delightful children, well educated, but with hands extended for American dollars. That never seemed to end in almost any circumstance.

As we waited, Skip and Charlie talked about their experience trekking up to Mt Everest base camp—they never made it. The portion between Namche Bazaar and Tengboche Monastery was too difficult, and they had to turn back. The very strenuous trekking they described caused those of us signed on for the post-trip extension to wonder whether we would be able to make it. I felt that if these men in great physical shape had had difficulty, what would happen to the rest of us?

Suddenly a siren blared. "What's that?" Mark, Bill, and I asked in unison. The travelers discovered that the siren was only the first one of four to announce the arrival of an incoming flight. The first siren meant that the plane had departed Kathmandu and would arrive in twenty-two minutes. Siren number two meant that the plane would be landing shortly. The third siren indicated that it was time to clear the runway of motorcycles, bicycles, children, and pedestrians. The fourth and final siren instructed people to clear the cows—yes, cows—off the runway before the plane landed. Watching from the small terminal, I thought that I would consider the term *runway* at this airport a loose description, at best. It was nothing but a long grass field.

"The simplicity of the warning system actually works well for the Nepalese," Skip said.

"For sure, there are no U.S. Federal Aviation Agency rules to follow." added Mark.

With the wait finally over, Gopan gathered his group. "Get your backpacks and go to the airplane through the security checkpoint," he said, pointing to a small shack with two entrances, women on one side and men on the other.

I awaited my turn, keeping my mouth shut, but wondering why only the women's carryon bags were opened and examined. The men quickly walked through their side of the shack and out the door to the plane. On exiting, I told Mark and Bill, "After three days on the river and two days in the jungle, I can't for the life of me imagine anyone wanting to touch anything in my backpack. It's just plain yucky in there."

The Lumbini Airways twin prop plane flew us back to Kathmandu.

15

Touching down in Kathmandu, I felt I was coming home. I had missed the city and Hotel Vajra, a sanctuary of peace and familiarity. The view from the air of Swayambhunath Temple's whitewashed dome and golden spire reminded me that I couldn't leave Nepal without visiting that complex, also known as the Monkey Temple. Mark, Bill, and Betsy asked me to join them for dinner, but with time slipping by so quickly, I decided to visit the temple instead.

I left the hotel and gave full attention to navigating the streets, and that was exactly what was needed. Drivers with horns blaring took hidden curves at high speed and slammed on brakes to avoid pedestrians and animals—if possible. One careless step or a moment of inattention could be my last. When I finally reached the steep bank of steps leading up to the Monkey Temple, I suddenly remembered that no shorts were allowed in the temple. Not believing I had walked so far for nothing, I returned to the Hotel Vajra, showered, and turned in early.

I slept until four o'clock, meditated, then dressed in long pants, and arrived back at the base of the Swayambhunath Temple steps by quarter to five. I started to count each step as I climbed, but eventually lost track and just concentrated on executing the long, steep stairway. At the last step, I looked down, dizzy and feeling as if I'd been on a stair-stepper.

The moment I walked on the temple grounds I imagined I had stepped into the middle of a circus. Monkeys scampered everywhere—climbing up the stretched prayer flags, stealing corn left at the Buddhist worship stations, fighting over a dropped cracker, jumping on statues, and chasing one another. Pigeons fluttered overhead, watching for corn scattered by visitors. Dogs fought. People walked clockwise around the stupa, spinning prayer wheels as they prayed. The parade was endless.

I appeared to be the only tourist among worshippers or the exercise enthusiasts who ran up and down the steep stone steps as a fitness routine. For a fleeting moment, I thought of joining them to get in shape for the Himalayas in a couple of days, but soon dismissed the notion. Just being in the mix of humanity and animals and music coming from loudspeakers was enough stimulation.

I returned to the hotel in time for breakfast and journal writing before joining my friends for an optional excursion we had all signed up for, a flyby of Mt. Everest and surrounding mountain peaks. When we reached the airport, the news was good—clear blue skies meant the plane would fly and offer unobstructed views.

While waiting, we struck up a conversation with Sam, a ranger from the Grand Canyon National Park Service. Tall, thin, and clean but a bit scruffy, Sam explained that he'd been sent here to establish a resource management program in a remote area of western Nepal. Its primary focus was to train naturalists. He was traveling with a ranger from Lasson National Volcanic Park in California and one from Minuteman Park in Boston, and they'd been advised to hang out in the airport both before and after their scheduled flight date. Flights in and out of western Nepal were unpredictable, but they were supposed to leave today.

While my friends talked with the ranger from California, I blurted out my vision and the Bengal tiger sighting to Sam. My excitement of meeting English speakers trumped my reticence. Sam appeared to understand my excitement or acted as if he did. When he asked what came next, I outlined our trek from Lukla to Tengboche Monastery with nights at several lodges. Sam interrupted enthusiastically, "You must meet the owner of Namaste Lodge. She's terrific, but I can't remember her name."

"We'll tell her you said hello," I replied, but the boarding call cut short our conversation.

After the small Buddha Airlines plane took off, the hostess offered cotton balls and small hard candies to lessen travelers' ear pressure. Mark, Bill, Betsy, and I looked at each other, eyebrows raised, wondering how cotton balls could prevent discomfort from air pressure.

More convincingly, the flight attendant pointed out the different mountain peaks in the Himalayas. Mt. Everest's summit had a wispy cloud, almost as if snow were blowing off the peak. I realized our cameras couldn't capture the beauty or magnitude of these mountains, and the price of this flight was money well spent—especially with clear blue skies as a perfect backdrop to Mt. Everest, the only peak we would probably be able to identify later in our photos.

Taking turns, we walked up to the cockpit for a photo through the pilot's shaded windshield. As the plane made the banking turn back toward Kathmandu, we were pushed into our seats, and the Himalayan range loomed large and awesome before us.

"I can't believe this feeling of being so small near those huge mountains," Bill said.

"I'm getting psyched for our Tengboche Monastery trip extension," I added.

Back at the hotel, the entire group boarded a bus for another tour of the countryside. I told Betsy that we needed to become expert on catnaps in buses if we wanted enough sleep on this fast-paced trip. Gopan hadn't said, but the group had mistakenly assumed that the village we were to visit would be close by, and little walking would be required. The bus ride took more than an hour, and the walk was a two-hour hike through small villages and terraced fields, down hills on rocky paths, up dusty roads, and over two bridges. "The first rule of traveling—expect the unexpected," I thought.

We hiked past fields of marijuana, and Gopan warned us not to try taking any away with us. Marijuana's easy availability had attracted people who adopted an alternative lifestyle in Kathmandu in the 1960s and early 1970s. I said that I liked adventure, but wasn't ready to try that—or to experience the inside of a Nepali jail.

Mark had a better idea: "How about sitting in the middle of a marijuana field, and I'll take a picture of you?"

"You can forget that, too. I can see myself explaining to my bosses that I was just walking along and before I knew it, I was in the middle of this field of pretty plants."

Mark videotaped (sometimes I thought he slept with it under his pillow) people in villages without electricity, radio, or television, where farming was done by hand and hoe. The children were very shy and hesitant to be photographed, but when Mark replayed a video for them, their eyes widened with amazement and smiles crept across their faces. He wanted to video two adults with a child who, at first, demurred, but then relented. Upon replay, they started giggling, then laughed out loud. It may have been the first time they had ever seen an image of themselves. A small boy started following Mark yelling, "TV man, TV man!"

Bill speculated that somewhere the boy had seen television and connected Mark's video camera with a TV screen. "We didn't see a single antenna in the village," he said, "but they knew about television; probably from school."

Hiking down a long, steep, stony path, we met an older group of school children returning home. A young boy around thirteen started practicing his English with Betsy and Bill. I followed behind, listening to the questions they asked and the boy's responses in excellent English. He told us that his father worked at the Agricultural Bank in Kathmandu. I felt that the very bright, personable boy was headed toward future success. He left us to run home and change out of his school clothes, but soon caught up with us again to resume talking with Bill and Betsy.

The group, most of whom had not brought along water, stopped in a tiny village for a soft drink. Several men sat on benches outside the small store, and a group of children played nearby. Apparently they knew about Americans and cameras, for the men told the youngsters to stand in a line and get their picture taken. Four boys and two girls stood erect and very formal, arms at their sides. One little girl in a flowered dress and a white bow around her long dark hair posed with a tight-lipped smile; a little boy in a purple shirt and gray pants with a broken zipper, had purple shirttails hanging out of his fly opening. The children stood very quietly, unsure of what to expect.

Everyone took photos and Mark videoed the scene with his camcorder. On the replay, the children gathered around Mark, their eyes glued to the screen. The little girl in the flowered dress threw her head back in happy laughter. Suddenly, the previously aloof men wandered over to join the excitement. Mark replayed the video repeatedly as more people came out of the store to see. Now, everyone was smiling, including the visitors. Finally having to move on, we said our goodbyes and returned to the dusty road, this time with a group of children following. Mark, the Pied Piper of Nepal, had substituted his camcorder for a magic flute and a polo shirt for medieval garb, but the children were the same.

I spotted two bulls peering at me over a brick fence. Their horns were painted with red dye, and each had a red dot on their foreheads. Without a doubt, these animals were blessed and revered. Across the road, a school had animals, flowers, and an airplane painted on its exterior wall. The plane had the English word *Airplane* written on it, and *Wel-come* was written above the school's entrance.

Six older boys were playing ping-pong on an ingenious table, a slab of concrete supported by columns of red bricks at each corner and a wall of bricks in the middle for support. Instead of a net, a row of end-to-end bricks crossed the middle of the slab. Amazing improvisation, but the ping-pong balls must have been a valuable commodity. The boys played intently without much yelling, while younger boys patiently waited their turn.

Nearing the end of our hike, large trucks barreled down the dusty road. Mark, Betsy, Bill and I scampered to a safe position as far off the road as possible to avoid being hit. Seeing the cloud of thick dust billowing up behind a truck, we inhaled deeply and held our breath until the dust settled. Not one part of my body remained free of dust.

Once back in the bus, we returned to Kathmandu through a section of the city we had not seen before. Just past Queen's Park, a May Day rally sponsored by the Communist party was in progress, red banners fluttering in the breeze. I began to recognize familiar landmarks as we drove and realized that the internet office was nearby. I asked Gopan to drop Bill and me off to check our email. He only agreed after Bill assured him that we knew the way back to the hotel. We did, sort of.

I had finished and was waiting for Bill, when a young college student named Tashi asked for help understanding an email in English. When I complied, the conversation turned to our trek. After I outlined our route, he asked if we were staying at the Namaste Lodge, and excitedly proceeded to tell me about the wonderful woman who ran it. "I can't remember her name, but give her my greeting when you get there."

This was the second time that day I had heard about the same nameless woman. I thought that the lady must be a powerhouse and knows everyone in Nepal. In casual conversations with both an American and a Nepali, she had been mentioned. I assured Tashi that I'd tell her he had said hello.

Bill and I decided not to hail a taxi but to walk back to the hotel, using a map we'd found in the internet office. We went down a street on which workers were digging to lay sewer lines and flicking stones to one side with pickaxes. We tried to dodge the stones, but when one hit Bill, he remarked that if this had happened in the States someone would sue.

"That's life in Nepal," I answered. "We just have to understand it and watch our step."

This was the night Gopan had planned a farewell dinner for the group at his home. A light rain began to fall as we waited for the bus in the hotel courtyard. I saw a familiar face, that of Kanti, the artist and director, whom I had met two weeks ago. As soon as he saw me, Kanti unexpectedly gave me a big hug in front of all the travelers and guided me to the side.

"You can't believe how much our talk meant to me," he said. "I was even contemplating suicide, and just your listening with compassion helped me through the tough time."

He invited me to visit the art gallery immediately, but the arrival of the bus intervened. As I boarded, he called, "The play was very successful."

"I'll see you when we come back from the Himalayas in a week," I answered.

What was that all about? Where did you meet him? What's the story? were some of the questions asked after my curious companions were all aboard. I gave a quick account of our morning meeting. No one needed to know the entire story. I was just happy that I had been there, and that things had improved for Kanti.

As we traveled, the rain fell harder. Gopan's new house, built to withstand earthquakes, was located down a muddy, unpaved street in a neighborhood still under construction. A barricade halted progress of the bus, and we had to walk a couple of blocks down the slippery street, managing to stay on our feet. We slipped out of our muddy shoes in the foyer before entering the living room.

Gopan showed us pictures of his Hindu wedding ceremony while we enjoyed those wonderful crispy French fries he thoughtfully served as an appetizer. The dinner was a bountiful smorgasbord of Nepali dishes, the likes of which we would not find in the Himalayas.

After dinner, Gopan gave each of the travelers a present wrapped in paper. As he handed one to me, I jokingly proclaimed that it was probably a Ghurka knife. A strange look passed over Gopan's face that made no sense until I unwrapped my gift. It was, indeed, a Ghurka knife, but just not any Ghurka knife. It was a glass bottle shaped like a knife that contained Nepali rum. I gave him a hug and thanked him for the wonderful trip, "a two-week, life-changing experience."

Gopan just smiled, shaking his head in wonder.

16

The seven travelers planning to go on the weeklong Tengboche Monastery extension, included the four of us friends; Pete, who no longer had to identify a day by what his wife served for breakfast; and enthusiastic Dick and his wife Pam, who was less enchanted with Nepal. We met our Sherpa guide the afternoon before our departure from the Vajra hotel in Kathmandu. Nalin, dark-skinned, thin, and short, greeted us in the courtyard. Pacing back and forth, he said that he came from a village in the Himalayas and had been a guide for several years. He told us what we could expect on the Himalayan trek and emphatically stated, "No alcohol on the way up. I can tell immediately who has been drinking. Don't do it."

He also issued duffel bags, sleeping bags, and water bottles. I mentioned that I'd like to have a purple duffel, my favorite color. Bill teased, "Purple? That's going to matter when you're trying to get up the mountain?"

"Well, it does to me."

Nalin told us to go to our rooms, and he'd meet each of us there to assist in selecting only the items needed for the trek. The rest of our belongings would remain in the hotel storage room until our return. When he got to Betsy's and my room, he reminded us to take only one set of long underwear and a few pairs of socks.

"Maybe so," I thought to myself, "but I'm taking my purple light-weight long johns *and* my aqua medium-weights. I hate being cold. I may throw in more socks, too."

I had guessed intuitively that it was unwise to cross Nalin outright. His eyes sparkled when he laughed and he could be jolly, but he could turn on a dime to seriousness. I made a mental note not to get on his bad side. Still, I intended to follow my own thermometer on clothing selection.

The next morning, it felt as if we were leaving on a separate vacation totally unrelated to the past fourteen days. Our clothing was more utilitarian, and our mood was heightened with apprehension about what lay ahead mixed with the thrill of adventure—trekking in the Himalayas.

I told Mark, "I'm so fortunate to be able to afford this trip and to get time off from work. How many people actually have such an opportunity? It will be magical, I just know."

Our purple, green, and blue duffels stowed, the magnificent seven climbed on the bus again, this time heading to the Kathmandu airport to board a flight into the Himalayas. Fortunately, the weather was clear so the plane could land at Lukla, a village nestled between high mountains; otherwise, we would have had to wait out the weather in Kathmandu.

I called in angels for protection and surrounded the plane, crew, and passengers with light. By this time, the group had come to expect this little service from me, and, in truth, a few of them had adopted similar rituals. The hour's flight to Lukla was only slightly turbulent; the landing, however, was an unbelievable experience.

The graveled runway in Lukla started at the edge of a cliff with a sheer drop of several thousand feet and ran a breathtakingly short way to the foot of a hill. The plane actually plopped down on the runway ready to brake and avoid slamming into the hillside. Then it had to maneuver into a turnaround area on the right where it was immediately surrounded by a crowd of trekkers impatient to fly back to Kathmandu. As we climbed out of the plane, angry voices of weary trekkers argued about which group was scheduled for the plane's return trip. Police were there to keep order and stop fistfights that commonly broke out. The unpredictable weather led to unpredictable flights and flared tempers beyond control.

Only a month earlier, the Nepalese government had decided helicopters could no longer accommodate trekkers, only transport cargo. There had been no helicopter crashes and no deaths, so the reason to stop passenger service could only be surmised. Even Nalin didn't have a clue. The new ruling stretched already full transportation schedules. Trekkers knew they might be delayed because of weather, but this was a new impediment.

"That's why we have a guide to tend to problems like these," Betsy commented.

Bill, Mark, and I were less confident. "We might be facing the same problem in a week," said Bill.

Our group had collected belongings and started to gather on the turnaround for a picture to mark the beginning of our trek when a new plane began its takeoff. Mark dashed down the runway after it, camcorder in hand, to capture its lift-off from the brink of the abyss. A skillful pilot managed once again to pull up and off the abbreviated runway.

Nalin waited patiently, with all our cameras hung around his neck, for his trekkers to reassemble for the group pictures. Trekkers still waiting for planes watched the tedious effort to record a trek's hopeful beginning and laughed. They had nothing else to do. Our distracted efforts provided comic relief. The whole tone of our trip was set: laughs, pictures, and more pictures and more laughs.

From the landing area, our group walked up stone steps to the whitewashed, two-storied Himalaya Lodge looking for a restroom. I asked the lodge owner, if there were any places in Lukla where we could send emails. He gave directions to the Ghorka Airlines office in the Khumbu Resort down in the village. We four walked down the hill toward the village where stone and wire fences blocked our way. We climbed over them and finally arrived on a packed dirt and stone main street.

The directions were perfect, and we had no problem locating the Khumbu Resort; however, the term *resort* is deceiving in the Himalayas. It was functional—no luxurious entrance, reception area, or spa welcomed us. Inside we finally found a thin young man with a moustache dressed in a vibrant red shirt and black jacket. He escorted us back a dark, narrow hallway to a small office in the rear of the building, actually a small room with precious little space to navigate in. To send emails, the fellow turned on a generator to produce enough electricity to run the computer or make a long distance call. We composed our emails and sent them, hoping for a reply when returning in a week. While we were taking turns at the computer, the young man asked if we knew of anyone who had lost film. Because only thirty minutes had passed since we had landed, to our knowledge no one in our group had misplaced any film.

Leaving the office and going back through the hallway, we passed a large common room with a stove in the middle, on top of which rested a large pot of tea. An inspiration suddenly surfaced in my mind. Known to friends for my indifference to cooking, I decided to initiate a series of cooking photos through the Himalayas. Informing Bill of my idea, I asked him to photograph me at the stove pretending to cook as proof of my newly discovered ability. The guys obliged, and the series began. I could hardly wait for other cooking opportunities. My son would never believe it. Once he had begged, "Mom, please, I want a TV dinner, I just can't eat your cooking tonight."

Lunch at the Himalaya Lodge was an egg, a sandwich made of strong-flavored yak cheese, vegetables, and mangoes. Afterwards we took up hiking sticks and backpacks, and the trek officially began. The group of seven, plus the hired Sherpas, quickly walked through the village and soon entered sparsely populated areas. The dirt trail, compacted by centuries of Nepalese foot traffic, and more recently that of trekkers, was the link for news and delivery of goods from one village to another. Twisting through the countryside, ascending and descending, the trail followed the terrain. In places, it was wide as a road; in others, barely accommodating two abreast. Rocks littered the trail; some loose and others partially embedded, the latter more troublesome for anyone not paying attention to the trail. Occasionally Buddhist prayer stones and flags occupied the center of the trail. Nalin told our group, "When you see a prayer stone like this on the trail, the tradition is to walk clockwise around the rock and prayer flag, or else bad luck will follow."

"I'm going around it several times," Mark suggested, "not to take any chances."

From the trail, we saw waterfalls cascading down high mountainsides. Hundreds of feet below, flowed roaring rivers and streams fed by milky-colored glacier melt. The higher we trekked, the fewer terraced fields were carved from the mountain. Stone homes untouched by modernism, shoulder-high stone walls, and fluttering prayer flags strung between buildings greeted us in small, neat villages.

In one village, a child toddled along the central street trying to keep his pants with broken elastic from falling down while he bent over to pick up pine cones, cradled in his other arm. Either the pine cones or his pants fell down. He couldn't control both, but he didn't stop trying, his little bottom shining from beneath his shirt.

Once, while ascending, we encountered Sherpa porters carrying hundred-and-fifty-pound loads, wearing only flip-flops on their feet. Keeping their heads down to balance the weight, they ignored the trekkers and kept up their momentum. Their bulky loads were as tall as the small men. We trekkers stayed out of the porters' way and wondered at their strength.

As our cameras captured their feat, I thought, "How can anyone call flip-flops protection from a harsh path and cold weather?"

We stopped so often to take pictures that, according to Nalin, a camera was constantly going off. As a group, we were inclined to document every memorable view or event. Dick, was extreme, even in this group. Moreover every time he found a subject who talked—whether in English or not—he said, "Can I take your picture? Now, ready? One, two, three!"

Every single time Dick said the same thing, like a programmed robot. Retired on a modest income, he had saved for years to go on this trip with his wife Pam. He said it was his lifelong dream, but the rest of the group sometimes doubted that it was Pam's dream. Understanding his enthusiasm, she had probably become immune to her husband's constant repetition, but it drove everybody else crazy.

As we hiked higher, more suspension bridges began to appear on the route, and I bragged to Mark and Bill that "those bridges" didn't scare me anymore. I said that I could cross them like a Sherpa.

"Let's just say you're more comfortable crossing them than you were two weeks ago," Mark said.

Sometime later I stopped on the trail and looked around. I was alone and heard no voices of my fellow trekkers. I didn't remember walking ahead of them or lagging behind. Where was everyone? Not even a porter was in sight. The only sounds were those of nature and of prayer flags fluttering on a flagpole nearby. For a moment, I felt as if my body was drifting into the air to join the prayer flags. I felt an odd sensation but couldn't identify it. Suddenly a shout from Bill pulled me back to reality. "The altitude," I thought, "it must have been the altitude."

After the uphill climb was over, we descended 900 feet to Phakding at an elevation of 8,660 feet. As we crossed a sturdy wooden bridge over a ravine, the three-storied, stone Namaste Lodge, our destination for the night, came into view. Our descent meant a tough day of trekking uphill tomorrow, but meanwhile, lemon tea and cookies awaited us in the courtyard of the lodge.

As we drank tea and conversed with male trekkers from India at the next table, Pete moaned, suddenly realizing that he had lost his film. Mark and Bill remembered that the manager of the internet office in Lukla had asked us if anyone in our group had lost a bag of film, and told Nalin what had happened.

"I already heard about the bag of film," Nalin said, "and I've sent a messenger down to Lukla to bring it here."

I thought to myself that it took us four hours to get up here from Lukla. How in the world would he go all the way down there and get back by tomorrow morning before we leave? I didn't see that happening.

Betsy and I climbed three flights of creaky wooden stairs to our assigned room. As I unpacked, I glanced out the window and saw three young men in a stream below. Two of them had a rough-hewn, L-shaped wooden carrier harnessed around their shoulders and back. The third was picking rocks from the stream bed and stacking them carefully on the carriers. Thinking Mark and Bill would be interested in a scene so reminiscent of ancient days, I called them to come and see. Mark, of course, brought his camcorder. While filming, he always narrated his clips in some nonsensical way, and this was no exception: "We have now arrived in Betsy and Sahara's room for a panty raid. In the stream below, you will see our accomplices preparing to haul away the hundreds of panties we will soon toss from the window…"

It was good to have Mark's humor again on a daily basis. He was back to his old self—although Mark would never like 'old' to be used in a sentence about him. I thought once again, "What luck to meet and travel with brothers so good-natured."

When they left, I pulled out my Packtowl, soap, and a change of clothes and headed to the shower downstairs. This might be the last chance to wash my hair for a few days. As I waited in the shower line, I noticed a thin young woman of medium height with dark hair and glasses behind the counter. I asked if she were the lodge manager.

"Yes, I'm Durga."

The Suitcase Wife

I gave the two messages—from the American park ranger and from Tashi. Durga remembered both and enjoyed hearing from them. Freshly showered, I dressed in black tights, white shirt, and a dark green Polartec, the latter to be my constant companion for the next week. I went to the courtyard outside to dry my hair and write in my journal.

While recording the Lukla airfield episode, I laughed aloud, then quickly glanced around to see if anyone had noticed. Some of the Indian trekkers at a nearby table were staring at me. Feeling the need to explain—one of the things I didn't like about myself—I told them the chaotic story, and we began to discuss our respective journeys. The Indians' destination was Mt. Everest base camp. My story about sighting the Bengal tigers fascinated them, but soon we all gave attention to Durga. She had come outside, pulled a harmonica out of her pocket, and started playing Nepalese folk songs.

The Indian trekkers and I clapped and tapped our feet to the music. "TV man" Mark arrived with his camcorder. Durga urged one of the Indian men to dance and me to dance with him. Loving to dance, I was easy to persuade. The rest of our group came out to investigate the source of the music. Betsy and Bill were first to join the dance, and the Indian trekkers stood up to enter in. I tried to entice Nalin to dance, but he hurried away. The woman manager of the guesthouse across the trail heard the music and came over with her harmonica. As the two women played and the others danced, villagers emerged from their homes to watch. I invited them all to dance, but even the village children were too shy.

Bill wanted the three former Philadelphians to try to do the Mummers' strut in honor of the annual New Year's Day parade there. Mark and I were game to make the attempt with Bill, but we soon admitted failure after finding there was no way to reconcile the rhythms of Nepali and Mummers' music. That still didn't stop us from having fun making fools of ourselves—until we realized our humor couldn't be understood, or appreciated, by people who knew nothing of Philadelphia. We figured that maybe the altitude had started to affect us.

Durga had planned a delicious dinner of rice, lentils, vegetables, and apple turnovers. At one point the conversation at the table with my fellow travelers turned to how I had begged everyone to dance. I explained that I normally would be self-conscious.

"But this time I felt as though I should just do it and not be so concerned about what people think. We all had fun even though it touched on silliness, right?"

That night, I brushed my teeth by flashlight and trotted to the bathroom one more time before turning in. The thought of inching my way down three flights of steep, narrow steps to a path in total darkness except for the beam of my flashlight didn't thrill me.

I reflected on the construction of the Namaste Lodge. Although its exterior was built entirely of stone, the interior was wood. The beautiful patina of stairs, floors, tables, benches, and walls was due to the rubbing of hands and tread of feet over many years. Nevertheless, a careless match or flame could send fire racing through the lodge.

No candles allowed, only flashlights—a rule easily followed.

17

What a beautiful night. Snuggled inside bedding and wearing my jacket to stay warm, I peered out the window at the gigantic stars shining in the Himalayan sky and the spectacular lightning bolts flashing across it. Seeing stars and lightning bolts simultaneously seemed incongruous, since the sky was very clear. Sleep evaded me. My body began to twitch, and after three hours, it still had not stopped. Meditating didn't help. A vision of prayer flags with a wall and another of a prayer stone had appeared, and I had had one dream of swimming buck-naked in a river, then searching through some bags on shore. The meaning of all escaped me, but my dreams were obviously getting wilder, at least in my mind. Of course, I never mentioned dreams to my traveling companions; first, because I rarely knew what they meant and, second, because no one else really cared.

In the morning, we left Phakding after the Indian trekkers had already gone. Durga had told us that a big party with alcohol drinks was planned to celebrate our return from Tengboche. Nalin warned us again to avoid alcohol on the ascent.

"You can drink when we come down."

After we left the lodge and were beginning to fall into the rhythm of hiking, my mind began to wander. I mused to myself that when someone says *party*, I'm right there, but how much more fun was it possible to have in a few days, when I'm having such great fun right now?

Outside Phakding on the trail to Monjo, we crossed a rickety suspension bridge the width of five wood planks with chain-link sides. The cables holding the bridge up over the chasm served as handrails. White, blue, green, yellow, and red prayer flags, flapping in the wind, were attached to the handrail cable on one side of the bridge. The cables were anchored in cement at both ends, but the bridge still swayed as we walked across it, one at a time. Bill, curbing his instinct to follow closely behind when I crossed the bridge, said, "I'm taking pity and letting you to cross the bridge alone, but only this time, you hear?"

"Yeah, yeah, I hear you," I called back.

We passed several workmen building a rest stop with stones, similar to the ones we had seen being carried out of the stream yesterday. "Do you think those stones are the same ones the men gathered yesterday?" Mark asked.

"Where else would they have taken all those stones? It makes sense, doesn't it?" I answered.

Taking advantage of the beautiful scenery, I stopped often to catch my breath, which was growing shallow. Nalin had strongly advised us to stop often and drink water to avoid altitude sickness.

"I want you to drink more water," he said, coming up behind me.

Our durable water containers had been filled with boiling water at the lodge. By morning the water had cooled for us to drink on the trail. We'd been warned constantly to drink only boiled water or sealed bottled water. Our entire group had listened, not needing to be told twice.

"Yak train coming," someone yelled. In the Himalayas, yak trains moved at a formidable speed, but the deep-pitched clanging of the bells around their necks warned of their approach. As soon as they were heard, anyone on the trail scampered out of the way. Mark, Bill, Betsy, and I hugged the side of the mountain at an extremely narrow section of the trail as they raced by. Bill commented that he actually felt the yaks' hair on his arm as they passed.

When we arrived in Monjo, the lunch stop, my first question was: "Bathroom?"

A finger pointed through the kitchen, out the back door, and with a flick of the wrist, up a small incline. Seeing the wooden shed ahead, I commented to Betsy that it couldn't possibly be the bathroom. But it was—the first of many just like it. Opening the door, I just stood and stared, unable to speak or breathe. Memories flooded back. As a kid growing up in the country, there had been an outhouse in the backyard. My grandmother had had a two-seater at her cabin in the Blue Mountains of Pennsylvania. Those outhouses with crescent-moon doors were first class in comparison to this one at Monjo. It had a rectangular hole in the floor, an Asian-style toilet that required straddling the hole and aiming accurately. I saw that their idea of flushing the toilet was throwing a handful of straw down the hole.

This trip would never get five stars.

"I'm putting this experience behind me," I told Mark and Bill, meeting them as I came out.

"Please tell us we didn't just hear that comment," Bill said.

I scrubbed my hands with an antiseptic wipe, and as we returned through the kitchen, I saw another opportunity for the cooking series. I asked one of our guides, who was standing in the kitchen, "Could I cook, but only pretend to cook? I just want a picture of me cooking."

At first the guide put his hands on either side of his head, as if he didn't quite understand or know what to think. Then he started laughing and translated my request to the cook, who handed me a fork to turn the bread frying in a pan. The young cook had a bigger smile on her face than I had on mine. Bill snapped the picture, and I was out of the kitchen before any cooking skill could rub off on me. Making reservations at a restaurant was more to my liking.

Before entering the Sagarmatha National Park, we stopped to show our trekking permits to an official. Sagarmatha is the Nepali name for Mt. Everest. The park borders Tibet with Mt. Everest as its main attraction. Bill, Mark, and I knew that Lhotse and Ama Dablam were just as spectacular, because we had seen them from the air. Now we anticipated seeing them from the ground. We had to cross back and forth over the Dudh Kosi River several times on suspension bridges, even once over a deep gorge, but my fear of heights appeared to have dissipated.

Another small bridge, just above the surface of the flowing water, was in disrepair. Rocks, logs, and thin planks patched it together. With the upcoming monsoon season, its days were numbered, but its picture-postcard aspect provided a reason for me to stop and drink water and catch my breath. I told Mark that I was struggling to breathe and still not accustomed to hiking this much and up these mountains.

"I hate it when we lose altitude, because I know we'll have a tough climb back up," he answered.

Staying focused and concentrating on the present helped me to continue. The group was joking about surrounding ourselves in light and angels. Pete even asked me to put some light around him. I assured him I would—especially around his knees. Bill wondered why I didn't just levitate over the river. I told him that I wasn't quite ready to yet. At least the banter helped divert my attention from the physical challenge I was facing.

This was a very tough trek of six and a half hours. The air was definitely thinner, making breathing difficult. My heart continued to pound. Fortunately, my leg muscles weren't a bit sore; all my condo-step training back home and trekking in the Annapurna range last week had paid off. Camaraderie with my friends kept me going, as did the encouragement of our guides. My labored breathing was decidedly slowing my pace. Mark and Bill gave fair warning that they were pushing on and would see us later.

Betsy and I kept our own pace, trailing behind. A bathroom break became necessary after all the water I had drunk. While looking for a secluded place by the side of the trail, I asked Betsy if she could guess how close the group of hikers we had passed on the trail might be now, but she couldn't. With few options for privacy, I squatted. By the time I heard Sherpa porters coming down the trail, it was too late to stop. I thought, "First leeches, then stinging nettles, and now porters. I have to believe Sherpas hunched over, one-hundred-and-fifty-pound loads, won't notice me."

Betsy and I continued up the hill, met Bill and Mark at a small deck overlooking the mountainside. We trekked together into Namche Bazaar. Water-driven prayer wheels along the trail and prayer flags strung across the town from one hill to another greeted us. Passing on through town, Mark, the shopper, eyed tabletops crammed with Himalayan and Buddhist memorabilia. Storefronts with colorful T-shirts decorating its walls, waited for the next buyer, probably Mark. A short distance up a hill in Namche we reached our overnight destination, the Himalayan Lodge. The four of us sipped lemon tea and rested.

When the others came in sight, I hung out a second floor window, and yelled, "Namaste!"

Everyone laughed. Even Nalin loved the special welcome, but, always the tour guide and protector, he yelled back, "Be careful."

Our assigned rooms were on the third floor, the bathrooms were out front in a brown shed with a corrugated metal roof. Showers were outside in the back under a rusty roof. Finally in our rooms after the arduous trek, I collapsed on the bed until the luggage was delivered. Then, with clean clothes in hand, I headed for the shower while there was no line. I turned on the hot water and lathered up, but the hot water stopped—with the temperature outside around forty degrees and rain dripping through the roof. Quickly drying and dressing, I ran up to the kitchen and burst in, "I don't have any hot water for a shower, could you please turn it on?"

The words were barely out of my mouth when I noticed that the kitchen personnel were heating vats of water on the stove, presumably to dump into a large tank near the door. Persons showering regulated its flow by moistening themselves, soaping up, then turning on the hot water to rinse.

"Sorry," I apologized, "now I understand."

I later told Bill the "no hot water" story, and concluded, "Of course, no one was in line for the shower or they would have found out how things worked before they got undressed."

The brown shed offered more challenge to the trekkers: as bathroom usage increased, the condition of the toilets deteriorated. I had figured one trip to the brown shed just before going to bed would last the night, but at 12:30 a.m., I had no choice but to make another. Fortunately I had gone to bed fully dressed to stay warm. I put on my boots, grabbed my flashlight, and made my way down three flights of creaky wooden stairs, wondering why I was always on the third floor. The real challenge in the pitch black darkness was carrying the flashlight and toilet paper, closing the door, and hitting the hole in the floor—while holding my breath.

"I can't believe I'm the only one who had to visit the brown shed last night," I complained to the others the next morning.

Several shamefacedly revealed that they had employed various other containers and emptied them discreetly that morning. Mark summed up the enduring lesson that we all should remember.

"Drinking tea for dinner is a diuretic."

18

Arising early to trek, Betsy and I quickly packed our duffels, and Betsy offered to pack my sleeping bag. I thanked her, but said I'd do it as soon as I found the strings to tie it up. Betsy laughed, holding up a small bag, "No, you just stuff it in here."

"You're kidding, right? Not this whole sleeping bag into that little thing? Can't be done," I said.

When I told the story on myself at breakfast, as an indication of how little hiking and camping I had done, I added that I had always thought camping out was staying at the Budget Inn instead of the Holiday Inn.

On the trail by a quarter to eight, we soon passed another lodge where our Indian friends from Namaste Lodge were staying. The Indians had decided to spend an extra night there to acclimate before setting out, but they waved and wished us well. The trail followed the contour of the terrain with views of steep, snow-capped mountains overlapping each other for miles on end. Struggling to breathe, I often ignored the scenery to concentrate on trekking. Stopping for brief water and rest breaks helped me to enjoy the majesty of the Himalayas.

We hiked uphill for hours, reaching 11,800 feet according to the most recent reading of Nalin's altimeter watch. Occasionally we encountered other trekkers, two of whom caught my attention with stylish dark hair and designer glasses. One of the young men from Singapore carried a golf club. I casually asked, "What can you do with that club up here?"

"It's useful as a walking stick until we get to Hotel Everest where I'm going to hit a golf ball from the highest resort in the world." the young man answered.

"Which club is it?"

"A four iron."

"Yeah, I should have brought my four iron, too, since I can't do anything with it on the golf course," I laughed.

The young man unzipped his backpack and showed me two yellow golf balls and tees, inspiring a photo opportunity—golfing at 11,800 Himalayan feet. "Would you mind if I hit a ball?" I asked.

He readily agreed, handing me a ball and asking if I needed a tee. He also asked permission to take my picture, possibly wondering if the American in hiking boots, cargo pants, and layered sweaters, with long, dark hair in a ponytail and a hankering to hit a ball off a mountain were crazy.

"No, thank you. I'll just hit it off the trail," I said.

Mark's ever-present camcorder recorded my backswing and follow through. My swing felt good. But I didn't hit the ball. Missing a shot usually upset me, but I had decided at the last minute not to send the ball out to litter the environment. Resolving the dilemma between respecting the environment and the thrill of launching a golf ball from a Himalayan mountainside, however, left me only to envision, as consolation, the yellow ball arcing cleanly through the thin air.

Nalin rushed over to warn me to take care not to fall down the mountainside. I hadn't been paying attention, but the trail had narrowed, and my left foot was just inches from the edge of a steep drop. Understanding his concern for clients' safety, I apologized. Nonetheless, my swing had looked and felt great: straight left arm, head down, good turn of the body, and perfect follow-through. "If I could only replicate it on the golf course," I said wistfully to Mark.

I thanked the Singapore trekkers, and our group continued on the path. As I walked, I called in my angels and visualized a surge of energy. Encounters with mountain goats, Sherpas with funnel-shaped reed baskets full of wares, and ubiquitous yak trains gave me welcomed opportunities to rest and drink water more often. We stopped for a tasty lunch of noodles and vegetables, but I was more tired than hungry.

The afternoon trek was even more difficult. Lack of oxygen continued to make my body tire more easily. On the strenuous uphill climb to Tengboche Monastery, I could only go a short distance before stopping to breathe. My heart pumped wildly trying to push more oxygenated blood through my body. Bill suggested that I take one hundred steps, stop, rest, catch my breath, then start again. Betsy and I both followed his advice; but as we neared Tengboche, the distance between rests became shorter and shorter. Soon we were down to forty steps before stopping, but my body was screaming for oxygen, and my head ached.

Mark and Bill reached the monastery gate well before Betsy and me, but they waited to welcome us to 12,950 feet above sea level. We arrived huffing and puffing, hardly believing we'd made the tough five-hour trek.

When the group reached the lodge a bit late, we found that our rooms had been given to other trekkers. Bill joked that the rooms must not have been guaranteed with a credit card, but neither Betsy nor I was amused. All we wanted was a place to lie down. Nalin immediately negotiated for rooms at the nearby Himalayan View Lodge. I wondered if a pattern were emerging: first the Himalaya Lodge, then Himalayan Lodge, and now the Himalayan View Lodge; Namaste Lodge was the only odd man out.

Nalin had done his best under the circumstances, but Betsy's and my so-called room was more like a cubbyhole. Our bed was a wooden platform the size of a double bed covered by an inch-deep layer of foam. I took the outer side, so as not to crawl over Betsy in the middle of the night. "It can't be as bad as it looks, can it?" she said.

Afternoon lemon tea and cookies were being served in the dining room, and we figured at least we could get warm there. The weather was miserable—cold, misty, and cloudy—surrounding mountains completely hidden from sight. The Tengboche Monastery was barely visible. That's how bad conditions were. Large glass windows wrapped around three sides of the dining room offering, on better days, views to diners seated at tables and benches. The fourth wall had glass cabinets with shelves holding bottled water, beer, and canned goods for sale. A wood-burning stove in the center warmed the room full of guides and trekkers, some huddling close to the fire to drive the cold from their bones. Though I coveted a stool near the stove, Bill and Mark waved us over to a table.

Soon we discovered that the two men had been assigned the entire second floor of a separate building with scenic views in each direction through large windows, much roomier than our place, but no more luxurious. As soon as the men heard about the cubbyhole, they suggested that Betsy and I take the extra bed in their large quarters. Worried about what people might think, we declined, a mistake we were to regret before that cold night was over.

Nalin's group sat and talked with Keith, an Australian, and his rosy-cheeked Sherpa guide. Keith had curly blond hair and a few days' growth of whiskers, sort of scruffy looking, I thought, but then who was I to talk. Everyone's concern was the bleak weather and hope for its improvement tomorrow morning. It occurred to me that if we had seen the elusive Bengal tiger in the jungle, why not clear skies in the Himalayas tomorrow? I stood up, tapping my spoon on the teacup for attention, and confidently stated, "I ask that everyone here think about clear skies for tomorrow morning. Send that out to the universe, and we *will* have clear skies tomorrow."

I received *"here-we-go-again"* looks from my group. Undaunted, I turned to Keith and said, "Well, it does work. I've seen it work."

"I understand exactly what you are saying," Keith replied.

I thought, "Whether he meant that or not, I can't tell. At least he's gracious."

Midafternoon, Nalin's trekkers left to tour Tengboche Monastery, which had burned down in 1989 and been rebuilt as a beautiful stone structure. Taking off our boots before entering, we admired the walls vividly painted with deities and symbols, but the great statue of Buddha, a magnificent golden color, overwhelmed everything else in the room. Following the tour, we stopped by the gift shop to buy T-shirts. Mark was ready to bargain, but Nalin said, "No bargaining. Those screen-printed shirts help provide funds to finance their new sewer system installation."

Having used their present system, I gladly contributed my share to the project and chose a shirt bearing the image of Tengboche. Mark was still undecided after the challenge of bargaining was removed. "Has there ever been a gift shop you haven't wanted to leave some American money in?" I teased.

"I can't think of one right now," he answered.

As we left the monastery, I asked Nalin if I could come back there to meditate tomorrow. He told me that prayer sessions began at six thirty. When we reached the lodge, I got my journal and went to the dining room to sit next to the stove for warmth. By now, I was wearing my medium-weight long johns under black wool pants topped by cargo pants; and two shirts under my green Polartec jacket topped by a red windbreaker. On my feet, I wore silk socks, then rag wool socks, and finally a pair of heavyweight wool hunting socks. Trying to put on my hiking boots was an ordeal. From head to toe I ached from the cold and still felt my body temperature dropping.

I decided to forgo showering. The thought of removing even one layer of clothing was repugnant. As it turned out, everyone had decided against a shower after seeing the facility. It was in a wooden shed, about six by four feet in size, with a wooden door for privacy. A roof of corrugated metal with a large red bucket in the center covered the shed. An eight-rung ladder leaned against the roof.

Bill figured out the shower routine: "One first gets a large bucket of hot water from the kitchen, carries it across the courtyard and up the ladder, and pours it into the red bucket. Then one climbs down the ladder, enters the shower, undresses, lathers up, and prays to have enough water to rinse off."

"Do you really think the water would stay hot?" I asked Bill.

I wondered who could possibly be that desperate to shower. No one in our group seemed to be rushing to do so.

At dinner I barely touched my food; nothing looked or tasted good. After a couple bites, I just pushed the food around on my plate and remembered that I hadn't been hungry last night either.

Later I sat near the warm stove with our porters, conversing as much as possible without a common language. I soon gave that up and concentrated on keeping warm until time to go up and snuggle into my sleeping bag.

There was no comfort during the excruciatingly long and cold night. After only three hours of fitful sleep, my body began to shake uncontrollably. My teeth chattered and I alternated between shivering with cold and burning up. I had a terrible headache and felt nauseated, listless, and completely disoriented.

"It has to be altitude sickness," I told myself. "I had worried so much about getting it that I manifested it. I put too much energy into negative thought and, sure enough, it has happened."

19

Finally morning arrived. I still felt bad, but at five o'clock, I quietly slipped out of my sleeping bag so as not to disturb Betsy lying beside me on the wooden platform. Picking up my hiking boots, I tiptoed out of the room into the courtyard where the snow-covered peaks of Mt. Everest, Lhotse, and Ama Dablam all towered before me.

Stunned by their sudden appearance in the cloudless sky and awed by their majestic beauty and power, I forgot my own ailments and sank down on the steps to revel in the view. "Trying to transmit the magnificence of Mt. Everest," I thought, "is like explaining the Grand Canyon to someone who's never been there. Both want experiencing; descriptions always fall short."

When I spotted Bill and Mark coming toward me, I excitedly threw both arms aloft, "Need I say more? Behold our wonderful clear skies!"

I reminded them again that I had meditated last night about clear skies before sleeping. Even Bill admitted that he had had a feeling just before going to bed that we were going to see clear skies. Truly this morning was the first in the past twelve days that Tengboche Monastery had enjoyed a clear sky. Many trekkers and photographers hoping for spectacular views had come and gone in the past, without seeing what my friends and I now saw.

When Betsy joined us, we walked around the grounds to experience the glorious views from every angle and take photographs we hoped would convey some of the majesty of the mountains back home. Keith, the Australian we had met last night, joined us and suggested that we go up a nearby hill for more views of the mountain peaks. Nalin, who noticed the small group starting up the hill, quickly followed us.

As soon as I started to climb, I began struggling to breathe and became more disoriented with each step. Just as I felt exhausted, chilled, and unable to go on, Nalin caught up with us. As soon as he saw me, he asked how I felt. With tears in my eyes, I mumbled, "Not too good; I think I have altitude sickness."

Nalin immediately told me, "I want you to eat a bit of food and get down from this mountain as quickly as you possibly can."

Raising his voice so that the others took notice, he continued to lecture, "Why didn't you wake me up during the night when you had problems? That's how people die—they go to sleep and never wake up."

I dragged myself back through the courtyard to my room. Our porters had left basins of water for ablutions. I brushed my teeth and washed my face with extreme effort, then climbed back into my sleeping bag, assuming warmth and rest would help; but neither came. In a sudden moment of clarity I thought, "I have trekked all this way, up stone trails, through yak dung, across suspension bridges, and I am not going to lie in bed feeling sorry for myself."

I got up and pushed myself to take more photographs of the awesome scenery, reasoning, "This opportunity will probably never enter my life again, I need to make the most of it." But my usual enthusiasm was clearly flagging.

At six thirty Bill, Mark, and I walked up to the monastery for the early morning prayer session with Buddhist monks. Mani, who had assisted in making my cooking photo in Monjo, was our guide and ushered us into the monastery as soon as the doors opened, pointing out three seats for us on the side. Mani knew the monks, and everyone knew Mani. Respected by the locals, he had served as a cook at Mt. Everest base camp for nine months. Bill, Mark, and I sat quietly, listening to the chanting of the monks until Mani retrieved us. Breakfast was ready, but I had no appetite.

When our group was packed and ready to move on, Nalin pointed out our afternoon destination, the Everest View Hotel several mountains away. Built in 1937 as a resort catering to a Japanese clientele, it was on the same elevation as Tengboche Monastery, and the clear skies offered wonderful views of the hotel through our binoculars. I shuddered, knowing that the trek there would be difficult in my present condition. Nalin, however, had other plans for me at the moment; he had assigned a porter to accompany me and carry my backpack. After he explained that the seriousness of altitude sickness required my immediate descent, Mark volunteered to go down with me.

"Thanks, Mark, I appreciate you in coming with me. I hope the trip down will be easier; because I really feel sick."

The three of us began our descent. Although it had taken us five hours to trek the same distance uphill on the previous day, going downhill took only fifty-five minutes. While waiting for our group to arrive, my headache and nausea dissipated somewhat, aided by another photo opportunity for my "cooking series." Young men were washing metal dishes outside the restaurant where the group had eaten yesterday.

"Could I have my photo taken with you, helping to wash the dishes?" I asked.

One of the washers spoke English well enough to ask me politely what state I lived in. Thinking once again that Nepali schools must drill their students on U.S. states, I answered, "Alabama."

He laughed as if I had answered correctly and nodded, "Yes, you can wash the dishes."

Sitting on my haunches as the young men did, I took my place in the line of dishwashers around one side of a large, battered metal trough. The English speaker gave me a dirty mixing bowl with one hand and with the other, a bar of soap and shredded white packing paper. Mark stood ready with camera. After scrubbing one bowl, I walked off the job, saying dramatically, "I quit, without notice!"

The young man translated, and all the dishwashers laughed appreciatively. Only later did I realize that we had eaten from those same bowls only yesterday. I concluded that I hadn't come to Nepal to worry about hygiene.

When the rest of the group arrived, Nalin could tell that I still suffered from altitude sickness, even after descending a couple thousand feet. He offered to continue having my heavy backpack carried, but I refused. As soon as we came to an uphill climb I began to experience breathing difficulty. Giving up, I asked Nalin to have someone carry it. Mani got the assignment.

As we trekked, a helicopter and a small plane flew by. Up to this point, we had not seen any aircraft in the Himalayas. Nalin groaned.

"When we see this, it is very serious," he explained, "It means someone has died."

Word traveled fast in the Himalayas, even without the benefit of phones. Nalin soon learned that a Japanese trekker had died from altitude sickness.

"For some reason," Nalin said, "many Japanese tourists die in the Himalayas. This trekker had never even told his guide that he wasn't feeling well."

This information had come so quickly and accurately that Bill and Mark were astonished by Nalin's line of communication, however it worked. They both looked at me with relief.

During lunch break, everyone voted to hike to the Everest View Hotel at 13,000 feet for more mountain views. I was uneasy about my ability to continue, but Nalin assured me that he thought I could do it, because the ascent wasn't so steep as it had been to Tengboche Monastery. Trusting his opinion, I went along with Mani still carrying my backpack in front and his own in the back.

On the trail we stopped to watch four boys playing a game of pitching bottle caps into a two-inch hole they had dug in the trail. While each boy tested his skill, the others huddled around the hole to observe carefully. As we'd seen before, the boys played quietly, with no fighting or arguing. Another youngster dressed in jeans, purple sweatshirt, and red hat carried a basket by a strap around his forehead like a Sherpa. He also stopped to watch the game.

The trekkers took time for frequent rest stops and water breaks. I succeeded in reaching the grounds of Everest View Hotel, the resort for wealthy and/or elderly Japanese that hadn't worked out as planned because flying directly up to this altitude caused too many physical problems for visitors. Although discouraged by the sight of thirty stone steps looming before me, I slowly plodded up to the hotel's entrance.

By the time Nalin's group stepped out onto the hotel's sweeping rear terrace, fog and clouds had rolled in, blocking any chance to enjoy the surrounding mountain views. Our luck that morning with clear skies and great views was not to be repeated. The only option before we left was to have a drink at the highest hotel in the world, and that turned out to be a very expensive glass of mango juice. Transportation costs to supply these remote areas pushed up prices. I confessed to Betsy my happiness that everything from now on was downhill, because I didn't think I could spend one more night at this altitude.

We passed the hotel's helicopter pad, as we headed to lower elevations. Mountain goats speckled the mountainsides, and we trekked past a teahouse with a sign reading "Push the Door" emblazoned on its gate. The Syangboche airstrip above Namche looked desolate without any air traffic.

At a crest overlooking Namche Bazaar, Mark, Bill, and I paused to look down on the town, reminiscent of a miniature electric-train village. Mark remarked, "This gray sky and cold damp temperature feels like snow."

I agreed, saying, "I hope we do get some snow tonight."

I heard no agreement with that wish. We began our descent down a steep trail that appeared nearly vertical. Suddenly my right foot slipped, and I began sliding down the trail of loose dirt on my feet—fast—as if I were snowboarding, but without the board. Mani attempted to grab my arm to stop me, but my momentum carried both of us down the hill approximately twenty-five feet. Fortunately we stopped without injuries. Poor Mani hadn't stood a chance of stopping me since I towered over him and was much heavier. Mark, behind us, couldn't stop laughing. After it was over, I thought it funny too—but scary, considering the steepness of the hill.

Nalin offered to lead anyone who wanted to join him to a small national park's visitor center at the top of another hill in Namche. Betsy and I went with him to see simplified displays telling the story of the surrounding area and the Himalayas. Buddhist items, Nepalese clothing, and household objects rounded out the exhibit.

On our way back to our lodge, we passed a military installation where no photos were permitted and heard a voice asking, "Where are you from?"

Betsy and I couldn't stifle our laughter. Dick had clearly blundered into the military installation, not bothering to read the signs. He always asked that question of every single trekker he'd seen during the past three weeks. A short distance ahead of us, Nalin perfectly imitated the next question in Dick's series of queries: "Can I take your picture?"

That was followed by "Ready on three. One, two, three!"

Betsy and I, laughing with Nalin, realized that the guides observed the trekkers' idiosyncrasies more than they let on.

After the room Betsy and I had shared at Tengboche, our room assignment back at the Himalayan Lodge in Namche bordered on luxurious: a queen-size bed and a single bed in a room located in the attic, directly over the kitchen. Its warmth, thankfully, penetrated every cell of my body. The bone-chilling coldness I had experienced yesterday was gone. Remembering our last stay here, I decided to drink absolutely no tea tonight to avoid creeping down four flights of stairs to the nasty outside latrine.

When I peered out of my bedroom window the next morning, snow dusted the surrounding mountains—again, a wish come true.

After a brief trip to the village for one last opportunity to buy colorful souvenirs, the group left Namche for Phakding, our day's trek destination. Lagging behind the scattered group, Mark, Bill, Betsy, and I met a cute, petite blonde woman and Mark purposely asked her, "Where are you from?"

When she answered, "Canada," we laughed, confusing the young woman, who didn't see what was so funny. Before telling her goodbye, he couldn't resist asking if he could take her picture.

We laughed again while Mark explained to the woman that it was a private joke, quickly adding that we were making fun of a guy in our group constantly taking photos of strangers.

Her eyes sparkled, "I'm in one of his pictures; he's a man in shorts." All five of us bent over laughing.

The group soon passed through a small village where a bull was standing in the middle of the road. Cautiously ceding the bull his territory, I hugged the edge of the trail, prompting Bill suddenly to shake the sleeve of my red jacket and yell, "Look, *toro, toro*, red jacket, red cape!"

A nearby group of trekkers from England thought his antics funny, but I wasn't amused: "Thanks, Bill, for being a pal. I look forward to seeing you in a *corrida*."

Along the trail, we encountered several bridges essential to the supply system which were undergoing badly needed repair before the upcoming monsoon season. Five men were working on an almost dysfunctional bridge supported by two heavy-duty cables anchored on each side of the river. They were looping a more flexible cable over the main cables with about a three-foot drop between loops. In the bottom of the loops, they placed new planks of wood to span the open distance between the two main cables. When several base planks were in place, more planks running in the opposite direction were put over them to serve as the walkway of the suspension bridge. At the far side of the river, there was still no bridge at all, only the two stretched main cables. Men on the bank attached planks to a makeshift pulley to supply the repairman working high over the river.

"Can you believe we've been walking over so many bridges built just like that?" Bill commented.

"Is that guy working out on the bridge wearing a safety harness? If so, I don't see it," added Mark.

Departing Sagarmatha National Park, I noticed a soldier with a gun and wanted my photo taken with him. He reluctantly agreed after Nalin translated my request, but the soldier refused to let me hold the rifle. That's where he drew the line. I couldn't blame him, but my philosophy was just to keep asking until someone says *no*. It can lead to interesting situations.

When we were crossing the rickety old suspension bridge near Namaste Lodge in Phakding, a yak train and their Sherpas overtook us. We held to the bridge's cables for dear life while the animals passed. There were no sides to prevent one's slipping into the river below, and I actually felt the yaks' fur graze my arm in passing, they were so close. I prayed that with all the weight on the old bridge wouldn't make the cables snap.

Bill wondered when the new bridge, more substantially built of metal would open for traffic.

"If we make it across this old relic," Mark answered, "the Chamber of Commerce better be assembling to dedicate its opening. This thing won't survive the next rainy day, much less monsoon season and yak wear and tear."

The Namaste Lodge welcomed us back. Durga had promised us a party and what a party she threw. We would be the last tourist group staying at the lodge before the monsoon season started. Candles, outlawed earlier, now flickered in bottles as table decoration. Nepali wine, Chinese whiskey, Nepali rum, and Tuborg beer flowed freely. We sat at oilcloth-covered picnic tables lining the perimeter of the dining room leaving an open area in the center. The food was superb. Durga, an excellent cook, served tomato soup, potato salad, rice, noodles, and spring rolls with vegetables. Fruit cocktail and a chocolate cake completed the meal. I sampled Nepali wine, too sweet for my taste, and chose a bottle of beer.

Dishes were barely cleared from the tables, when music began. Mark asked Nalin if they would sing their national anthem, and the Nepalese proudly responded for their guests. Then Durga pulled out her harmonica. One porter started the dancing, making another exceptionally shy porter join him; both young men danced well. Durga pulled me onto the floor to dance with one of her male friends, a man from the village, who wore jeans and a white polo shirt and was several inches shorter than I. I didn't catch his name, but obviously he was well chosen—we both loved to dance.

He smiled and laughed until the music stopped, then told me that I looked just like his older sister Dee-Dee, and before long, the Nepalese were all calling me Dee-Dee. Between dances, I asked Dee-Dee's brother what he did for a living.

"I was the supervisor in charge for the new bridge."

"The new bridge just outside of town? When is it going to open?" I continued.

"Yes," he answered. "It opens in two days."

"Just in time for the monsoon season, that's great news." I especially loved the way the answer to Bill's question had come on a dance floor.

At the next break, he gave me a thumbs-up, saying, "You are good dancer."

"Thank you, I like to dance," I said, as one never to refuse a turn about the floor.

The Suitcase Wife

What most Nepalese really wanted, however, was a party. The trekkers were only an excuse to gather and celebrate. As more villagers arrived, one man dressed in colorful clothing and a hat, none of which matched, began dancing a bit. Well into the whiskey, he and Nalin began singing, alternating improvised verses to a villager's harmonica.

We enjoyed watching them dance, play, laugh, and have a great time together. Some trekkers retired early, but I, seldom known to leave a party early, and my three friends stayed, afraid we'd miss something. Had we left, we would have missed an episode with a particularly difficult guest.

The woman, accompanied only by a Sherpa, was traveling to Mt. Everest base camp. She began hounding Durga's husband for a big candle to take to her room, "How do you expect me to see?"

She continued to badger him, "But you promised me! Why can't I have a candle in my room? A large one! You promised!"

He had already stated the policy of no candles in rooms, explaining that the old dried wood interior of the lodge could be a tinderbox. However, she was absolutely relentless and wasn't satisfied with his explanation. Her negativity grew more annoying to everyone. We all thought, "Lady, just shut up and go to bed."

The party broke up at nine forty-five.

20

"No headache this morning," I announced jubilantly on our final trekking day into Lukla. Durga served us another hearty breakfast and, when we were ready to leave under cloudy skies threatening rain, tied a creamy silk scarf around our necks for good luck and safe journey. Mark whispered to me, "I hope this is the last scarf we get, or my luggage will be overweight."

Overhearing, Bill remarked, "Like always, you'll just give me some of your stuff to carry home."

Durga joined us on the trail as far as her father-in-law's home, and she, too, had trouble keeping up and breathing because of the altitude. She said that she had not been visiting for a year, because they were so busy at the lodge. Stopping at an unbelievably picturesque site, we posed for a group photo before a two-story, gray stone house with sky-blue trim in a bright, grassy green, rock-strewn field with a snow-fed stream meandering past and a mountain in the background. One of the porters greeted me as Dee-Dee. I was sorry I hadn't gotten the nickname before last night, because it was much easier for them to say than Sahara.

Farther down the trail, Nalin stopped to show off a reforestation project, desperately needed in Nepal to replace the thousands of trees harvested annually, in part, to support development of the tourism business. On terraced slopes, long raised beds of dark moist soil were planted with pine seeds and covered protectively with brown straw. Other beds holding saplings in progressive stages of growth showed the development of the project. The trekkers were pleased to know that efforts were underway to preserve the forests of the beautiful countryside we had been walking through and seeing at such close range.

The Suitcase Wife

Three-quarters of the way to Lukla, the rain began to fall, lightly at first, but increasing as we drew nearer. The stones grew slippery, and dirt turned into mud puddles. My hooded red jacket was ultimately overwhelmed by the cold rain, and I was miserable. Reaching Lukla's main street challenged us all to dodge the animals and the slippery mud puddles that sucked at our boots.

As we approached Khumbu Resort Bill, Mark, and I separated from the group to retrieve our emails. Unfortunately both its generator and printing capabilities were down, but the agent remembered us and promised to deliver our emails to the Himalayan Lodge.

Soon Betsy and I were standing in the doorway of our assigned room staring at the thick mattresses, fresh linens, warm blankets, and our private flush toilet and recalling the presence of strong, hot showers.

"Does this not feel like a five star hotel after days in a sleeping bag and a few tepid showers?" Betsy commented.

I couldn't have agreed more. After reorganizing my duffel bag and luxuriating in a hot shower, I joined Betsy, Mark, and Bill around a table on the grass lawn overlooking the graveled airstrip. The rain had stopped but had already caused cancellation of more flights out of Lukla, creating a backlog of trekkers needing lodging for the night. The Himalayan Lodge was overflowing, and the scene in the lobby was chaotic.

The promised emails arrived and were read, but basically it was a time to do absolutely nothing—or watch two nearby dogs sleeping away the afternoon. Later I mentioned casually that I was getting hungry and craving a garden burger with onions and tomatoes. About that time Nalin came out to direct his group through the throng of trekkers into the lodge owner's private dining room where our dinner included vegetables, french fries, pineapple, and—to my delight—a garden cutlet with onions and tomatoes, exactly as I had described.

Talk was all about getting "socked in" and being unable to fly to Kathmandu. I joked that I would love to email my boss, saying that I was stuck in the Himalayas and couldn't get back to work. After dinner, the lodge owner turned on his television, thinking we would like to see the shows. Almost immediately, young porters from isolated Himalayan villages gathered to peer in the windows, eager to watch television, which still amazed them.

Noticing that our sturdy host was fighting a bad cold, I offered my cold medicine, which I no longer needed with our departure imminent. I walked across the grass and past the still sleeping dogs to get the remaining capsules, then returned to explain how often to take them and to say good night. As soon as I settled into my cozy bed, I discovered why the dogs slept all day—they had to bark all night. One bark produced a swelling antiphonal chorus of others.

By daybreak it was obvious that limited visibility would preclude flights to Kathmandu for the time being. In addition the phone line was down and Nalin couldn't even call to change our flight from Kathmandu to Bangkok for the next day—no phone, no generator, no email. Only one flight had left Lukla yesterday before the rain, and all of yesterday's cancelled flights had priority today. Since transportation from Lukla stopped after five o'clock in the afternoon anyway, we figured that tomorrow would be the earliest we could leave. Even that scenario could worsen if clouds rolled in that afternoon, as they often did.

Mark had stayed in bed reading, but the rest of us sat around the picnic table to see whatever happened. Clouds finally dissipated and flights resumed, but only one Lumbini Airways plane was flying the Lukla turnaround; the second plane had "technical" problems.

Bill calculated, "If only one flight left Lukla yesterday and eight were cancelled and three flights flew out this morning, then another eight flights must depart before our turn would come. The turnaround time leaving Lukla for Kathmandu and returning is an hour and forty-five minutes. Therefore," he said, "if we can get out by eleven o'clock tomorrow morning, we still might be able to make our connection to Bangkok."

The Suitcase Wife

As we sat idly watching for flights, a business opportunity idea bubbled up. I suggested a cottage industry to make and sell T-shirts at the Lukla airport for trekkers. The shirts' message could be: *I was socked in* Lukla, Nepal. "The Nepalese could make money selling T-shirts like the I-survived-Hurricane-Andrew ones that popped up just hours after it hit South Florida."

Pete said, "You have too much time to think, and I think you're just bored."

After further consideration, Pete and Bill decided a T-shirt should read *Socked-in at Lukla*. The *Nepal* wasn't necessary; if anyone knew anything about Lukla, they would know it was in Nepal. "Go for the intelligensia with more grammatical direct-ness and a little snob appeal," said Bill.

"Remember that complaining woman we saw at the Namaste Lodge?" he asked Betsy and me, "I wonder how she's doing on her trek to Mt. Everest base camp?"

"I wonder if that woman's Sherpa has pushed her off a cliff yet?" Betsy commented. "Maybe a yak did him a favor and butted her off."

"Would that be considered a Yak of God?" I quipped.

Groans and hisses followed, but I persisted, "I know that was bad, but sitting around here waiting for planes is messing up my mind."

Nalin joined us breathlessly, "Two Lumbini planes are now ferrying trekkers out. There may be a chance we can get out today."

With a wave of his invisible wand, Nalin had conjured up seats on a chartered plane—but only six were available, and we numbered eight, if Nalin were counted. While we'd been sit-ting around and blathering, major wheeling and dealing had occurred between the lodge owner and Nalin to get his group out today. Perhaps even money had changed hands to increase the opportunity. The air was apparently thick with intrigue.

The owner himself approached the table and whispered, "Pack now. Get down to the plane quickly."

Nalin added, "And be quiet as you go."

We hurried to our rooms, threw belongings into bags, and headed down to the tarmac shouldering our own duffels and not waiting for a porter. Resolving the problem of more passengers than plane seats still remained. The plane had not yet arrived, and Mark suggested that the fairest method to determine who stays behind was to draw straws. "The person with the shortest straw loses."

Everyone agreed. Mark, still trying to be fair, said, "Since Dick and Pam are a couple, they shouldn't be separated. We should leave them out of the draw, and the remaining five draw straws."

Everyone agreed again, but I also thought quietly, "Dick wouldn't offer to stay, of course. He's happy with Mark's idea."

Mark picked up pieces of reed and clutched them in his fist with only the tops showing. I drew first, a long straw, but long enough? Two more straws were drawn, both long. Bill drew the next to last straw, the shortest thus far. Mark held the remaining straw and slowly opened his fist to reveal a long straw. So Bill would have to stay.

With his jovial persistence, Nalin negotiated to get Bill on the plane, without success. Then suddenly a seat on a small helicopter mysteriously materialized at the cost of two hundred and seventeen dollars. Bill didn't have that much money in his pocket, none of us did. Collectively Mark, Bill, Betsy, and I began pulling money from pockets, passport holders, and backpacks until our pooled resources bought the seat for Bill—but with an undetermined departure time.

We, waving goodbyes to Bill, boarded the plane and taxied off the end of the runway back to Kathmandu. Our Himalayan experience had ended, but Bill's still persisted.

When we landed, the bus driver loaded our duffels and set off to the Hotel Vajra. Near the area of the email office, Mark and I hopped off the bus accompanied by a guide to lead us to the hotel. By this time, I felt that I could walk to the hotel blindfolded, but I didn't object to the guide's company.

The Suitcase Wife

While Mark responded to a waiting email, I talked with the woman attendant, asking if she would give Tashi a message, the next time he came in, from "the American woman who helped him." When the attendant promised to do so, I said, "Tell him that she met the manager of the Namaste Lodge, and Durga is, indeed, a wonderful person, who asked about him."

Mark and I left the office with our guide, but on the way to the hotel, he got lost and we ended up at the Monkey Temple. "So much for our needing a guide," I whispered to Mark before taking over and eventually leading us to the hotel.

After settling in and showering, Mark, Betsy, Pete, and I met at the Sunset Bar on the rooftop one last time. We had barely given our drink orders when Bill stepped through the doorway.

> Hey, everybody, I'm back. About an hour after you flew out of Lukla, my helicopter arrived. There was too much weight to fly with three passengers and the pilot, so some guys decided to siphon gasoline out of the helicopter's tank. One of them sucked the siphon to get it started, and spit the gasoline out of his mouth after it began to flow. Then we loaded for lift off, but my duffel didn't make it and I don't know when I'll get it. I hope it's still with Nalin waiting to get to Kathmandu. The helicopter really struggled to get off the ground, then the pilot just barely skimmed the treetops and the mountains, in case he had to set it down fast because of low fuel and too much weight. I'll never forget that crazy ride.

Betsy, Mark, Bill, Pete and I had tickets to Bangkok the following day. Though I had never trekked before, I felt good about my adaptability and awed by sights I had seen. My fellow travelers expressed similar sentiments. I decided that perusing endless outdoor catalogs, page after page, and ordering stuff had prepared me for almost everything, except altitude sickness.

21

As leaving wondrous Nepal drew close I wanted more T-shirts to emblazon its name at home on my nephews and friends. Betsy and I strolled toward the market, knowing we were near when we passed a butcher shop with a skinned goat draped across a table. With directions from several vendors, we found a T-shirt shop. As soon as we stopped, the owner began to display shirts he pulled off the shelves at a feverish pace. He would shuffle rapidly through stacks of shirts to find any size mentioned. Having seen Mark bargain so often, I decided to try my hand and asked the price of my favorite style. He assured me that it was "only two hundred fifty rupees."

"What if we bought three?" I asked.

"Two hundred and thirty each."

I countered, "Two hundred."

"Two hundred twenty."

"Last offer, two hundred ten."

"Okay," he agreed.

I was happy, and he seemed pleased. Since I had no idea whether I had made a good deal or not, Mark would likely retain his crown as King of Bargaining. We walked back to the hotel, passing the same goat draped over a table but now joined by a headless calf on another table.

Nalin—with Bill's duffel—had maneuvered to arrive in time to load the group into the bus and escort us to the airport. He continued to shepherd us through check in like the good guide he was. He knew the ropes, had connections, and was worth his weight In gold in tight situations. After hugs and goodbyes Pete, Mark, Bill, Betsy and I walked through immigration and boarded the plane to Bangkok. Even the runway, rumored to be built over a field of garnets, didn't attract my interest. I was ready to head home.

An overnight layover in Bangkok allowed time to explore the city. Clearing customs, we walked the short distance to the Amari Hotel where thick, luxurious towels and icy bottles of mineral water soothed our weary bones. At the hotel's featured Thai lunch buffet, my thoughts drifted back to my Aunt Luci whom I silently thanked for expanding my world and introducing me to travel and new foods.

With so few hours in Bangkok before flying to the States, we hired a driver to take us into the center city. We were grateful for credit cards, because pooling our money to get Bill out of the Himalayas had taken most of our cash. The driver dropped us at the Patpong market where aisles of stalls offered silk scarves, knock-off watches, and practically anything that could be sold, even sex. A sign like a menu outside that stall listed each sexual act available and its cost. Mark wanted to photograph the sign, but a man, angrily waving his arms, chased us away.

Bill announced that the car was waiting. As soon as the driver spotted us approaching, he turned on the air conditioning.

After a fitful night's sleep, I woke ready for good food. I crowed to Betsy that I'd lost about ten pounds and needed breakfast. "The guys can catch up with us. They'll be late anyway."

Not an ounce of fat was noticeable on my body, well toned after the trekking and some meager meals. The breakfast buffet featured Chinese and American food, so I had both: smoked mackerel and red snapper, sushi, fried rice, pancakes, fruit salad, and eggs.

Mark, Bill, and Pete soon joined us. Later Pete said goodbye. When he hugged me, he commented that he bet my journal was unlike anyone else's on the trip. I smiled, saying that he might be right:

> I wrote about my own feelings and exceptional moments on the trip—hardly anything about food or shopping or weather. Maybe I saw experiences through different eyes—not better or worse—just different. Safe travels home, Pete.

Mark used his credit card again to hire a car and driver for four hours, but at the Chao Phraya River we pooled our remaining cash to take a longboat ride. Before boarding, I asked where the bathroom was. A pointed finger and a flick of the hand directed me through one room to a back room. In the first room, a man was sleeping on a cot. The back room was empty. Thinking I had misunderstood the pointing finger, I went back to ask again and received the same direction. Baffled, I returned to the back room, now noticing a partially missing floor plank that must be the bathroom. Squatting over the opening, I saw the river directly beneath. River pollution must be incredible, and I resolved to warn my three companions.

Traveling in the longboat, we saw people playing, washing dishes and clothing, and bathing in the river. "Pollution aside, how could anything even look clean?" Mark quipped, "If you fall in the water, Sahara, you're on your own. I'm not saving you."

A smaller canal, branching off from the Chao Phraya, was home to a floating market selling food and flowers of every imaginable color. Steeply pitched roofs with turned up corners and intricate gold, blue, and red decoration adorned small temples along its banks.

Soon we came to a snake farm and watched grown men, who should know better, catch snakes with their teeth. Fearful of snakes, I turned ashen and cringed when one of the men brought a snake over to me. I admitted to my friends that he had chosen the right person to elicit a response: "If I'm asked whether I fear heights or snakes the most, the answer is snakes."

Going back on the main river, we passed the Wat Arun or Temple of the Dawn, its middle section covered in scaffolding for cleaning. As soon as we docked, our driver retrieved the car and drove us to Bangkok's famous weekend market housed in buildings and stalls that covered many acres.

Unfortunately the first area we visited offered animals for sale. Among the sad dogs and mournful cats, we saw brightly colored parrots, small squirrels, large cages full of yellow, green, and blue parakeets and exotic animals we didn't recognize. Saddened by the caged wild things, we were walking toward an exit when Bill spotted a pinball machine. Mark immediately challenged me to a game, which inspired raucous cheering and partisan taunts. Mark won with 97,000 points, but at least the gang was happy and cheerful again.

Stopping at the hotel to pick up our luggage, we headed to the airport. I almost emptied my wallet for the airport tax upon leaving Bangkok. Left with only a dollar, I was quite uncomfortable until I could use my credit card again. "Next time I'm taking twice as much money. It's too scary to travel with a dollar to last all the way to Atlanta," I thought.

In Los Angeles, we said goodbye. Betsy's flight left first. Before they flew off to Philadelphia, Mark and Bill promised to keep in touch. Hugging them, I said, "I had the time of my life, and I'm going to miss you guys. What a great time we had together."

In truth, I was thinking, "I know how these promises work out. They never amount to anything, and eventually good intentions fall by the wayside. I'll never hear from them again."

I remembered Betsy's earlier comment that she had replaced her fear of suspension bridges, with the fear of people from Pennsylvania. Now I hoped that she was wrong.

Over the next few months Mark, Bill, and I kept in touch through emails and cards exchanged at Christmas. My expectation that our contact would fade after the trek didn't materialize. We continued to be friends, albeit at long distance. In late winter, Mark emailed that he and his wife Megan had decided to visit China, Tibet, Hong Kong, and Bali that summer and asked if I would like to join them. Bill, it seemed, had a prior commitment and couldn't go.

Remembering what fun it had been to travel with the two brothers, I first wondered how Mark would be with a wife at his side, especially one so uninterested in adventure travel. She, along with Bill's wife, had opted out of the Nepal trip, but this trip must appeal to her or she wouldn't be going.

I emailed Mark that I would see if space remained on the tour and when I could schedule a three-week vacation, figuring it would be easier to get time off in summer than it had been for spring trekking. That left what, for me, always seemed to be the final question: whether to spend that much money. The China trip would cost more than Nepal, where buying opportunities were few. However, within a week I emailed Mark: "I'm good to go. What's next?"

A flurry of emails over the next few months kept Mark and me busy with getting visas, researching travel books, and deciding how much money to take. We didn't want to run into unexpected cash problems like we had in Nepal. We decided to meet in Vancouver, Canada, before catching our flight to Beijing. I planned to arrive a day early to relax, begin adjusting to time differences, and see Vancouver, a city I had never visited.

On the appointed morning, Mark wakened me with a call to say that he and Megan had arrived and suggested that we meet for breakfast at nine o'clock. As I dressed, questions raced through my mind: Will we still be friends after not seeing each other for a year? Will I still want to travel with him? Will I like Megan? Will she like me?

The Suitcase Wife

I waited in the hotel dining room for them—apparently Mark still ran late, as usual—but as soon as we saw each other, reconnection took over. Mark introduced Megan, who was a foot shorter than Mark with short brown hair and brown eyes; she was outgoing and quick to laugh. Moreover she, too, had been born and raised in Philadelphia. What was not to like? I soon felt the trip looked promising.

When we were seated and the waitress had gone for coffee, we decided what to order, then began polite conversation. The waitress returned for our order and Mark, gesturing toward Megan, "My wife would like two eggs over easy and bacon, and my suitcase wife," looking at me, "would like the same."

Megan burst out laughing and Mark and I joined in, tears rolling down our cheeks. After initial puzzlement even the waitress smiled, not really understanding the joke until Mark explained it. At first, she hadn't known how to react, but then again, neither had I. Mark's humor had broken the ice.

The breakfast episode set a tone for our whole trip. Subsequently we often referred to me as Mark's "suitcase wife." On the Yangtze cruise, Megan extended the joke by presenting to me a string of pearls, "Mark and I want you to have these for taking care of him when he was so sick in Nepal—nothing but the best for Mark's suitcase wife."

Mark added, "Don't worry, they weren't expensive."

I understood the subtle pecking order.

Later in Bali when Mark was buying a skirt for Megan, he kidded with the women vendors that he had to keep both of his wives happy, then asked me what I would like. Gesturing toward Megan, he said, "This is my real wife, and she is my other wife," causing giggles. Mark kept a straight face.

Leaving Bali and landing in Los Angeles, I said goodbye to Mark and Megan with a sigh of relief. We had enjoyed one another's company for three weeks, but the tour itself had been very fast-paced and tightly scheduled. I had definitely decided that I preferred the more challenging and less structured adventure trips on which anything might happen and usually did. Apparently Mark and Bill agreed, because during the next few years, we enjoyed wonderful trips to Cambodia, Vietnam, Thailand, Mongolia, and Egypt.

When I came home raving about what fun we had or how much we had learned or other glowing trip reports, I sometimes detected a hint of disbelief or suspicion in my audience. It was almost as if they were thinking, "Oh, sure, they just travel together for love of adventure, travel, and friendship. That's impossible. It can't be that innocent."

But it wasn't impossible. That's why Bill, Mark, and I had continued taking trips together. Each brought a different dimension to the friendship that even others traveling with us enjoyed. Mark and Bill were good brothers and I was a good companion. I took the teasing as the "suitcase wife" in stride and enjoyed finding humor in situations with the brothers. A committed caring for one another's well-being, especially encouraging during difficult hiking or when one fell sick appealed to me most of all. We felt we could count on one another in times of need and feel safe when traveling in third world countries.

Although living at a distance from the brothers, I looked forward to planning our next trip together when all our schedules allowed. I wouldn't change a thing about our enduring friendship.

22

"We are on our final approach and will be landing shortly in Islamabad, please fasten your seatbelts."

The announcement roused me from memories of past trips to wonder what this one would bring forth. I looked around the cabin and saw that, as the plane approached landing, women passengers were quickly arranging scarves over their hair. During the three-hour flight from Abu Dhabi to Pakistan, most of them had removed their head scarves.

As in Dubai, Mark's long legs led the race to immigration, the baggage carousel, and customs. Afterwards a man who identified himself as our driver was waiting to drive us to the Serena Hotel in Islamabad's diplomatic area. According to him, it was the best hotel in the city. Security was tight with a tall, black iron fence surrounding the hotel's grounds and a guard station just outside its barricaded gate. As we approached it, a guard ordered the car to stop for inspection. Bill whispered, "Jeez, can you believe all this security? Look at those spikes on that barricade."

Five guards inspected every part of our car, even using a mirror on a pole to examine underneath the vehicle. Only after the absence of explosives or weapons was assured, did the steel barricade recede into the ground, the fence gate open, and access to the hotel grounds clear. "But look up that driveway to the hotel," I exclaimed.

An obstacle course blocked a direct route to the entrance. Six-foot-long, staggered concrete highway dividers filled with flowers required the driver to drive slowly around each to follow the inclined driveway. The Serena's entrance, where guests were delivered was above ground level. Before leaving the premises, the driver deposited our bags at another security point to be searched once again. At the registration desk, Bill, Mark, and I showed our passports keeping quiet unless spoken to.

Finally two musicians playing Pakistani instruments welcomed us wary travelers through an arabesque entrance into the lobby with marble walls and floor and a fountain gurgling in the center. A sparkling chandelier, tall lamps, candles, and thick oriental rugs completed the picture.

Alex, our tour representative, was waiting for us. Dark haired and a tad overweight, he was Brazilian and worked for a travel company based outside Pakistan, but he employed native guides in accordance with local regulations and language skills. After polite inquiries about our trip, he suggested that we meet shortly to review our itinerary, "which had some changes."

Mark, Bill, and I looked at each other: "Now what?"

Before leaving the United States, we had been notified that the portion of our trip to Peshawar and the Khyber Pass had been canceled because of terrorist attacks. They were considered too dangerous for tourists. I had looked forward to seeing the Khyber Pass, an important trade route and military post linking Pakistan and Afghanistan. It sounded so romantic. Perhaps I had read too much Rudyard Kipling. I hadn't known enough about Peshawar to regret it's being off limits.

Now, Alex gave us more disappointing news. Travel to the Swat Valley had been canceled yesterday, because the Taliban had killed some police officers near Mingora where we were scheduled to stay. I had so looked forward to seeing the Swat Valley known as "the Switzerland of Pakistan," with its clear lakes, tree-covered mountains, and beautiful meadows.

Alex said, "My home office and our Pakistani guide felt we should change to another interesting itinerary, rather than risk a serious problem. We'll be traveling east of the Swat Valley on the Karakoram Highway, going into Baltistan, better known as 'Little Tibet,' in the far reaches of northeastern Pakistan."

I had read in one of my travel books that portions of the Karakoram Highway were "full of potholes and rather rugged." I wondered to myself, "How rugged really? This might be harder than it sounds."

Alex assured us, "The trip will be very safe with no excursions into dangerous areas. The Pakistanis as a whole are very friendly in spite of the terrorists who grab headlines throughout the world."

Mark, who had been growing increasingly restless as Alex spoke, said, "I always thought travel adventure. . . oh, never mind, not important," he concluded abruptly.

That meant that Bill had connected with an unnoticed, but sharp elbow poke. He and I both knew Mark's taste for adventure and realized that this was no place to proclaim it. We had decided to be more discreet on this trip. Even Mark's wife Megan, before he left, had made him promise not to rile anyone: "I know how passionate you are about things that matter to you, but please try keeping quiet."

When Alex had finished and left, we commiserated about missing the Swat Valley and hoped there were to be no more changes. I said, "I just loved the name Swat Valley."

"The Pakistanis need to stand up and swat the Taliban and reclaim their land," Bill added.

We signed up for a truck-painting tour the following morning, and Mark and Bill went to their room, while I went to meet Harriet, my trip roommate. When I knocked and walked into our room, Harriet was already unpacked. She was shorter than I, slim, wore glasses, and spoke with a slight accent.

"Hi, I'm Sahara. I can't place where you live by your accent?"

"I live in Canada, but I was born and raised in Argentina," Harriet replied.

"Oh, that makes sense. Isn't that disappointing we can't go to the Swat Valley now?"

While introducing ourselves and chatting, Harriet pushed her brown hair from her eyes as she casually peered over my shoulder at the construction site facing the hotel and noticed a man in dark blue pants and shirt walking back and forth while the workers were busy at their jobs. Reaching for her binoculars, she suddenly asked me, "What is that man carrying?"

After closer observation, she continued, "I can't believe it. That guy in the blue uniform is carrying a machine gun and patrolling the construction site. Isn't this wild?"

Obviously security at the hotel was of high priority. I quickly picked up the phone and called Mark and Bill in their room, "Look out your window. Do you see that guy in a blue uniform walking back and forth at the construction site? He has a machine gun."

23

The next morning Harriet slept in, but Mark, Bill, and I woke up early and headed for breakfast in the dining room before our special truck-painting tour and visit to the Lok Virsa Cultural Museum. Fellow travelers began to introduce themselves to us, obviously trying to figure out the relationship between the two men wearing wedding bands and the woman with none, traveling together. We three enjoyed watching the curious faces, but we intended to keep the mystery alive for a bit longer, not mentioning a word about the "suitcase wife."

Kimmitt, our Pakistani guide for the day, arrived to chauffeur the three of us on our morning tour. He was slight of build and free of facial hair with hollow cheeks, and dark hair and complexion. Fluent in several languages, he introduced himself. His eyes sparkled when he spoke, and the sunglasses pushed up on his head were of the latest fashion. He lived in both Islamabad and Skardu in northern Pakistan, traveling between the two for work and to visit his girlfriend.

Bill, Mark, and I were his first clients, as he was near the end of his training as a tour guide. His laugh came easily and he wasn't afraid to answer sensitive questions about his country. He drove a small blue Toyota, a departure from the white Toyotas seen everywhere. In the course of the tour, we would discover that Kimmitt was to accompany us for the entire trip until we reached the Chinese border.

When we left the hotel's lobby, Bill and Mark were dressed conservatively in tan slacks and dress shirts, and I wore a long-sleeved blue polo shirt, khaki cargo pants, and a head scarf that coordinated with my outfit. Mark did say rather loudly,

The Suitcase Wife

"Hey, do you see that guard standing up in that tower over there? I think he has a machine gun."

We wanted to make sure no one in earshot missed seeing him. Other guards dressed in dark blue trousers, light blue shirts, and wide silver belts were also carrying guns and patrolling the front driveway. A guard in blue trousers and white shirt speaking on a cell phone appeared to be the supervisor. When Mark and I began to take photographs, a guard quickly approached us, "Please do not film near the gate."

"Okay, no problem," replied Mark, honoring the pact we had made before arriving in Pakistan, "No pushing the envelope; we'll be low key this time."

On the way to the truck-painting factory, Kimmitt drove through Rawalpindi, Islamabad's sister city, where the airport was located. A sign read: "GOOD BYE, Thank you for visiting Islamabad International Airport." Litter and trash covered both sides of the road, and men milled about with no apparent vocation.

At least at the factory, men and young boys had jobs, although Bill, Mark, and I soon saw that the work was hard and dangerous. A supervisor told the visitors, with translation by Kimmitt, that the truck-painting industry employed sixty thousand men. He said that boys begin as early as eight years old to learn the trade. If they didn't do well, the boys, some of them orphans, were out of work and have to find different employment.

The workers were oblivious to the visitors until we showed a genuine interest in the process. They worked under the hot, blazing sun at tasks that appeared tedious and dirty. Their arms were covered with paint, but they still took pride in their job. I thought, "In the end, the fumes from those paint cans and the repetitive motion required will probably shorten their life expectancy. I'd bet that paint is lead-based, but I'm not going to ask."

We learned that a paint job costs approximately two thousand dollars and takes eight to ten weeks to complete. The vehicle is out of service the entire time, producing no money to support its owner. The owner determines what kind of elaborate design he wants on his truck. Sometimes they choose famous people like cricket legend Imram Kahn, soccer champ Pele, and Princess Diana or religious symbols, military heroes and equipment, and even the Mona Lisa. As Bill, Mark, and I traipsed around the open-air factory, we even saw lush landscapes with waterfalls and deer adorning trucks' sides and rears.

Mark concluded, "Only the lack of imagination could determine a boring design."

I viewed the workers as true artists, taking immense pride in their work and marveled at the kaleidoscope of colors, ranging from hot pink wheel rims to lime green hoods, and truck bodies decorated with designs made from red, orange, green, blue, and white reflective tape cut into intricate shapes. Men cut the reflective tape into leaves, figure outlines, and shapes of triangles, diamonds, circles, and trapezoids of various sizes, some only an inch in height; then pasted them into geometric designs over the entire truck.

"Can we even imagine the patience it takes to do this job?" asked Bill.

"This is nothing less than spectacular with the patience of Job *factored* in," added Mark.

"Mark one," I laughed, licking my forefinger and running it down an imaginary blackboard to acknowledge Mark's pun, one of the reasons I enjoyed traveling with the guys.

Bill earnestly pressed on, "Anyone has to see this production to appreciate all the work entailed in creating "jingle trucks." How could I adequately describe the truck-painting process to anyone? It's mind boggling."

Jingle trucks were named for the sound they made as they drove down the road. To achieve the "jingle," chains and medallions were inserted through holes predrilled in the truck's chassis at the bumpers and sides and welded into place. The chains, hanging down from the chassis, clanged against each another as the trucks motored across the landscape. A burly, slightly balding man with a beard and arms stained baby blue up to his elbows, squatted on his sandals, painting the jingles. Hot pink, lime green, and baby blue jingles alternated along every foot of a bumper.

Walking back to the car through the factory, we admired elaborate woodcarvings made to decorate the trucks' exteriors and saw another section devoted to upholstering their cab interiors in fabrics woven with gold and silver threads. I crawled up into a truck's cab, wanting to know how it felt to ride so high off the ground. Before we left, Mark and I took photos, and I regretted not having my Polaroid so I could have given pictures to the workers. "What a tough life they have."

On the drive to the next stop, I kept looking at my fingernails. Thinking aloud to the boys, I said, "What do you think my nails would look like if I had to pull the backs off all those tiny reflective tape pieces and stick them on a truck? There must be thousands and thousands of them in a design."

"Knowing you, you'd need more than just a manicure," said Mark. "You'd need therapy."

"You're right, I wouldn't have patience either."

Kimmitt said that the jingle trucks are Pakistan's natural treasure and unique to that country. Bill wondered if there weren't some way for Pakistan to promote their national treasure, because the workmanship and creativity of the industry were so outstanding. Unfortunately Kimmitt had no answer, but neither did the government. We would encounter jingle trucks throughout the areas in which we traveled.

The next destination, the cultural museum, required only a brief stop, so Kimmitt drove the blue Toyota to an overlook above the city, commanding an entire view of Islamabad. We enjoyed the impressive panorama a few minutes before driving down to the King Faisal Mosque, the last stop.

Kimmitt told us that the mosque held 85,000 worshipers outside, 15,000 inside, and another 200,000 on the surrounding grounds.

It's the largest mosque in Pakistan and South
Asia; the sixth largest in the world; and the tallest
in South Asia with its four 260-foot minarets. The
mosque is supported by the late King Faisal bin
Abdul Aziz of Saudi Arabia.

We removed our shoes, and I tried to cover my hair with
a scarf.

"How do I look?" I asked as the scarf started to slide off
my head. Mark and Bill just shrugged, their silence meaning
"whatever."

Lacking time, we moved quickly over the grounds, then
collected our shoes—gold-sequined sandals for me—and
quickly posed for photos before returning to the hotel for a
tour of Islamabad with our entire group.

While we waited for the tour bus, Alex said about the
guides, "I'd like to clear up any confusion. Throughout our trip
along the Silk Road, local guides are required. Their knowledge adds to your experience. We also have national guides
in each country who stay with us for the entire time. Having
many guides might seem strange, but you'll understand each
has a different function as we go along."

The bus arrived with Ali, our Islamabad city guide, welcoming us. Slender with a quick smile, he pointed out that just
a few short blocks from our hotel was the Red Mosque. "Do
you remember hearing about it, a month ago, when Islamic
militants and the Pakistani military clashed?"

As the bus reached the Red Mosque, Ali continued,

You'll notice it's no longer red; it's now white.
After the clash with the militants, the government
decided to paint it white. While the celebration
was taking place at the mosque, Islamic radicals
smuggled in red paint and brushes and they had
the mosque half painted red again before they

were discovered. Security had checked pockets and people themselves before entering. How the militants had managed to transport red paint and brushes is still puzzling. The only possible explanation was that underground tunnels radiating out from the mosque served as supply lines.

"Unless security allowed them through," I thought.
"Where there's a will, there's a way, we say," offered Mark.

24

"It's too early," I grumbled when the six-thirty wakeup call came. While Harriet and I hustled to pack our duffels and get to breakfast, I complained that I hadn't slept well—or long enough. Alex was pushing hard to load passengers and luggage for an eight o'clock departure. He advised, "Since there are American tourists in the group, please tell anyone who asks about your nationality, that you are Canadian."

He also warned everyone not to tell anyone our next day's destination as we headed toward China.

Alex's caution suddenly reminded me of advice I'd gotten from a friend and former government official upon learning that I was going to Pakistan. I leaned across the aisle to relay my friend's opinion to Mark and Bill as we left Islamabad. His advice had been direct and unequivocal: "Do not trust anyone, even if they appear to be nice."

It seemed that Alex, our national Pakistani guides Abdul and Kimmitt, and even Rashid, the bus driver, couldn't get out of Islamabad fast enough. Abdul was married with two children; he hovered around five eight, with skin the color of creamy cappuccino and dark wavy hair. His wife's good cooking coupled with meals on the tours had probably added a few unwanted pounds. His serious nature contrasted to his fun-loving cousin Kimmitt.

Rashid, at nearly six feet, was taller than most Pakistanis, and sported a dimple in his left cheek and a sparkle in his dark eyes. He was quite reserved and understood more English than he let on but preferred to concentrate on his driving skills. Mark, Bill, and I preferred that, too.

The Suitcase Wife

Our medium-sized bus finally entered the famous Karakoram Highway (KKH) outside the city. Alex explained that by the time we crossed the border into China, we would have traveled the entire length of the KKH, which follows one ancient caravan route on the Silk Road. He added that if we had gone to the Swat Valley, we would have missed a portion of the highway.

"Well, at least, we can claim that we did the entire route," Mark assured his seat companions in the back of the bus.

Alex continued, "We'll be going through some incredibly beautiful scenery, but the road is very rugged. I want to warn you of that ahead of time. That's why we can't have a larger vehicle."

We headed for the Baltistan area, located in the extreme northeast of Pakistan. According to Abdul, "This particular area of Pakistan is not accustomed to tourists, only to mountaineers who travel there to climb K2, the second highest mountain peak in the world, second only to Mt. Everest. Because of the terrorist attack in the Swat Valley, this will be the first tour group to stay in and explore Skardu and Shigar, both towns in Baltistan."

I knew about the Baltistan area from reading Greg Mortenson's *Three Cups of Tea*. Abdul, who had grown up in the area had heard about Mortenson's work with town elders to build schools for both boys and girls in northern Pakistan.

The bus had barely advanced along the KKH, when we reached Abbottabad. The town had a military installation and Abdul warned us not to take photos as we passed, for fear the bus might be stopped. Years later, hearing the news of Osama bin Laden's demise, Mark, Bill, and I were astonished that we had passed close to his refuge where he had lived undetected, so close to the Pakistani military base.

We stopped after only twenty miles on the KKH at Taxila, considered a top travel destination in Pakistan. Getting off the bus and into the ruins, the group listened to the guide's lecture:

> In 1980, Taxila received an UNESCO World Heritage Site designation. It was an important religious center until invaded by many conquerors, including Alexander the Great. Early in the twentieth century, ruins of three ancient cities were excavated along with numerous stupas and monasteries. Jaulian, the Buddhist monastery, was the most famous structure and for the purpose of preservation, you'll find its stucco sculptures inside the museum.

Being respectful and paying attention to the local guide was becoming more difficult as Bill, Mark, and I fought jet lag. Hot, dry, and dusty, we shuffled through the ruins, trying to pay attention to the guide. We did admire the ancient alcoves with bas-relief sculptures incredibly rich in detail after thousands of years, but our energy level still dropped. Looking at each other with half-closed eyes, we realized that all we wanted to do was get back on the bus and rest.

Once we had gotten back on the bus, we couldn't ignore the dangers of the KKH itself. The serpentine, stone-strewn dirt road chiseled from the mountains with a thousand-foot drop into the Indus River precluded relaxation. Each time we hit another rut. Bill gasped, "Where are the guardrails?"

Rockslides often delayed passage, shrinking the road's one-and-a-half lanes to a single lane. We splashed through rivulets formed by small waterfalls cascading down the mountainsides, and actual paved sections of road were few and far between. The Karakorum Highway offered as many thrills as an amusement-park ride. I held onto the seat in front of me for dear life, trying not to succumb to the temptation of looking out the side window at the sheer drop to the river below.

The leftovers of a recent rockslide had narrowed the road to one lane. It was there we came face to face with a huge jingle truck. Neither would back up and allow the other to pass. It was a standoff; Rashid and Abdul got off our bus and tried to negotiate a solution. Meanwhile more and more vehicles lined up behind both truck and bus, and confused drivers joined the melee.

Eventually our bus driver conceded, and all the vehicles behind our bus backed up to a wider area allowing the jingle truck to pass. Rashid had decided that the young truck driver was too inexperienced to back up. Mark whispered to Bill and me, "Isn't that wonderfully reassuring news—a truck driver who is unable to back up a big truck? Wonder what else he can't do? So much for safety."

When the jingle truck and line of vehicles were past, our bus continued up the KKH. Bill confessed that this drive, though harrowing, was also pretty exciting. Mark agreed, and I added, "No one back home would ever believe such a roller coaster could exist."

We drove through a village virtually destroyed by the earthquake of 2005, and after three years, many of its buildings still lay in ruins. It was easy to understand why rebuilding would be slow in so remote an area. Alex pointed to a destroyed building and said, "When the earthquake struck at 8:00 a.m., this school's concrete roof collapsed, killing two hundred students and their teachers. They had no chance to escape. It was such a tragedy."

The group still had a long journey before arriving in Besham for the night, and I requested a "potty break." I had anticipated that in a landscape so rugged and void of population, there would be no bathrooms, but as I told Mark, "There are certainly enough large boulders to provide privacy."

For most of the travelers, this created no problem. When the bus stopped, it was women to the right, men to the left—except for one self-conscious, plump woman in the group.

She waited until the other women had returned to the bus, before deciding to get off. That was the first of many times she pulled the same trick. Later, Harriet and I called her on her tactic, which often delayed our getting on the road. Eventually she did improve.

Mark, Bill, and I sat near one another on the bus and conversed with fellow passengers, some of whom were still curious about our relationship. We were forthcoming about our friendship based on a mutual love of travel and a shared preference for an adventurous edge to it. We readily described highlights of trips we had made together, ending with our fortuitous, luxury-laden four days in Dubai. Some could understand the arrangement, and others couldn't, but we didn't worry about the "others." We told of packing all the Hermes products from the hotel and promised a show of "everything we raked off the shelves. It's a stash!"

Exhausted from a ten-hour ride, we finally arrived in Besham. A quick meal led to bed, but for me, no sleep. The hotel's spartan accommodations offered no air-conditioned relief from the hot, sticky night. Pushing deeper into Pakistan, Bill, Mark, and I had understood that lodging choices would become more rustic, but the Burj Al Arab's and the Serena's opulence faded into distant memory. Alex had said that travel on the Karakoram Highway tomorrow would mirror today's ride. Mark had commented, "Now, that's something to look forward to. To think that terrorism was once our worst worry; it pales in comparison to traveling on the Karakoram Highway."

The five o'clock wake-up call couldn't come soon enough for me; I had tossed and turned all night. Even my breathing exercises failed to encourage sleep. I grumbled to Harriet that it wasn't going to be a good day. After breakfast, we had driven only a short distance, when the bus stopped dead in the middle of the road, a large herd of goats leisurely strolling up the highway blocking its passage. Normally not so grumpy or so sleepy, I couldn't resist saying to Harriet, "Didn't I say it wasn't going to be a good day?"

The KKH hugged the Indus River, its water a chalky, brownish gray. Occasionally milky pale-blue raging streams passed through towns or villages and fed into the Indus. In one village, homes had been built into the steep-sided hills bordering the stream, with some extended over the stream itself.

I pointed out one house and said to Bill, "Look at that roof; it substitutes for a yard. A goat is grazing on some hay up there; a wheelbarrow is sitting on a dirt pile, and the wash is drying on a clothesline."

Rashid dodged goats, people, and colorful jingle trucks carrying wheat, coils of steel reinforcement cable, fuel, and sacks of potatoes. Mountains with scrub vegetation and plenty of rocks rose steeply up from the road. I said, "If Afghanistan looks anything like this, no wonder Osama bin Laden has never been captured. This terrain could hide anyone."

At this point on the KKH, towns were few and far between. The ones we did pass through were strangely similar: No women were on the streets. Abdul explained that they weren't allowed in public unless covered from head to foot and escorted by a husband or male relative.

I admitted, "This is not for me—no freedom to come and go as I please, waiting for someone to accompany me. You've got to be kidding."

Most spectacular was the scenery with craggy mountain ridges and snow-capped mountains in the distance. Rashid stopped the bus at an overlook where three mountain ranges—the Himalayas, the Karakoram, and the Hindu Kush—were all visible. I grinned, thinking back to our experience in Nepal several years ago, and told Mark and Bill, "They are truly beautiful, so long as I don't have to climb them."

Two hard days of traveling, brought us to the northern Pakistan town of Gilgit. After dinner, though exhausted,

Harriet, Bill, and I wanted to find a store selling school supplies we could take to a needy school in Shigar, our destination for the next day. We asked Alex for directions, but he only knew that there was a store somewhere in town. Carrying the pooled money of several fellow travelers, we walked purposefully through town on a mission to find the store. Arcades of storefronts, fashioned from concrete pillars and flat concrete roofs, displayed household items and clothing. I tried communicating with locals to locate the store, "Do you know English? We're looking for school supplies."

The older shopkeepers merely shrugged their shoulders, either indicating their lack of understanding or pretending that they didn't. Harriet told me as we walked, "Here we are, two white foreign women unwrapped and accompanied by a white male. No wonder they won't talk to us."

I finally said, "Let's think: where would young men work who might know English? How about that telecommunications shop at the end of that street? Remember how Kimmitt and Abdul are always on their phones. Let's try it."

As we entered the door, four young fellows greeted us in English. Bingo! I could hardly believe it. After explaining what we wanted, one of the young men told me he would lead us to the store. Winding through a labyrinth of streets, he asked me where I was from. I impulsively thought to tell him the truth, but the stern warning not to admit to being an American came rushing back to mind. I told him I was Canadian. Immediately the young man asked, "Would you like to make a phone call home to Canada since I can make foreign calls on my cell phone?"

I could have kicked myself for lying to such a nice person. The lesson from this experience convinced me to ignore instructions and tell the truth; it didn't pay to lie. Now having to make up a lame excuse, I said, "Thank you for your offer, but my brother is at work."

The young man not only guided us to the school supply store, but stayed with us during our spending spree and translated. I asked if I could come behind the gate to choose the supplies. When they agreed, I joined the Pakistani sales-men as we pulled tablets, ABC books to learn English, colored pencils, and regular pencils off the shelves.

Our purchases filled two boxes and cost fifty-three U.S. dollars, later confirmed by Alex as a bargain. With goodies in arms, we shook hands all around with the Pakistani men, bid-ding them goodbye and thanks.

Later thinking back on the shopping spree, I was amazed at how bold I had been to slide behind the gate, head uncov-ered, and talk directly to the men. I chalked it up to another adventure with everything flowing smoothly to make it happen. Surprisingly I had felt no hostility from the locals.

25

The Karakoram Highway of yesterday would pass as a major, well-maintained thoroughfare compared to the stretch of road leading from Gilgit to Skardu. Another tough day of riding in the bus brought the kind of thrills to and squeals from its occupants usually found at a Six Flags park. Bill, Mark, and I, all sitting on the side closest to road's edge, were watching the swiftly flowing Indus River hundreds of feet below. Bill remarked, "Anyone ready for some fun rafting down there?"

"Too dangerous for me, Bill. Go for it," I answered. The roiling water would render the danger of upsetting into a disaster. Fortunately rafting wasn't planned on this trip.

While I was looking down toward the roadbed, suddenly a huge hole covered with exposed steel rebar materialized under the right side of the bus. Only black space could be seen beneath the worn rebar, and Rashid had just driven the bus over it. "Ohmigosh, did you see that?" I yelped excitedly.

"Yes," answered Mark, "and I can't believe it. This is wilder than yesterday—worse road condition, and the road is even narrower."

I noticed a cable stretched across the Indus River and attached to the mountains on either side, with something attached to the cable moving slowly over its expanse. Puzzled, I wondered what in the world it was. With binoculars we could see a man sitting on a stick with his ankles crossed, holding onto a heavy-duty clip snapped over the cable; while his friends on one side of the river payed out a rope allowing him to slide across the river. Without benefit of a bridge nearby, the ingenious idea saved time and made an easier, albeit much scarier, way to cross the river than scaling narrow mountain paths until he came to a bridge.

Occasionally a small community of stone buildings with green, terraced fields carved from the mountainside and large trees provided a welcome relief from the usual starkness of rocky crags. Bill asked me if he could borrow my camera to photograph some of the "cool layers of stone."

"Have at it, my friend," I said, knowing that, as a lover of rocks, photographing them sent him to heaven.

Abdul pointed to the steep mountainside on the opposite side of the river and said, "Look hard. Do you see any holes in the mountains?"

I saw inconspicuous holes, barely noticeable from a distance, and faint paths reminding me of rabbit trails. Abdul explained that the holes were entrances to gem mines, and the main path running along the mountainside was a transportation route for men who worked in them. Barely discernible along the path was a cluster of small, one-story stone buildings that housed miners. "Actually," I thought, "I can't think of anything but mining that this rugged landscape could offer humanity, unless it was a place to hide."

Again rockslides had blocked the road, and bulldozers had heaped rocks and debris into mounds, clearing a path for vehicles. At one narrow section, the bus once again came bumper to bumper with a jingle truck loaded high with sacks of potatoes. Both drivers refused to give ground. A heated argument escalated with Rashid in the bus watching the potato-truck driver approach, waving his hands and arms for emphasis. Alex, assuming that money could be a deciding factor, spoke to the truck driver, but it didn't work. The driver was defending his right of way. Alex had incorrectly judged the situation.

Alex's and Abdul's next tactic was to explain that the bus was full of tourists, who needed to get to Shigar. The potato-truck driver realized that tourists brought money into this hardscrabble Baltistan area. He walked back to his truck.

In Pakistan, vehicles drive on the left side of the roads, like the British. Rashid and our bus were on the inside lane closer to the mountainside, which normally would have the right of way. The truck driver adamantly refused to backup and allow our bus to pass, because that would push his weight load too near the edge of the road. A slight shift of load could tip him, his truck, and the potatoes over the side into the river. As soon as Rashid realized the situation, he backed up to a slightly wider spot allowing the potato truck to proceed safely. Both drivers waved to the other in passing.

I was fascinated by the sudden resolution. "And isn't it interesting that the driver wouldn't directly accept money but, indirectly, he acknowledged the importance of tourist dollars."

Once again traveling the road, we passed a crew doing repair work. "Did you notice those men working down below the edge of the road trying to repair its shoulders," I exclaimed. "They aren't even wearing safety harnesses. How dangerous is that? One wrong step and they'll be rolling down the mountainside."

A short distance down the road, a highway construction roller that appeared to be broken down on the inside lane and a scraper pushing rocks a short distance away left only a narrow passage. Concerned about safety, Alex told us, "Because traveling closer to the road's edge is very dangerous, I'm asking everyone to leave the bus and walk ahead to a safer location down the road. Leave everything on board, and Rashid will drive through this narrow place. We'll board again on the other side and continue."

Mark observed, "With all these delays, I wonder when we'll get to Shigar."

I wondered the same thing, but the walk felt great, even for a short distance. I'd been on the bus much too long. Without more delays, the van drove through Skardu on our way to Shigar. I noticed a sign to Shangrila at a fork in the road. "There's another Shangrila in the world to go along with every other country that claims one," I laughed. "Every country chooses its own spelling, too; however, I'm still looking for the one that will bring me eternal life."

The Shigar Fort, recently reopened as a hotel, was to be our base for the next two days and offered amenities comparable to high-end hotels. Its location in this out-of-the-way rural area surprised me, until we discovered that it was operated by the Serena Hotel chain and read its brochure: "The Shigar Fort Residence is a unique heritage conservation project which offers guests the opportunity to experience the restored architecture of a 17th century Raja fort-palace, while enjoying modern amenities and services."

I stopped reading after learning that Hassan Khan, the twentieth ruler of the Amacha Dynasty, originally constructed the fort mainly of stone.

"What else would he use with untold millions of rocks all around him?" I was clearly tired after a long day of bumping over rocks in the bus.

Assigned a room to myself, no roommate, I followed a porter along a convoluted route to my room and ducked under a low doorway to enter, thinking, "I need to remember about this low doorway."

The planked floors polished to a deep satiny finish required the use of slippers provided by the hotel to avoid scratching. Antiques in the room probably also needed special care. I sat on my bed and sympathized with the poor porter who had to hoist my duffel and climb a narrow spiral staircase to reach my room. Seeking to end the day peacefully, I found the outdoor garden and gazebo overlooking a pool with the relaxing sound of a waterfall. Mark and Bill joined me in the gazebo for a few minutes before dinner spent rehashing the crazy day.

Without the usual early wakeup call, Mark, Bill, and I slept late the next morning. The two men eventually ambled down for a leisurely breakfast in the trellis-covered courtyard.

I arrived at the table holding the top of my head, "Can you see any blood? I forgot to duck down enough and nailed my head on the door near my room. Ouch! I just knew I was going to hit it before we left this hotel."

No major harm was evident. We finished eating and by mid morning, joined several of our group walking into Shigar. Dusty, narrow streets led past children in schools and women scrubbing clothes in troughs by the roadside into the heart of the village where men managed their businesses. Two clean-shaven, well-groomed men in one store worked at portable sewing machines, with their legs extended under a low table. Behind them, shelves displayed bundles of fabric. Across the street, two men, each wearing a *shalwar kameez*, shook out a bundle of pants and small colored hats to sell. The older with a long, picturesque white beard graciously allowed a few photographs. A pile of fabrics in pale blue and purple, mauve, and grays lay at his feet.

A few steps away, another shop sold tennis balls. "Tennis balls?" I asked. "But I haven't seen any tennis courts."

The yellow balls, we were told, were for youngsters' cricket games. Remembering the appointment to deliver school supplies, several in the group purchased some of the balls. Bill said, "Let's not forget about soccer balls. The kids would like them, too."

Down a shaded street, we encountered a wizened old man, or perhaps he just appeared older than his years. His typical native dress was dingy and faded, and a brown *pakol* or wool hat covered his head. Only the tips of his chin hair were tinged with white, while the remainder of his beard was jet black. When he smiled, deep lines etched around his narrowed eyes and his empty gums were exposed. He rested the white bag he was carrying on a low windowsill and posed for pictures, enjoying every minute of the attention.

Our destination was a mosque. The on-site guide said that the Amburiq Mosque was built in the fourteenth century by Amir Kabir Sayyed Ali Hamdani and was the first mosque in Baltistan area. After years of decay, it had been restored by the Aga Khan Cultural Services of Pakistan, using methods of stone and mud construction appropriate to its era. I remembered that the same organization had restored the Shigar Fort Palace and created the small boutique hotel in which we were staying. I'd read in the hotel brochure that the foundation had won a UNESCO award for excellence in 2006.

We stepped into the mosque's courtyard, where the guide pointed out a sycamore tree that was around seven hundred years old. Its trunk measured seven feet in diameter. Our entire group was to gather there and wait for a complete tour of the village led by Tariq, a local man who normally guided expeditions to K2 base camp.

26

Tariq arrived wearing a pocketed vest over traditional clothes and over his close-cropped hair a blue baseball cap with "Alaska" stitched on it. Shorter than most Pakistani men, he had a large dimple in his right cheek and unwrinkled skin, despite his extensive exposure to the harsh weather in climbing K2.

For some unknown reason, I felt compelled to ask Tariq if he had heard about Greg Mortenson and his book, *Three Cups of Tea*. He looked at me puzzled. I rephrased the question, "Have you heard of Dr. Greg?"

"Yes, Yes! I know Dr. Greg. He's a very nice man and built many schools for the Pakistani children. I have met him," Tariq said excitedly, "and one of his schools is here in this village."

He was very proud of the fact he knew Dr. Greg and pleased to meet someone from the United States who knew of him and what he had accomplished. Clearly I had made a new friend. I couldn't believe my luck in following an impulse and seeing happy results.

Mark looked at Bill and whispered, "I guess that answers the question of what school gets the school supplies. Want to bet we take them to Dr. Greg's school?"

I pulled out my camera and asked Tariq if I could take a photo. I had begun traveling with a Polaroid when I visited remote areas and enjoyed seeing an unsuspecting subject startled by the camera's whirring and shooting out a piece of paper. Upon handing the blank sheet to the subject, he/she would flip it from side to side with a puzzled look, trying to figure out what was going on. I always knew who had seen a Polaroid camera before, because they would shake it to develop it faster. But when the uninitiated watched an image begin to appear, it was a magical moment, a mystifying experience.

As the group walked down a dusty lane towards the school, I chatted with Tariq, who spoke English well. Suddenly I stopped, miming to a group of several men that I would like to take their picture: by first pointing to the camera, then to the men and circling my hand to indicate all of them. Four clean-shaven men and one bald man smiled and nodded, indicating their permission. With camera raised, I was about to push the button, when a man with a black beard screamed in Urdu, one of the languages in Pakistan. I didn't need to know Urdu to understand that he was angry at being photographed. Shocked and taken aback, I didn't know what to do. The first words into my head came out, "What did I do? Did I just start an international incident?"

In a matter of seconds, Tariq quickly jumped between me and the man with the beard. They were arguing and yelling at each other. Sheepishly I stood wordless, not knowing what to do. When the argument died down, Tariq casually walked to me and quietly said, "Let's go."

He motioned for me to continue down the lane away from the episode. Still shaken and confused, I asked, "Tariq, what just happened back there? What did I do? I only wanted to take their photo."

Tariq replied, "It was nothing."

"That, was not just nothing. What happened?"

Not answering immediately, Tariq finally said, "You saw the man with the beard?"

"Of course," I quickly replied.

"That man is very conservative. He is Taliban. We don't agree with the Taliban."

I shook my head, unable to speak. "I can't believe this just happened," I thought.

The group moved on. Later Neil, a spry gray-haired retiree from Connecticut who was in the rear, told Mark, Bill, and me that the man with the beard had continued ranting and shaking his finger at the other men in the group who'd wanted their photo taken. When I told him that the man was Taliban, it all made sense.

"You can chalk it up as another experience that I survived to tell about."

At the end of a dusty lane was a sign: "In the Name of Allah Almighty - Visitors Welcome! - Jafar Abad Community Girls School - Start May 2000."

We had finally arrived at the school with the supplies neatly wrapped in boxes tied with red twine. Kimmit had carried them from the bus.

Young girls greeted us with a song. They were dressed identically in loose-fitting emerald green tunics over white pants and white scarves covered their heads. Some had fingers dipped in henna. Undaunted by the earlier episode, I took each girl's photo as they sang, placing every one the camera ejected in a line on the teacher's desk while I took the next. The girls closest to the desk watched in amazement as the images grew more distinct, while they tried to concentrate on singing.

When the school supplies were presented, the headmaster said his thanks with a smile. His eyes widened as the supplies stacked on his desk grew taller and taller. After my earlier experience, I felt better when he asked for a photograph with his daughter, a student at the school.

Walking back through the village on a different lane, I had a feeling the Polaroid camera wasn't finished for the day. I asked a group of children if I could take their photos and a brave little boy agreed. As the others watched it develop, they wanted pictures, too. One child ran from the lane to a nearby house with his photo in hand, and the next moment, a mother was pushing five children in ragged shorts and tops out the door.

As I took pictures, I noticed that the mother had inched closer to the lane, but stopped short. When the children ran back to the house, the woman caught my attention, looked directly at me, and patted her right hand over her heart, nodding slightly. The "thank you" she expressed could never be duplicated or more appreciated, for it had come from the heart and across wide differences in culture.

For lunchtime, Alex had arranged transportation back to the hotel. When our group saw a tractor pulling a cart approaching, the first of several quips was, "Hey, Alex, nothing but the best for your group, eh?"

Tired and hungry, Bill, Mark, and I quickly climbed into the cart for the dusty, bumpy ride back to Shigar Fort. I remarked that I hoped we didn't meet any more Taliban on the way back. "What would they think of us now?"

Actually local Pakistani men laughed and seemed to enjoy watching foreigners bump along in a cart. Mark stopped videotaping and asked Bill, "Wonder what was hauled in this cart yesterday? You'd better hand me your antiseptic gel. I'm not videoing anymore until I use it."

"Like we're ever going to see your film anyway," I kidded Mark.

Although Mark usually had his video camera in hand to capture our adventures, we had never seen the results from any of our trips together over the past nine years.

As we walked to the entrance of the hotel, I stopped to talk with Rashid, who was washing the dust-covered bus. Walking on, I noticed a woman washing clothes by a small aqueduct and two young girls playing nearby. A male relative of the mother seemed to be their escort. I held up my Polaroid and pantomimed a request to photograph the young girls. As the girls scampered away, I suddenly thought to photograph the man first and let him see the process. When I did so, he insisted that the girls come back and pose. The man and mother seemed happy to receive the photograph, nodding their heads and smiling.

The remaining distance to the hotel wasn't as pleasant. A group of young boys returning from school walked alongside me, talking to me in English. When I turned off around the corner of a building, I felt little stings on my legs and back. At first, I ignored them, then another volley came, and I spun around in time to see boys disappear around the corner. I glared at one boy who had walked with me and he looked terrified, but it wasn't he throwing the pebbles. My mind shot back to that warning before coming: "trust no one." Things weren't so friendly after all.

Following lunch and a brief rest, Alex suggested a hike to Kari Dong, the ruins of an old fort dating back to the eleventh century, at the top of a nearby mountain. Apparently only Mark, Bill, and I thought that a perfect way to spend an afternoon. We all enjoyed the physical exercise, though at times I had difficulty keeping up with the men. When we encountered a steep undefined trail, the hike became more dangerous. Small rivulets crossed the trail, gravel slipped under foot, and the incline increased sharply. The guides determined not to climb any farther. I gasped, "Thank goodness, this was about as far as I could go."

Bill and Mark's response was to tease me as usual with: "Oh, you're such a girl!" I had heard that too often over the years to be upset.

When we reached the village, a polo match was in progress. Mark, Bill, and I climbed into the concrete stands to join the local men and several other members of our group. Three-man teams faced off against each other; and goals brought cheers from the fans.

Ever-ebullient Neil decided to teach the Pakistanis to do the "wave," but something was definitely lost in translation: jumping up, throwing your arms into the air, while

The Suitcase Wife

yelling "yeah-yeah-yeah" in sequence didn't quite translate into Urdu. It didn't matter, all the polo fans laughed, delighted to see Americans doing their strange customs. I, sitting on the top bleacher, kept my eye open for the Taliban fellow, "If he thought photo taking was too radical, these antics might put him over the edge."

27

I was ready for breakfast before my travel companions the next morning, so I approached a woman with her head respectfully covered who was sitting alone. I asked if I might join her, and the woman introduced herself as a health-care professional from Islamabad. She had read that Fort Shigar had been restored as a lovely hotel.

When I mentioned the previous day's encounter involving a member of the Taliban, the woman, glancing cautiously around, said in a soft voice, "The Taliban is infiltrating Northern Pakistan from Afghanistan and settling in small communities like this. By offering help and financial assistance to mitigate the hand-to-mouth existence in such places, the Taliban expects a repayment of loyalty."

I listened intently. Looking around again, the woman continued, "Sadly, if the villagers keep accepting their help and don't defend themselves against situations like your encounter yesterday, such occurrences will probably become more commonplace, and more Taliban will come; it's certainly a bad situation."

Slowly raising a clenched fist to her chin, she said, "You will see when a Taliban member enters a barber shop, he first grabs his beard at the chin to determine whether he can have it cut. If the beard extends from the bottom of his fist, it may be trimmed; if not, it must remain at its present length."

After finishing breakfast, I wished her a pleasant weekend and thought once again that meeting interesting people was another reason to travel.

When I told Mark and Bill of my breakfast conversation, they wished that they had gotten up earlier. The guys encouraged me to talk to strangers when we noticed someone wanting to make contact. For some reason, people weren't hesitant to engage me in conversation or offer assistance. I was approached more frequently when alone, and if the guys were close by, they joined the conversation.

Once again, I was reminded how lucky I was to travel with them. Deep down, I knew Mark and Bill adored their wives, and the wives felt so secure in their marriages that they allowed their husbands to travel for as much as four weeks with me and not feel threatened.

Hopping in the bus, we left for the market in Skardu, the last large town before mountaineering expeditions headed up to climb K2. At the crowded market, Mark, Bill, and I separated for our own errands.

Following my breakfast conversation, I was fixated on beards—whether men with beards were or weren't Taliban—and speculated whether a beard was ready to be trimmed. I realized that my questions probably bordered on profiling, but I was curious as I walked through the market.

Looking in one storefront, I saw a tall young man with a day's growth of beard leaning on a shovel before the biggest mound of dried apricots I'd ever seen. The pile was higher than the man's shoulders and perhaps twelve feet wide, touching both sides of his store and extending about eight feet out from the back wall. I gestured by stretching my arms up high and bringing them down to waist level, meaning that I'd never seen so many apricots before.

The merchant didn't speak English, but he understood the gesture and offered me an apricot. After tasting it, I wanted more. Wisely I chose a much smaller bag than the one requiring the shovel to fill. Walking away, I wondered how many rodents lived at the bottom of the pile. I couldn't imagine the man's ever reaching the bottom, but I sure hope my apricots came from the top.

Dust wasn't confined to back lanes of the market, but swirled over the market's paved streets; there was no way to avoid it. I ran into Mark and Bill shopping for postcards and a camcorder tape. Mark needed more money and asked me how much I had with me. Our guide had earlier advised us to carry only a small amount of money and be cautious at all times.

"I don't have enough to pay for all that," I said.

The three of us pooled our money to pay the bill. Mark laughed, "That's what friends are for—money. Especially you, Sahara, since a suitcase wife is supposed to carry enough money for us."

I refused to demean myself by responding.

Following lunch in Skardu, we journeyed to Shangri-la, not to experience paradise on earth, but to visit a resort centered around a DC-3 airplane. I couldn't help thinking, "Shangri-la's image—synonymous with peace, tranquility, and transcendence—doesn't quite fit with the idea of a DC-3 sitting in middle of a landscaped lawn overlooking a lake."

The transformation of the airplane into a coffee shop didn't quite jibe either. In the 1990s, according to local legend, the DC-3 crashed during takeoff from the Skardu airport but suffered little structural damage. The owner of the Shangri-la resort, who incidentally was a high-ranking military officer, purchased the plane and brought it to rest in the resort. We agreed that we could check that site off our list, if it had been on the list to start with. The revised itinerary clearly required that the guides fill out several days with some sort of activity.

On the way back to the Fort Shigar Hotel, Abdul, speaking from the front of the bus, told about his arranged marriage and meeting his bride, then entertained questions. Everyone listened intently and was amazed to hear that Abdul's parents had made the arrangements when he was just five years old. Divorced for many years, I couldn't imagine an arranged marriage. "Perhaps," I thought, "I'd have been better off if I'd had one."

On second thought, I realized I would've had to marry someone my mother and father chose, and that would mean disaster from the get-go. I'd rather make that decision, whatever the outcome. Our introspective driver, Rashid, commented that his marriage had also been arranged, but offered no details. Kimmitt, at least ten years younger than Abdul, knew that marriage questions would soon come his way. When they did, he answered with glee, "I'm not like these old guys. I'm not going to have an arranged marriage. I'm more modern."

Everyone burst out laughing. Later he admitted that he had a girlfriend at the university in Islamabad but he didn't see her often, because he was just finishing training as a tour leader. I was fascinated that a young man in this largely traditional culture could show his independent streak.

The following morning, after leaving the hotel at six o'clock and facing a long dusty, bumpy ride, Alex announced that we would be returning to the original itinerary this afternoon in Gilgit, where we had shopped for school supplies. He wanted to complete the nine-hour ride from Skardu and arrive at Karimabad in the Hunza Valley by nightfall.

We faced the same scenery, the same road, the same rough ride we had had three days ago heading into Skardu. Bill summed it up, "There's only one road in and one road out. It's that simple."

After bouncing on the potholed road, a rest stop was needed, and the bus pulled into a tiny restaurant. Alex stated, "Here's the deal. You have two choices. First option is resting in the restaurant and having tea; second option is walking up the road and being picked up by the bus after we leave."

I immediately said, "I'll take option two, walking. Anyone join me?"

Surprisingly, no one else wanted to walk, not even Mark and Bill. I couldn't believe it, "A chance for some good exercise, and you want tea?"

As I left the restaurant, Alex cautioned, "Just be careful on the road."

Caution was the operative word, as I discovered walking on the treacherous road with no guardrails or sidewalks and massive jingle trucks kicking up dust. I wondered what I'd been thinking, but I wasn't ready to call it quits. I was in no mood to hear the guys saying: "Oh, you're such a girl!"

Looking down at my flip-flops, I could only imagine how dirty my feet would get. "Too late now, keep moving, it'll all work out," I advised myself. "You were bored sitting in the bus with another seven hours to go, plus you need the exercise."

Qualms set to rest, I committed to walking as far as I could before the bus reached me, even in gold-sequined flip-flops. When the jingle trucks passed, I kept to the side of the road closest to the crumbling shoulders and drop off, closed my eyes, and turned to avoid the full blast of a dust cloud. The few Pakistanis walking nodded as they passed, but never spoke.

On a winding section of road, I stopped to photograph three jingle trucks closely following each other. Suddenly, the leader stopped on a hill, and its driver signaled me to come closer. I ran through two inches of pulverized dust in my flip-flops to speak to them. The drivers didn't want to talk; they wanted to see their photos and have more taken up close. At least, I figured that's what they wanted from their pointing to my camera and back to themselves.

Looking back over my shoulder, I thought, "How dangerous is this? Three huge trucks parked at the crest of a hill in the middle of a one-and-a-half lane road with the drivers stopping to have their pictures taken."

I quickly snapped a few shots with my digital camera and displayed them to boisterous laughs coming from mouths with missing teeth. At the approach of another truck, they hurried off. I waved and continued my hike, reflecting that if I'd stayed back at the restaurant, I would have missed another amazing experience. My fellow travelers were surprised at the distance I had covered before the bus picked me up. It didn't seem all that far to me, but my dirty feet disagreed.

Continuing on the serpentine road, we reached Gilgit in time for lunch, after which red and baby blue jeeps with canvas roofs and doors, and open sides waited to take us to see the Kargah Buddha, a short distance west of town. After a few kilometers, explosions startled everyone in the jeeps. Not knowing the source of the blasts or if we were under attack, we all ducked but were soon relieved to find the explosions were for new road excavations, not a terrorist attack. "I'm sure happy it wasn't anything serious," Bill said, and I added, "That was scary."

A few miles down an unpaved, but well-constructed road with stone embankments, a Buddha looked down on us from high on the side of a stark mountain. Carved in bas-relief into the mountainside, the Kargah Buddha dated from the seventh century. From the road, we needed binoculars or a good zoom lens to see the fine detailing. Alex asked a series of questions: "How was it carved on the sheer mountain? Did they use scaffolding? Was the carver dropped by rope from the rock overhang and suspended while he chiseled? Did those parallel holes on either side of the Buddha once hold a protective shade?" There were no known answers, but Alex wanted us to think of different possibilities.

Back in Gilgit, the group walked with our guides to a suspension bridge, much sturdier and wider than the ones Mark, Bill, and I remembered in Nepal years ago. Long as a football field, the bridge was suspended by massive cables and allowed only small vehicles to cross its wood-planked roadbed. Jingle trucks were forbidden. Pedestrians, jeeps, small cars, horses, bicycles, and motorcycles squeezed onto the bridge. A quarter of the way across, we turned back, feeling the sway of the bridge as we walked. I thought, "Now, that was interesting, but let's get a move on."

We returned to the bus, ready for our next destination, Karimabad. Remnants of rockslides on the Karakorum Highway slowed our progress. Even though it had been reopened to traffic, passage was treacherous and narrow. Abdul said that one bad rockslide had just happened within the past couple of days. The KKH was the lifeline for the residents of Northeast Pakistan, and it opened quickly to resume transport of necessary food and supplies. At best, passage was slow and difficult through these rugged and inhospitable mountains.

At last Pakistan's twelfth highest mountain, Rakaposhi, came into view and our destination in the Hunza Valley was near. This area was considered a Shangri-la, too. I was satisfied that real Shangri-la was within the person, not a physical location, but others believe a specific place bestows inner peace or, at least, exemplifies it. I wasn't about to debate the issue. "This trip is for fun," I told myself.

28

The following morning Mark, Bill, and I received news of a bus bombing in Islamabad's sister city of Rawalpindi. The truck-painting factory we had visited only five days before was located there. Bill feared those interesting tours would be cancelled just as the Swat Valley tour had been. "We were lucky to have seen the fabulous truck decorating when we did."

Mark predicted, "Now, with some radical trying to make a statement, more tourist dollars will be lost in Pakistan, and it's only a matter of time until the entire country is affected."

A leisurely wake-up call scheduled at the Baltit Inn for the next morning suited me fine, and I took my time showering before breakfast. Later in the morning, the group assembled for a hike through Karimabad to the Baltit Fort, strategically situated on the highest hill overlooking the area. Abdul introduced the fort guide, Ali, who, like many other Pakistani men was thin, short, dark-complexioned with black hair and dressed in a pure white *shalwar kameez*. How long would it stay white with dust everywhere?

We listened to Ali explain a chamber where rebellious men lived in total darkness for several days. After release if they had not changed or shown they had learned a lesson from the ordeal, they were exiled to China with no hope of returning. I wondered if there were any men who didn't get the message after such treatment, but I knew the guide would have no answer to that question, so I kept silent and continued listening.

Ali led us into a low-ceilinged room where everyone sat on benches while he presented a slide show of elderly people from the area who had achieved longevity—some as much as

The Suitcase Wife

118 years and one man said to have grown a second set of teeth. A murmur at that information indicated the tourists' interest in an anti-aging Shangri-la. Unable to resist, I announced proudly that my grandmother, at age 105, enjoyed good health and added, "But she'd sure like to grow a new set of teeth."

I wandered through the fort looking at rooms designed to illustrate daily life in the fort—kitchen, storeroom, one room that served as a mosque with colored glass panes offering spectacular views of the mountains. My interest and attention were starting to wane, and I asked Bill if he wanted to go outside to see the scenery.

From a vantage point in the parking area, we could view the surrounding town below and switchbacks leading up to the fort and a nearby glacier. The town's buildings were made of stone covered in cement and whitewashed. A few had pitched corrugated metal roofs, but most were made of cement edged with raised stones. They were flat and not completely square, some rounded at a corner, others five-sided, but from high above, they had a jigsaw-puzzle look, neatly fitting together. A few sported satellite dishes.

When we got back to town, Bill decided to go back to the hotel instead of window-shopping. Mark stopped at a mountain gear store to see their merchandise, and I found another shop to investigate. My eye caught a blue dress with lots of small silver medallions sewn over its surface and two-inch delicate chains dangling from the cuffs, neckline, and hem. I asked to try it on, but it was tight across the shoulders and chest. "Unfortunately, it's too small," I told to the shopkeeper, "but it's quite unusual."

Undaunted by the garment's not fitting, the shopkeeper plopped a matching helmet on my head, as if to complete the outfit. Medallions obscured my vision—but not too much—when I looked in the mirror. "It does look sort of cool and fun," I offered laughing, "but what if I wore it to the symphony? I wouldn't be able to move for fear of jingling."

The afternoon's destination required a jeep ride, and Mark suggested that we three ride together. Oncoming traffic was minimal, but the roadbed was like the Karakorum Highway—rutted, narrow, winding, rock strewn, and treacherous. Bumping along and hanging on the jeep's straps, Bill, Mark, and I were in high spirits, knowing that at the end of the rough ride a hiking opportunity awaited us. Sacks of potatoes, some as tall as a small child, stood ready to be sewn shut in one village.

A few miles on, we noticed thirteen large, flat baskets containing something red on the roof of a house. Abdul later told the group that we had seen tomatoes being dried on rooftops. It was the end of the growing season and important to preserve enough food to last the winter.

Finally the group arrived at the Hoper Glacier, though the ride *felt* longer than the hour and a half it took. Alex asked how many wanted to trek down to the glacier and back. Three hands shot up, but we were the only ones interested in a strenuous hike; the others chose to wait at the overlook. Looking down the side of the mountain, I realized the challenge. "Hey guys, I know going down won't be any problem, but, man, coming back up is another story."

Rightfully concerned about the trek back up—its steepness confirmed by the number of visible switchbacks—I took trekking stick in hand. Loose gravel on the faint trail made for cautious stepping as we descended; it grew colder as we neared the glacier. Mark asked Kimmitt, who had accompanied us, how far a drop it was to the glacier. After calculating, Kimmitt figured about seven hundred and fifty feet. It seemed like more.

When we reached the glacier's edge, we could look up the valley that the glacier partially filled as far as the eye could see. Bill, with his love of rocks and geology, was in heaven. "The experience of standing at the Hoper Glacier and seeing its majesty is without words. What an incredible experience. It's just raw beauty," exclaimed the usually taciturn Bill.

The Suitcase Wife

A steep climb up the glacier's side—equivalent to climbing a two-story building on wet, loosely packed gravel without benefit of a trail—remained as the only obstacle to a surface view of the glacier. Bending forward at the waist, to keep from falling over backwards, we clawed our way slowly up the side to the top. I was slower than Mark and Bill, but I made it, and it was well worth the effort. As we stood on the glacier's surface, Kimmitt said, "What do you hear?"

I said, "You can hear the ice crack and moan!"

"The glacier is moving," Kimmitt said, "but not to the extent we can feel it move. With the glacier moving, what we're standing on is crushed stone pushed up by the ice as it moves."

"No wonder it was mushy and tough to climb. That's so interesting." I said.

Bill explained, "The mushy part, as you describe it, Sahara, is actually rock flour made from pulverized rock and mixed with melting ice water to get this consistency."

"How did you get so smart? Your explanation makes it easier for me to understand," I responded.

Standing higher than the glacier surface at this point, gave Bill, Mark, and me an incredible unobstructed view as the Hoper Glacier zigzagged miles up and down through valleys, rising up the mountain to its snow- and ice-covered apex. Grays, blacks, dirty whites, brilliant whites, rugged mountains, rocks, clouds all combined for an Ansel Adams-like landscape photograph of dramatic vistas. Bill went crazy, "This is so cool. Look up that valley. I can't believe this!"

A close-up view of the glacier's rough surface with ridges fascinated us. Bill said that those were called fractures. I replied, "Well, Bill, it reminds me of spiked short hair with gel."

The guys rolled their eyes. We all took off our outer jackets for photos. I wore a green bandana around my neck; Bill's was red; and Mark's, blue as we posed with Kimmitt in the foreground of the glacier vista. Then it was time to go. "Time to slug it back up the mountain—I'm dreading this portion of the trek," I complained.

Mark agreed with me, but Bill, still exhilarated, couldn't wait for the challenge. "That's great, Bill, you can help me crawl up to the top," I laughed, with more than a tinge of truth.

Trekking up the switchbacks required discarding layers of clothing and frequent rest stops. After more complaining from me, we finally reached the top of the mountainside. Actually, Bill walked briskly up the switchbacks with no problem, as Mark and I had known he would. Both of us were panting. Bill won this race; Mark placed; I showed up. I was happy to finish on my own steam, without the guide having to carry me out.

We jumped back in our jeep for the dusty ride back to the Baltit Inn. A few kilometers later, two young boys with toothy grins, dressed in torn pants and T-shirts, hopped on the jeep's back bumper like little leeches, for a free ride to their village. The boys knew how to hang on tightly as the jeep bounced over rocks and ruts. They jumped off at the village, waving goodbye. This seemed to be a common mode of transportation in the area and fortunately it hadn't hurt anyone.

Soon we saw another group of boys riding a seven-foot tall grass pile atop a large field wagon pulled by a tractor. Two older boys sat on top, while three younger ones sat on the back. One little daredevil dangled on a thick branch protruding from the bottom of the pile, swinging wildly on the bumpy road. We concluded that kids everywhere just take risks without thinking they're risky. I would probably have been dangling from a grass wagon, too.

As we reached the outskirts of Karimabad, Rakaposhi and a series of mountain peaks appeared in clear view, with shadows cast by the angle of the setting sun. Cameras were readied for a quick round of pictures, but everyone wanted to hurry back to the inn and wash up. After dinner we intended to visit the internet café, about the equivalent of a long city block from the hotel, to catch up on the world and accumulating emails.

Later that evening, with laptops underarm, we climbed seven narrow concrete steps to the internet café's entrance. Though small inside, with most computers occupied, knowledgeable personnel connected our two laptops to the internet. Bill snared an available computer. We worked diligently until Mark asked if all were done. I needed more time and told the guys to go ahead. "See you tomorrow and thanks for a great day."

I got back to work and finally finished close to eleven thirty. I knew it would be a pitch-black walk back to the inn. Without streetlights, only a porch light at the Baltit Inn was barely visible in the distance. As I stepped out of the café door, I froze at the sight of the small red end of a cigarette glowing in the dark. Someone was sitting on the top step. Suddenly, a soft male voice quietly and slowly spoke in English, "Where are you from?"

In that split second, I thought, "Oh, no, what now? Here I am alone, without the guys for protection." My mind raced. How do I answer this question? Do I tell the truth? Tell him what country I'm really from? Or tell him Canada? Why does he want to know? After what seemed an eternity, I decided to breathe calmly and tell the truth.

"I'm from America," I answered.

The voice from the darkness slowly questioned me again, "America? What's it like living there?"

Once again, I hesitated, "Pretty cool and fun," wondering, if this answer sounded casual or might trigger a negative response.

The stranger's voice quickened, "I can't even imagine what it would be like to live in America. That is my dream. One day I will go to America."

I wished him good luck with his dreams and left, never once seeing a face, only hearing a voice in the darkness. I walked carefully back to the inn and crawled into bed.

29

The next morning, careful not to wake my roommate, I slipped into my jeans, T-shirt, and flip-flops and eased out the door to photograph Rakaposhi at sunrise. I saw no sign of Mark and Bill, who had said they wanted to see the sun rise, but I truly didn't expect to see them at this hour, unless it was mandatory. Walking down into the lower garden, I saw Rakaposhi, wrapped in shimmering golden orange as the early morning sun hit its slopes. When the sun rose higher, all vestiges of softness were swept away, but Rakaposhi was still beautiful.

Dissatisfied with the view from the garden, I walked toward the internet café; this time for a different purpose. I had noticed a ladder propped against its wall, and today saw three people standing on the roof. Thinking that would be a perfect vantage point, I looped the camera around my wrist and gingerly approached the rickety ladder made of branches lashed together. Cautiously I climbed the uneven rungs and, from the last one, pulled myself onto the roof, thinking all the while getting down would be even scarier. The men, it turned out, were Koreans who greeted me with a quick nod. From the roof, the view of Rakaposhi, unobstructed by electrical wires, was magnificent.

When I had finished photographing, I confronted the ladder again, first lying on my stomach along the edge of the roof, then swinging my legs and feet over the side to grope for the first rung, and, holding to the edge of the roof, transferred my weight to the ladder and descended. Back at the Baltit Inn, I still saw no sign of Mark or Bill, but was confident they wouldn't miss breakfast.

The Suitcase Wife

Jeeps stood ready for the morning tour, signaling we'd be driving over dusty, winding roads again. I exchanged my flip-flops for boots and joined still drowsy Mark and Bill for Altit Fort, three kilometers from Karimabad. Altit Fort still required a great deal of restoration, being provided by the Aga Khan Trust. The process offered work for local men.

As the group walked toward the fort, a large sign identified a building called the *Women Multipurpose Activity Center, a project of the Aga Khan Rural Support Programme – A Self Employment Project for Women – Promoting Women Entrepreneurship – A Path out of Poverty*. This concept interested women in my group, especially in light of the cultural disadvantages we had noticed over the past week. I observed that the sign appeared old and wondered if the original intent was operative, and if the center was still funded.

Looking up toward the fort, houses were pressed together creeping up the mountainside. Winding through narrow pathways, we passed small homes built with rocks bonded together with mortar. The homes had wooden doors and lintels, few windows, and outdoor ledges held cooking pots. Everything was clean and tidy. Small children stared at the foreigners. One shriveled woman in a flowered dress with brightly dyed orange hair sat on a street corner like the guardian of her neighborhood. From under a colorful hat she stared at each person walking by.

Commanding the steep mountain pinnacle was Altit Fort, now laced in scaffolding, but positioned as a sentinel. The original fort, built in the eleventh century, was older and smaller than the Baltit Fort we had visited yesterday. Without benefit of hardhats, we walked under the scaffolding throughout the work site. Our guide, eager to offer every scrap of information, said that Prince Charles and his wife had visited the fort a few years ago. I wondered if they were made to walk unprotected under the scaffolding also. Our guide pointed out a walnut tree, said to be six hundred years old, and Bill whispered to Mark and me, "If that tree still produces walnuts, I'd be surprised and sure would like to eat one of those nuts."

At the back of the fort stood a separate rock spire, with a relatively flat top approximately four feet square. It rose about seven feet distant from the fort, with nothing between the two but a sheer drop of one thousand feet to the Hunza River below. The guide bragged that two young boys from the village could jump across the void without a running start and safely land on the rock's top.

I knew that was all Mark had to hear to think that he could do it, too. And sure enough, he wanted to attempt it; at least he said he did. Bill and I objected, but he proceeded to measure off approximately seven feet and jump it to prove he could make it. The group's consensus was not to try; it was too close to call. "What if you measured short, or slipped on a pebble, or a gust of wind blew you off course," I argued, "one miscalculation, and it's over."

Brother Bill spoke up, "Mark, we're not a hundred percent sure you could make it. Sahara and I are counting on more trips with you." That worked.

We moved on to a new two-story stone school flying the national flag of Pakistan and an Altit flag. Surrounded by a stone wall topped with decorative iron fencing, we were impressed by the school's size and modern feel. Once inside, we saw a school overwhelmed by the number of children attending. The headmaster explained that they had two shifts because there were so many students. We noticed that the older students were separated into same-sex classes, but the younger boys and girls shared the same classroom. "See there, a little boy and girl are even sharing the same double desk. I'm curious as to when the shift occurs and whether it relegates young women to a less important status."

All the students wore uniforms: the girls, a green print *shalwar* over solid green trousers; the boys, dark gray pants with a blue shirt and a green necktie. Their backpacks held every textbook needed for classes; there were no lockers. When asked how many classes are taught in English, the headmaster said that in the fifth grade, only one class is taught in Urdu with all others conducted in English. "We have classroom rules in English, too," he said pointing to a list hanging on wall near the door.

Respect your teachers;

Respect your friends;

Speak English and Urdu Language;

Keep your class clean and tidy;

Speak truth and politly (sic);

Take your turn;

Do your Class work and home work on time;

Say Good morning/noon/salaam;

Say thanks for your teachers;

Be a good student;

Be Punctual.

"These rules need to be in every classroom back in the States, too," I said.

Before we left, the group made a contribution to the school. A pre-school class, led by two teachers, sang songs in both Urdu and in English. We were already convinced that education of both girls and boys would be the key to Pakistan's future. I whispered to Mark, "Those poor girls looked scared to death to sing to us."

Visiting schools wasn't at the top of our list but visiting rough and tumble places like our next destination was. Eagle's Nest located above Altit in the village of Duikar was best reached in jeeps unless one had several hours to hike up a steep, dusty road. It began as a camping site on a high mountain ridge and grew over the years into a hotel complex with unencumbered views of Rakaposhi, and the Hunza River.

We hiked a steep incline to an overlook, passing a smooth stone shaped like an eagle, hence the name of the complex. Bill, after inspecting the eagle and its texture, decided that it must have been formed by flowing water. It was hard to believe there was a riverbed that high up. We posed for photos with the spectacular mountain views as background before walking to the hotel for lunch.

Another spectacle appeared unexpectedly during lunch: the waiter's emerald green eyes. After trying my best not to stare, I finally succumbed and asked if I could take his picture. "You have the most beautiful eyes I've ever seen."

I hoped I didn't sound foolish.

He nodded but didn't seem embarrassed. His piercing eyes, enhanced by his black hair and dark complexion were amazing, and I hoped the camera would capture the full effect. It didn't. Fortunately Mark and Bill at another table hadn't heard my request or teasing would never end.

With nearly an hour remaining before the jeeps left Eagle's Nest, Mark, Bill, and I asked to walk down the road until the jeeps retrieved us. A young girl in a red dress waved as she passed us going up the hill. A cute little girl dressed in a filmy blue and white ruffled dress over trousers walked with a young boy still in his school uniform. Both smiled at the three foreigners. Seeing orchards, stone homes, fields of pumpkins and passing through villages greeting the people we met, Mark, Bill, and I enjoyed both the sights and the exercise.

In one village we spotted a white door with a burgundy fleur-de-lis and lettering reading, "Scout Office, WEL... "Perhaps the missing COME was due to spelling difficulty, running out of burgundy paint, or lack of time. We would never know the answer. Soon the jeep picked us up.

The Suitcase Wife

Today was our last in Pakistan; tomorrow we would go to China. We thought that the Pakistani people had offered wonderful hospitality and the country had stunning natural beauty. Concern remained about the economy and a stable political environment to safely raise and educate their children.

In China we could finally drink a beer, washing down all the dust we'd swallowed in Pakistan, but Alex warned our group, "Tomorrow's going to be a long journey. I never know what to expect getting into China from Pakistan, but be prepared. We're leaving early."

30

I was dreaming of a soft knock at the door and an attendant announcing the arrival of my tea. Instead, the phone jangled loudly at the ungodly hour of 4:15 a.m. After that wake-up call for our excursion to Tashkurgan, China, Harriet and I hustled to pack and eat breakfast. Warned of delays in customs at the Chinese border, the whole tour group was hurrying in hopes of shortening the predicted thirteen-hour journey.

The Karakorum Highway (KKH) didn't improve on its final leg into China. Still prone to landslides, the same serpentine, mountainside-hugging, one-and-a-half lane road was edged by steep drop-offs into raging rivers with only a few concrete stumps for guardrails. Ironically a concrete-block wall lettered boldly in black proudly credited the highway's construction to: "F. W. O. (Pakistani Army Corps of Engineering), The Builders of the KKH, Eighth Wonder of the World."

"Yeah, it's certainly a wonder," Mark joked, "A wonder that there aren't more deaths from its treacherous conditions."

As we entered higher elevations, the mountains grew steeper. Abdul said that in 1973 a landslide so massive had occurred here that it blocked the KKH for a week, spilled over the edge, and dammed up the river. The Pakistani Air Force, on orders from the government, dropped bombs to blast an opening in the rockslide dam to allow the water to escape before it built up enormous pressure. That prevented a break-through which would have killed many people. Peering at the terrain outside the bus window, I couldn't even imagine planes flying through the tight mountainous areas, not to mention bombing a dam with accuracy.

The Suitcase Wife

As we drove higher, Abdul pointed out that Pakistan was home to more than a hundred peaks above 23,000 feet. We stopped for a short break at the Passu Glacier. I noticed on a sign about the glacier that a Pakistani and Japanese expedition team first climbed it in 1978. The largest Pakistani climbing team had forty-six members, including ladies. Another expedition reached the summit in 1996. Its fifteen members included the oldest climber, age fifty-six.

"Imagine that, a fifty-six-year-old man—and even ladies—climbing. What is the world coming to?" I asked Mark and Bill.

Back in the van, only sixty-two miles from the Chinese border, we came to an unexpected stop at a milepost marker on a whitewashed base. A woman sat cross-legged with hands peacefully folded in her lap on the base. She wore a thick lavender sweater and matching trousers with a tangerine-colored silk scarf covering her head. Long black braids framed her face, weathered by life and the harshness of Northern Pakistan. She was carrying a backpack and waiting for a bus.

She graciously posed for several photos, but never looked directly into the camera and gave only a tight-lipped hint of a smile. Kimmitt asked in Urdu if she were heading our way and wanted a ride. The woman nodded, climbing aboard and taking the rear seat next to me. Almost immediately she began to talk. I quickly passed a note up front asking Kimmitt to come translate. With his help, she and I and others nearby exchanged questions.

When asked if she were married, the woman said she was, tracing with her finger the lines in her face. Pointing to my face and indicating fewer lines, she asked Kimmitt a question. She wants to know your age Kimmitt said. I told her, knowing from the curious look on her face that more questions were coming.

Kimmitt translated the first one, "Are you married?"

I replied truthfully that I was not. The woman's raised eyebrows showed surprise, but she was still not satisfied.

"Why not?" was the next question.

I thought for a second before answering. "Maybe, I'm too bossy," I offered to Kimmitt for translation.

The woman smiled at me, then laughed out loud, nodding her head.

"That's good," she answered.

Miles later, after the Pakistani woman had been dropped off at her destination, Harriet remarked to me that I had missed a great opportunity. "When the woman asked if you were married, you should have pointed to Mark and Bill and said that those two men were your husbands."

I marveled at the thought. "I can't even imagine the response of a woman living in a male-dominated country and a culture that allows a man to marry more than one woman, but you're so right; I wish I had said that."

When Mark and Bill were told the alternative response, Mark laughed, but Bill didn't appreciate it. "Lighten up Bill, it's only a joke," I said, "Remember, I am *only* the suitcase wife."

When the bus reached Sost, the last village before leaving Pakistan, our guides unloaded the luggage for customs inspection. Fortunately for me and Mark, the officials bypassed our luggage, but chose to check Harriet's and Bill's. "How do you always get to be the lucky one?" Mark asked him.

Inspections uncovered nothing but dirty clothing. Everyone was free to go, that is free to leave our transportation of the last ten days and board another vehicle. Alex explained that the Pakistani government authorized only specific vehicles to continue from its customs town of Sost to China—and this was one of those vehicles. We didn't understand his answer, but chose not to pursue the question. "It's the government's method of controlling security," Alex added.

The guides were already tying the luggage on its roof. Our first impression was of a second-rate bus painted Pakistani flag green with blue, dark green, and red waves on its sides. Side mirrors jutting out looked like insect antennae. The new bus bore mud-splashes, and the seats were caked with dust.

Alex directed the group to walk through immigration and passport control. In one office, I showed my passport to an official, who inspected it repeatedly and stated brusquely that it had expired. Leaning over the counter, I pointed out the expiration date and said, "There're still more than six months before the passport expires. There's not a problem."

As the official continued to examine my passport, the line behind me grew. Finally conceding that the passport was valid, he handed it back and waved me on. Before leaving the immigration and passport control building, another official reviewed all the passports again. This time I had no problem and fervently hoped that was an end to expiration nonsense.

We said a sad goodbye to our Pakistani guides and driver, thanking them for showing us their country and wishing them and their families well. Abdul, Kimmitt, and Rashid seemed to enjoy providing insight into the lives of their people and presenting Pakistan's natural treasures in exciting and challenging ways. I got Kimmitt's email address and hugged them all before boarding the bus. Sitting down with my eyes still teary, I hoped everything would be okay for them in view of escalating terrorist attacks, but I didn't have a good feeling.

The bus was barely on the road before stopping again to allow another official to review all the passports and check the validity of each visa and exit stamp. We made bets on how many more times we would stop at checkpoints before reaching China.

The KKH leading to the Khunjerab Pass between Pakistan and China soon proved to be even more difficult than its previous sections. The worn-out bus lacking shock absorbers added to our woes by failing to cushion the impact of the rutted Karakorum Highway. At one point the bus hit a bump so hard, we flew out of our seats by at least six inches before crashing back down onto their unforgiving surfaces. Sitting in the rear, I slammed down hard, jolting my back severely. I announced bitterly that I was moving my aching back up to the front of the bus until the road got smoother—"if that *ever* happens."

Grabbing seat backs hand by hand, I staggered to the front seat, complaining, "I've had enough of this damn rock and rolling with this decrepit bus trying to knock my back out."

I hoped that wouldn't happen with another ten days to travel. Actually the episode was a blessing in disguise. I now had a fabulous view of the countryside as the bus entered Khunjerab National Park, "The Paradise of Flora and Fauna – Join Hands For Conservation - Elev. ranging between eleven- and sixteen-thousand feet."

The tall, wispy trees bordering the highway made the land appear to me more hospitable than the endless rocks. That didn't last long, and the terrain turned rocky again, with cattle roaming free to graze on the sparse vegetation. The bus halted, waiting for the cattle to move off the road while their mustached herder, stick in hand, tried to hurry them along. Bill complained about idling on the road in our lumpy seats while the smell of diesel fumes grew stronger with each passing second. "How much longer do we have before we get off this bus?" he continued.

Everyone groaned when Alex told Bill that we were still miles away. At one point we were only thirty miles from the Afghanistan border, and Mark joked with Alex, "How about we make a detour? I'd like another stamp in my passport to rack up my count of countries visited."

In all seriousness, Alex told Mark that a detour would not be advisable. "No way," he concluded.

Approaching the Chinese border, the incline steep- ened, the temperature dropped, and the sky turned gray. At last a modern blue highway sign, hanging above the road, announced that the distance to Tashkurgan, our immediate destination, was 143 kilometers. To Kashghar, our subsequent destination a few days later, was 438 kilometers. Although we had no idea what awaited us at the border, this specific information appeared promising, and I called back to Mark and Bill that I was starting to smell beer.

Closer to the border, snowflakes began to hit the windshield. The bus passed two cyclists, a man with dreadlocks down to his waist and a young woman, both with heads down battling the snow as they pumped up the steep road to Khunjerab Pass. I thought, "Here I am complaining about this lousy bus, and those two are braving the weather on bicycles. At least, we're warm."

When we reached the pass, the snow had stopped, but it was still cold as everyone piled out of the bus for photos. The cyclists arrived a short time later. We spoke and learned that the man and his attractive woman friend had been traveling for two years since leaving their home in Scotland. Originally Istanbul was their destination, but as they traveled, they extended their adventure with no end in sight.

The Chinese didn't permit cyclists to enter China through the Khunjerab Pass, requiring that the couple backtrack down the KKH and board a covered bus to Tashkurgan where their adventure could resume. That was their only option. As the two turned back, Mark, Bill, and I pushed into our dilapidated bus for a cozy ride on to Tashkurgan. Mark pointed out a mileage sign, "Hey, we're only 4,300 miles from Beijing. If those cyclists have Beijing in their sights, it'll take them another two years."

A white pillar marked the China-Pakistan border, and Mark, Bill, and I saw it as a measure of road condition. The Pakistani dirt- and stone-based KKH, rutted and prone to landslides, became a double-laned macadam road named the Friendship Highway after it entered China. Chinese improvements had begun in the latter decades of the twentieth century, and the difference was like night and day. Mark and Bill compared the contrast in road surfaces to highways in the U.S. whose degree of maintenance varied from state to state based on money and priority. All I cared was that travel on the bus would be easier now, but I planned to keep my front-row seat.

Alex noticed me taking a photograph of a Chinese army watchtower flying several red flags and warned the group sternly not to take photos until we reached Tashkurgan. He emphasized, "We do not want to be pulled over to the side."

In the fifty-five miles before reaching the Chinese Passport and Customs office, we'd already encountered so many checkpoints that we'd lost count. On arrival we quickly obtained our luggage and stood in line beneath an interesting sign stretching from one side of the hall to other: "Respect the Passenger as the Master, as the Relative, as the Teacher."

Mark commented that the country was probably gearing up to host the coming Olympics. Navigation through customs was relatively easy, and soon we boarded a much newer bus than the aged Pakistani one. The three old friends sat down and looked at each other. Mark stated succinctly: "All right! We had a great Pakistan Silk Road adventure. Let's see what happens on the Silk Road through northwest China."

"I sense a difference in the two societies immediately," Bill remarked as we were passing through Tashkurgan, "Look at all the women walking on the streets—by themselves, with other women, and many interacting with men. Some of them are even wearing business suits."

I actually felt the oppressive weight of being a woman in Pakistan begin to lift as soon as we entered Tashkurgan. China's obvious inclusive attitude towards women was revivifying. I now realized that the societal norms of Pakistan had numbed me. Afraid of giving offense or drawing attention, I had unconsciously stifled my normal high spirits and enthusiasm. "I feel that I can breathe again," I thought.

The Suitcase Wife

Walking into the marble-floored, modern hotel in Tashkurgan, I immediately dropped my backpack at a small glass table and headed straight to the bar. I ordered the biggest bottle of beer available, a Sinkiang. My tongue was already anticipating the first taste of its bitterness and the touch of its pleasurable coldness. To wash away the dust of the trip, Mark and Bill joined me in clinking glasses. "Here's to a fabulous trip through Pakistan, to new adventures in China, and to the best tasting beer we've ever had," I said.

31

After a good night's sleep and a really hot shower, I boarded the bus for a short tour of Tashkurgan. Alex introduced our new China national guide, Tamer. My first sight of him was confusing—he didn't look Chinese, being wiry and thin with features more like Pakistanis. As always, I checked his teeth when he smiled; they were crooked and nicotine stained. Tamer said that Tashkurgan, meant stone fortress, and it was considered a dismal outpost along the Silk Road. A fort built there six hundred years ago was made of clay bricks, not of stone.

As we headed towards Kashgar, cemeteries lined the road, but they differed in terms of tombs. Graves with domed structures, Tamer explained, accommodate bodies of Sunni Muslims, while flat-roofed structures contain the bodies of Shiite Muslims. He cited several differences between the two sects, but claimed that they lived peaceably together and rarely discussed the topic of religion. In China, he concluded, avoidance of religious subjects works well in communities.

Bill and Mark wanted to know how schooling for Muslim boys worked. Tamer candidly explained that a Chinese government mandate allowed no boy under age eighteen to enter a mosque. In addition, the government refused to permit the building of sectarian madrassas for education of boys. All religious education was confined to the home. I could tell that my friends wanted to know if China was actively trying to quash religious contention that plagued nearby developing countries. They were too polite to ask directly. I couldn't blame them, because Tamer seemed quite comfortable with government controls of religion, perhaps because the frontier was a long way from Beijing.

The Suitcase Wife

The bus slowly ascended toward snow-covered mountain peaks framed by bright blue skies. Everyone enjoyed the ride in a spacious, comfortable bus in good working order. I realized that I wasn't worrying about my back anymore, and the altitude wasn't affecting me either. Approaching 12,000 feet, I remembered the altitude sickness I'd experienced in the Himalayas when I first met Mark and Bill.

The sudden spectacle of men on motorcycles herding yaks gave reason to stop the bus. Tamer and Alex, cautious as always, warned us to watch where we stepped. Cameras in hand, we carefully picked our way across the field avoiding yak patties. Two women sitting with a baby caught my attention. When I lifted my Polaroid they posed, and the camera ejected a photo. Before I told them to keep it out of the light for a few minutes, the older woman had tucked the photo under her jacket. "Yep," I thought, "she's had her picture taken before."

I figured the women's familiarity with picture taking was probably due to time spent out in the field near the road. Maybe they just wanted a more recent picture of the baby. At any rate they seemed to be enjoying the photo, and soon, an older herder approached wanting a picture, too. One more photo, and I headed back to the bus.

In addition to yaks, sheep and goats grazed along the road and even a camel. As soon as Bill spotted it, he called to me, "Look, Sahara, there's your favorite animal."

The trip to Mongolia with Bill and Mark had cured me of any affection I might have had for camels. To the amusement of our fellow travelers, Bill teased, "Remember the time your camel wouldn't go, so you got down and *pulled* him through the Gobi Desert?"

"Thanks for reminding me—again," I answered.

Harriet said that she'd like to hear my side of the story.

"We were riding camels in the desert, and mine wouldn't cooperate. I finally just got off, handed the reins to a guide, and walked toward the oasis where our vehicle was parked.

Halfway there, I met a young man on a camel with a string of three camels behind him. He thought I was in distress and wanted to give me a camel ride to the oasis. All I could think was: I'd just got off one foul-tempered beast that wouldn't behave and here was an offer of three more. I wasn't about to get *near* any more. I thanked him very nicely and shook my head in an emphatic 'no.'"

Bill and Mark had thought the whole episode was hilarious. I had to laugh with them but added, "I'll never ride a camel again. You didn't see me riding one in Dubai, did you?"

The words were barely out of my mouth, when the bus turned down a lane and a herd of camels came into view, not just any herd of camels, but camels with saddles on their backs. I shrieked, "I just don't believe this! I am not seeing stupid camels with saddles on! My worst nightmare is better than this."

Prudent Alex tried to swallow a smile as he explained our luncheon plans, "See that village in the distance over there? That's where we will eat, and this is the only way to get there," he said, pointing to the camels. "The narrow road and bridge cannot accommodate our bus."

"I don't want to ride a camel," I whined theatrically before capitulating and mounting, making sure to point out, "Getting on isn't a problem, that's the easy part."

The stuffed saddle made of heavy cloth was strapped between the camel's two humps, requiring us to sit between the humps, with our legs hanging down. The humps were rubbery and flopped to either side. I reminded Bill and Mark that we had had no saddles in Mongolia and just hung onto the mane until the camel got to its feet. While the three of us waited for the others to mount, Mark and I took silly pictures of each other. Suddenly my camel whipped his head around and, as if expressing annoyance of having me on his back, spit on my dangling leg—wet, green, smelly, slimy spit.

"Damn it! I told you I didn't get along with camels, and this just proves it. They don't like me, and I don't like them. This is the absolute last time I ride on these monsters. And, you can remind me of that anytime you want!" I ranted. "This is my only pair of jeans and I have to sit in them for the rest of the day."

Mark and Bill couldn't stifle their laughter, and they couldn't stop it. By the time we reached the village, dismounted, and I had wiped most of the remaining spit off my jean leg, I was speaking to them again. Lunch was in a home where two teenage girls, wearing vests embellished with sequined designs, served us sliced melon, tomatoes, cucumbers, rice crackers, and bread with a choice of green tea or peach juice.

I, along with Mark and Bill, decided to walk back to the bus, pleasing me. "Now guys," I gushed, "Isn't this is just about heaven? Walking is far better than sitting on a smelly, matted-haired beast. The camel-riding novelty is *so* over."

Our last stretch before Kashgar excited Bill, the rock lover. At one point, the bus pulled over so Tamer could point out a view in which mountains topped by snow, a glacier, sand dunes in the foreground, and a small lake could all be seen at the same time. Bill was thrilled by the variety of eco-systems in close proximity, while Mark and I saw it as a picturesque view.

The next section of highway, aptly known as "Tiger's Mouth," inspired awe in everyone. It was dangerous and narrow, with blind curves and accident-provoking switchbacks. The bus slowed to avoid a gap where part of the road had broken away and fallen into the deep gorge below. Large rocks sheared away from the mountain wall littered the highway, creating a driving puzzle for the driver.

Eyes sparkling, Bill was glued to the window. "Look up at those mountains. Do you see those red, green, and white rock streaks cascading through them? It's amazing. That's so beautiful!"

This scenery lasted for miles. Finally Bill asked to borrow my camera. "I really want to keep some pictures of these rocks," he said happily.

And I happily passed him the camera, "Knock yourself out, Bill."

Serious Bill became ecstatic over geology and geography; Mark loved shopping, supporting local economies, and making videos. I bordered on ecstatic about using my Polaroid camera and travel in general—when I wasn't on a camel.

Once out of "Tiger's Mouth," a Chinese passport control officer temporarily halted our progress. Alex collected our passports and, with Tamer, took them into the passport office. Several minutes later, they returned and announced that the officer wanted to see each person in addition to his or her passport. "It's different every time I come," Alex said. "Leave all your belongings on the bus and follow me."

On reaching Kashgar, we found the hotel conveniently located in center city, giving us an opportunity to walk the streets. Tamer told us that there was a mall close by that might interest us. Like any large modern city, Kashgar's storefronts displayed stylish clothes, pastries, and electronics. The mall, however, was totally unlike anything called a mall in the U.S. An unassuming entrance between two ordinary storefronts belied its true nature, but pungent smells of unfamiliar food cooking and a cacophony of strange noises offered hints. Inside, children raced through aisles, bicycles and whining motor scooters weaved in and out around pedestrians, and crowded open-air restaurants attacked the olfactory senses. Vendors heaved rotten produce into the street, butchers chopped at bloody carcasses, and knife-brandishing merchants hawked their sharp blades. The noise level and craziness ratcheted up progressively as we pushed farther into the mall. Having lived in New Orleans for several years, I compared the scene to Bourbon Street at midnight on Mardi Gras "and this wins, hands down."

A few steps from the mall's exit, civilization reigned again. Quiet returned, at least relative quiet, considering that we were on a major street of Kashgar. Here we saw our first example of "Chinglish" on a sign. Puzzled, we cocked our heads from one side to the other, seeing a man behind the wheel of a car with his mouth open and a "z" alongside his head, accompanied by the word "pleasedonotdrivetiredly." When we got the message, we laughed. "It does make sense, sort of," Mark said.

32

Happy birthday to you—happy birthday to you—happy birthday, dear whomever—happy birthday to you! The familiar tune dinged over and over throughout the night in Kashgar. Where was this bothersome music coming from? A nearby amusement park? Whose birthday was it anyway? Trying to figure it out, I was not only annoyed, but exhausted. My roommate Harriet, who could sleep through an explosion, hadn't heard a thing and was still sleeping when I left the room.

On the way to breakfast I thought back to Betsy, my roommate on the Nepal trip years before, and the camaraderie and adventures we shared. On this trip, however, the same connection with Harriet hadn't occurred. Harriet preferred spending time with others in the group. Having less in common didn't bother me in the least, since I had two great traveling companions already.

I walked into the large hotel dining room by myself, not seeing any fellow travelers. I strolled around the breakfast buffet viewing a myriad of Chinese dishes. Recognizing very little, I chose watermelon, a hardboiled egg, bread, and the standard green tea. I was usually adventurous in eating new foods, but not after a sleepless night. Bill came in and looked around, but told me, "Sorry, nothing looks good to me. I'm heading back to the room for a granola bar and hoping lunch will be better."

We soon assembled and went out with Tamer to explore a local market. "Excuse me, Tamer, but could you please tell me why 'Happy Birthday' is played all night long?" I asked. "It drove me nuts. Over and over all night."

He cocked his head attempting to figure out what I was talking about, then started laughing. "That is the street cleaner. It plays music as it cleans the streets."

With that mystery solved, we were to wander through the market and rejoin him in twenty minutes. Compared to yesterday's crazy mall, the market's streets were swept clean, but it was still early in the day. I walked down the market's main street lined by bicycles with large baskets and brightly colored motor scooters parked neatly side by side. Skinned animal carcasses hung from butcher shop hooks. A white-bearded artisan sitting behind a wheel sharpened a piece of metal, the beginning of a new knife. Around him metal boxes, rectangular trowels, cooking utensils, buckets, and mailboxes waited for life in a new home.

Everything was very orderly. Overhead, ornately painted second- and third-story balconies in a kaleidoscope of color and filigreed decorations sheltered those merchants in stalls underneath.

A young man making food steamers from long, thin wood strips caught my eye. He stood behind a small hand-made oven, pushing lengths of wood between brackets mounted on the oven's top. The fire inside caused the wood to bend into a circle, the first step in the process. The artisan didn't even watch what he was doing; it appeared to be second nature to him.

Bags of raw cotton and spices mounded in containers lined the street. Copper pots and utensils hung in neat rows. A wooden cart was heaped with tomatoes and greens, and a tricycle cart carried stacks of neatly folded rugs. From food stands covered with umbrellas, aromas of cooking mutton and onions, chicken, rice, bread, kebabs, and dumplings wafted through the marketplace as owners geared up for the lunchtime crowd.

I stood to one side, trying to look inconspicuous and observe the most interesting aspect of the market, the shoppers. Women in brocaded silk dresses and pantsuits with fashionable handbags, girls in denim skirts, women with head coverings and others with none, and women in high heels, sandals, and flats strolled the streets socializing and shopping. A pregnant woman with a ponytail stood by her scooter talking on a cell phone.

Muslim women, fully covered in black with only their fingers showing, shopped unaccompanied by an uncle or brother, unlike in Pakistan. Fascinated by their strict dress code, I couldn't even imagine what it would be like to conduct my daily public life fully covered. Photographing Muslim women proved elusive. They skillfully dodged my camera lens at the last moment, their timing impeccable.

We reconvened for our next stop, the Id Kah Mosque. Tamer told us that Kashgar's central mosque was built in 1442 and was the largest in China. The yellow-tiled mosque's capacity inside was a thousand worshipers with room for twenty thousand more on the adjoining grounds. Again he emphasized that boys under eighteen were not allowed to attend the mosque's madrassa. Tamer had asked us women to dress conservatively, meaning head covered and no shorts. My blonde bangs did escape my scarf, but I did the best I could. My face was visible, but the only other skin showing were my fingers and my glittery red-painted toes. The peacefulness I felt walking through the garden towards the mosque surprised me.

Inside we saw other tour groups dressed in shorts with bare arms and uncovered heads. "What gives here? I thought women had to be covered?" I asked Bill and Mark. Shrugging their shoulders, they gave me *that* look, the one that said, "Don't complain to us, see Tamer."

Alex was waiting for us back at the bus. He said that he had arrived late at the mosque and missed us, so he headed to the ticket office to ask if anyone knew our whereabouts. The man had told Alex that seven groups were touring, so Alex described Tamer, who had bought the tickets. The man had said, "Oh, yes, I remember him. In his group, all the ladies were dressed like Muslims. Very nice."

Lunch brought an unexpected experience, a wedding reception unlike any we had ever seen. Under a pavilion in the restaurant, men were dancing together on a raised, covered dance floor. The groom wore a navy blue suit, white shirt, red tie, and light blue sequined hat. A videographer filmed him dancing on this special day. The groom was enjoying the attention of all his friends who, casually dressed, surrounded him as sparkly confetti showered down on one and all.

When the music ended, the men drifted to tables to eat and toast the groom. Not one woman, not even the bride, was present. Women stayed home; they were not allowed at the celebration. A table full of the groom's friends noticed us and asked where we were from. When told, the men laughed and said that they had guessed correctly. "Are we so obvious?" I asked Harriet.

The next stop was the Aba Khoja Mausoleum built in the seventeenth century, considered the best of Islamic architecture. "The legendary missionary, Aba Khoja, and his descendants are buried there," Tamer explained, "and, supposedly, inside the mausoleum is the tomb of Xiangfei. She was captured by an emperor and taken back to Beijing to be his concubine. Xiangfei didn't want him. Eventually the emperor's mother either murdered or forced her to commit suicide, and she was returned to Aba Khoja for burial—or, so the story goes."

The entrance arch was covered in tiles of blue and white geometric design with an occasional tile missing. The mausoleum's exterior was also faced with tiles patterned in intricate designs and laid in stripes of emerald green, cobalt blue, rust, and golden brown colors. Tamer said that the exterior was beautiful, but many tiles were missing, and the Chinese government provided no funds for restoration, which depended on donations and entrance fees.

Bill and I looked around, and he concluded, "Judging from the scarcity of people on the grounds, the situation looks dire. They can't be collecting enough money at the front gate for upkeep."

Mark met us outside the entrance and said, "You won't believe what happened. While you were inside, five Chinese men came up to me and asked if I'd be in a photo with them. They wanted to shake hands with an American."

I said to Bill, "Clearly the committee of five recognized Mr. Wonderful American as soon as they saw Mark."

"No doubt about it," Bill agreed.

Alex offered the group two choices: head back to the hotel or have a Chinese massage. Only seven people, including Mark and me were game for the massage. Bill said, "See you back at the hotel."

At the massage place, we were all ushered into one room fully dressed and told to push our pants legs above our knees. I wished that I had known to shave my legs before coming. Oh well, too late. While our feet soaked in water, infused with Chinese herbs, male masseurs worked on the women's legs and females worked on the men. Their fingers dug deep to loosen knotted muscles and fists pummeled our backs, while the masseuses chatted and laughed with each other. The louder the yelp from a customer, the more they laughed. Mark told me it sounded like a conspiracy to provoke an outcry. "Wonder what they are saying about us? Do you think they know English?"

"They're probably talking about my hairy legs," I guessed.

Painful though it was at times, the massage lasted for one and one half hours and was a bargain at fourteen dollars, including tip. Mark and I both loved bargains.

The next morning, the agenda included the famous Sunday Kashgar Market. In operation for 2,500 years, the market drew an estimated 100,000 people weekly. Kashgar, once an important gathering post at the junction of the Silk

Road's northern and southern routes, had lost its importance but had regained it over recent years. The livestock portion of the market was the first stop of the day. A litany of cautionary advice spouted from Tamer and Alex before the bus emptied: "Don't approach any animals from the rear and get kicked. Watch where you step. Look out for vehicles. Return to the bus in an hour."

Bill, Mark, and I stepped into the melee of activity and sounds. The minute my feet touched the ground, I realized that I had messed up when I had slipped into my beloved flip-flops that morning. The worst possible footwear for the day provided absolutely no protection from the dust, tractor and truck wheels, animals, dung, and other people's feet. "This is truly stupid to be wearing flip-flops. I should have known better. What was I thinking?" I lamented.

Mark and Bill heartily agreed with me. I thought to myself, "Thanks a lot, guys. Whatever happened to sympathy?"

Nevertheless, the three of us thrust ourselves into the crowd of craziness. Tractors loaded with wooden pallets, a horse-drawn cart with two men holding a calf between them, double-decker trucks crammed with sheep, and a pickup carrying a bull with a makeshift blindfold clogged the dirt street. Bicycles with carts attached ferried produce to stalls; motor scooters, trucks, and carts drawn by donkeys dodged vehicles, pedestrians, tourists, and vendors. Bill, Mark, and I had to pay constant attention, not only to protect my feet, but also our entire bodies.

The day was going to be a scorcher, with temperatures already hot and not a cloud in the sky. Large umbrellas, some store-bought, others made with poles and sheets shaded vendors behind piles of onions, greens, carrots, potatoes, red and green peppers, and netted bags of tomatoes heaped on the ground, hoping an errant tire or hoof wouldn't squash them.

Eager to see the livestock, we followed the animal trucks. Owners were required to stop and pay taxes, considered "legalized robbery" by many, before entering the livestock market. An official in a blue uniform and brimmed hat stood with his hands behind his back, watching to ensure that no vendor slipped by without paying. The parade of people continued to stream in. A white horse, bedecked with fancy decorations, bells, and colorful tapestries, pulled a carriage holding his proud owner past the entrance.

Walking towards the corrals, we came upon two men discussing something over a fence, each surrounded by his circle of friends. The tall, younger man was bald and wore a white shirt unbuttoned almost to his waist. He was listening to the older man with a white beard who rested his elbows on the fence railing. The discussion quickly heated up. Suddenly the tall man screamed at the older man, lunged at him, and was restrained by men on his side of the fence. Another volley of angry words followed and another attack by the tall man; the older man's friends pulled him out of range. The tall man walked away, only to charge back screaming at the old man, and a series of shoves began.

It was a definite ebb and flow of raw emotions, which Mark and I documented with our cameras. Several European tourists came over to chide us for filming the episode, accusing us Americans of intruding on private business. As I said later, "Everyone was yelling, the Chinese at each other and the other tourists at us. It was hysteria."

When told about the incident, Tamer said that there was no problem with taking photos: "Photographing, especially with the video camera, probably caused the men to exaggerate their argument for a good show. Or perhaps one man sold his livestock at a cheaper price than the other man, stealing his customer."

Whatever had happened had made for an interesting day, and Mark, Bill, and I had once again timed it perfectly, being at the right place at the right time. Fortuitous timing seemed to follow us on our trips.

The Suitcase Wife

Sheep, of all colors, ranked as the largest commodity at the market. One seller tied all his black sheep together, followed by his twelve gray sheep tied together, then his beige sheep. The reason wasn't apparent to the casual onlookers when all the other sheep huddled together indiscriminately. Behind the sale area, men loaded the sheep on double-decker trucks. Two men hoisted a sheep up from the ground, while a man in the truck leaned over the side, grabbed it, and tossed it over into the truck "That guy's back must hurt by the end of the day," Bill observed.

Action never ended: a small boy pushed an errant cow away from his own cow's food trough; a donkey ate greens from its wooden cart tended by a young girl patiently waiting for him to finish. The side of the field opposite the animal area was lined with food stalls. "How appetizing is that? I remarked. "There's no way I could eat there without getting nauseous." Mark and Bill agreed.

The three friends looped around to the horse area, where, surprisingly, a lone woman was holding her own alongside many male horse traders negotiating sales. Suddenly, a cow pulled off the back of a truck startled a nearby horse led by a handler. As it bucked and spun around wildly, the man, yanking on the rein, tried to calm it. Tense moments ensued as he fought to control the frightened horse. Remembrance flooded back to me of being kicked by a horse while riding with Mark and Bill on the Mongolian Steppe—no broken bones, but I vowed to stay away from crazed horses. I backed away quickly despite my flip-flops. Mark and Bill backed up too, but Mark's camera was rolling.

Reconvening at the appointed time, the tour group hopped up on several two-wheeled carts pulled by donkeys, used for transportation between the livestock and main markets. Red blankets over the worn wood provided little comfort on the rough ride. The drivers switched their donkeys to move them down a four-lane highway congested with buses, motor scooters, vans, and cars. Whether planned or not, the drivers began to race each other. Finally, the police stopped the carts and asked everyone to jump off. Aching, we hobbled to the Main Market.

On the way, Mark, Bill, and I spied a pile of handmade brooms on the sidewalk. Mark asked, "Sahara, I think, as our suitcase wife, you need one to sweep the floor." I answered his smart remark in the negative. Bill, usually reserved, chimed in with, "Or, you could use it to fly home."

I thought of ignoring him, but laughed instead. "Actually, I could use it for my next quidditch match," I said.

After the last-minute instructions from Alex to be careful to count change and watch out for pickpockets, we were told to return in an hour. Mark, Bill, and I entered the market. To say it was large was an understatement. It was huge, acre upon acre, going on forever. Crowds shuffled through a massive permanent building shopping for shoes, clothing for all ages, cooking utensils, electronics, spices, and anything else they could possibly desire, a seemingly endless selection of products. Passing one booth, I saw bunches of dried reptiles and birds, their bodies spread open and attached to sticks. At the corner of the booth, gray snake skins dangled above a row of packets of pellets and spices. Jars filled with unidentifiable items lined shelves with small apothecary drawer cabinets beneath. I stared at the strange items, wondering whether they were medicines or potions but not ready to experiment.

Continuing to walk, we passed another medicinal remedy booth where a mounted head of a mountain sheep and a bull's head stood guard over large wide-mouth apothecary jars filled with coiled snakes, scorpions, dead lizards, frogs, lifeless worms, bits of bone, and broken shards of antlers. With Harry Potter still in mind, I informed Bill that the students at Hogwarts would have a field day here with all these ingredients for their potions. Always interested in how such items were used, I asked Mark if he saw any cookbooks for sale. Bill shot me a sideways glance, but no smile.

Leaving the orderly confines of the building, we stepped into a bizarre Never-Never-Land. Crowds of shoppers, shoulder to shoulder, slowly strolled through the outdoor market's narrow aisles of tarp- and umbrella-covered booths, looking for special deals. An enterprising vendor, instead of hawking his selection of clothing by voice, relied on an electronic megaphone set on a loop to repeat his message in a shrill voice. A short distance away, another vendor had a young woman with a megaphone at his side to offer specials on shirts. Shoppers congregated around his booth, adding to the difficulty of passage.

One booth sold nothing but flimsy plastic bags, hundreds upon hundreds in a rainbow of colors, packed in small, neatly stacked bundles. I stood amazed at the bright scene and wondered about the purpose of all those bags. We watched shoppers bargain for better prices. Little food restaurants strategically placed along the passageways waited for tired and hungry shoppers to rest and eat. Mark decided, "If someone can't find what he wants here in this market, he'll never find it. This market sells everything imaginable."

The deeper we wandered into the market, the more we were dazzled, until we reached its outer edges where vendors had thrown tarps on the ground, with little protection from the sun, to sell clothing and fabric. To me, it appeared that the quality of the clothing lessened as we neared the market's outer limits. Rather than being neatly stacked on shelves, crudely folded items lay scattered on the tarps. Business was still brisk, however.

With time running out, Mark, Bill, and I headed back through the crowded aisles toward the entrance and straight into the middle of an uncanny medicinal sideshow. "Oh, my God, look at this," Mark said with excitement in his voice and his camera filming.

Under a yellow, blue, white, and red paneled umbrella, a hawker had set up shop with items we'd already seen at other stalls. He was talking into a microphone covered in bubble-wrap plastic while a live snake and a lizard writhed in one of his hands. His audience appeared mesmerized.

At a healing booth a short distance away, the barker had a metal box with squirming, live scorpions two inches deep at his feet. He spoke into his microphone while a snake and four lizards crawled over his back, shoulders, and chest. The crowd was glued to the unbelievable sight. My fear of snakes rushed over me. I cringed as a lizard rested on the hawker's forearm while a snake slithered over his shoulder and down his chest to meet the lizard face to face. "Trouble ahead," I thought, but nothing happened.

If Mark, or I, or Bill had thought these two men had cornered the market on strange, it was only because we had not yet come to the next scene. In the back seat of a banged-up red automobile, a man, claiming to be a doctor with a reputation as a healer, offered his services. The car's windshield and back window were covered with boxes of dried scorpions, and two large lizards were resting on its roof, which made seeing inside the car difficult. A flurry of activity inside the car was causing it to shake. In full view of gawkers, a young woman emerged from the car with head bowed. A path opened, allowing her to depart. I angled for a better view. Litter trashed the car's interior, and the "doctor" sat slovenly on the ripped-up seat.

"What did he do, what treatment did he offer?" I wondered.

The good doctor adjusted his posture in the rear seat, waiting for the next client, poor soul. Even I, who had studied Reiki and occasionally practiced it, thought that this performance in the pandemonium of scorpions, lizards, and snakes was too weird to believe. I considered myself open-minded, but this was beyond understanding. Mark and Bill were aghast, but Mark finally broke the tension by asking me if I would like an appointment. "I can arrange one for you, and I'll even pay for it—for our suitcase wife, nothing but the best, you know."

We laughed, and we agreed that there would be no sessions with this "doctor" anytime soon. The healing extravaganza capped a hectic day at the famous Kashgar Market.

33

The huge statue of Chairman Mao with hand extended greeted hotel guests every morning from across the street as we opened the draperies. Today was my last morning wave to the chairman before our tour group left on its longest travel day to Kyrgyzstan. We had been promised a comfortable bus for the twelve-hour, hundred-twenty mile trip and were starting early to avoid a backlog of buses at checkpoints and border crossings. Mark, Bill, and I were curious to see if we would encounter as many passport-control stops leaving China as we did entering. Surely, it would be easier.

Once aboard the bus, all went well until an hour out of Kashgar when the smooth macadam road suddenly reverted to its former rutted, narrow, dirt self as we bumped along to the border. Tamer explained that politics were at the root of this problem: the Chinese government was upset with Kyrgyzstan's decision to allow the United States to build an air base in their country. As punishment, they refused to pay for any road construction, so the highway into Kyrgyzstan wasn't improved—and wouldn't be until the U.S. base was gone. Travelers had a long day of rough travel to the border.

Alex, as part of his effort to beat other tour buses and avoid long waits in line, had told us to pack all printed matter, including books and magazines, in backpacks instead of suitcases so luggage wouldn't have to be opened if the Chinese decided to check for dissident information. On the road early, our group arrived one hour before Customs and Passport Control even opened, but that wasn't enough. Two tour buses were already parked, suitcases unloaded, and passengers in line, waiting for the doors to open. We quickly joined the line and waited. Bill and Mark read books while I checked out other tourists.

When the doors opened, travelers with suitcases in tow began to be called to the first available desk by officials who thoroughly examined and stamped passports. Suddenly a uniformed young woman walked over to Mark, Bill, and me speaking in Chinese. The three of us looked blank, then signaled for Tamer. He came to the rescue, translating the official's concern that we were standing too close to each other and needed to spread out, keeping more space between. Mark and Bill determined that one floor tile qualified as appropriate space.

After completion of the visa and passport check, the group still couldn't leave. Luggage had to be scanned. Asked why, Tamer explained that the Chinese scan all suitcases to ensure that no Chinese dynasty artifacts are taken out of the country illegally. The process backed up queues of tourists, causing Alex more impatience even though he was familiar with the two-hour process. When suitcases and passengers finally were loaded and ready for the two-hour drive to the border, another official boarded the bus for one more passport check. The bus started, traveled a total of a hundred and twenty feet, and stopped again for—a passport check. I blurted, "What's going on here, why do we have to create jobs for a whole million of the Chinese people."

On the road at last, the great race was on. Of the three tour buses, which would be the first to reach the checkpoint at the border? The other two buses had had a healthy head start, and Alex and Tamer's bus had also made a short restroom stop. Before long, however, our bus sighted one of the others just a short distance ahead. Simultaneously, we lucked into a relatively smooth stretch of highway and sped up. After a short but thrilling neck and neck dash, our bus finally passed the other. The second bus's advantage was too great to overcome. It reached the checkpoint first, with Alex and Tamer's bus second.

Ironically, after all that expended energy, we all waited. Some official's lunch break had delayed him ten minutes. On arrival, he boarded our bus, made a cursory review of a few passports, asked Alex to identify the Canadians and the Argentinian, then nodded and left the bus. He waved Alex's bus around the first bus. That's how it worked: a certain number of yuans properly placed, tipped the process in our favor. Mark, Bill, and I agreed that whatever it took was fine with us, and Alex certainly knew when to spend his discretionary money. However, it did add a sleazy element to the race for the border, and I had loved all the intrigue and effort of the contest. All we questioned was why did the official only want the non-American foreigners identified? It was usually the other way around in China.

Our bus reached the Kyrgyzstan border first, winning no prize except a chance to get through the gate before other tourists. Mark, Bill, and I hastily grabbed our suitcases and dragged them to the gate—where another delicate situation unexpectedly developed.

Our new Kyrgyzstan guide Vladi, delighted to greet his Chinese friend Tamer, inadvertently put one of his feet through the gate, thus, into China—and he had no passport or visa! A Chinese soldier immediately rushed over to Vladi wanting to fine him, or maybe bribe him. The situation escalated with Vladi signaling an armed Kyrgyzstani soldier to join his confrontation with the Chinese soldier. More discussion followed, while Bill, Mark, and I stood with suitcases at our feet watching the incident play out. Apologies appeared to be made and accepted; perhaps a "fine" was paid. As soon as possible, we scrambled across the border and back into a bus before any more drama occurred.

Six-three, hazel-eyed Vladi sighed with relief about the border incident and smiled as he greeted the group. I immediately noticed his well-cared-for teeth. "Welcome to my country

Kyrgyzstan," he said. "That was some excitement back there, wasn't it? It all turned out well."

As we drove, Vladi mentioned that his profession as a tour guide for the past seven years kept him away from a wife and young daughter often, but he loved what he did. At some checkpoints, Alex only needed to show our collected passports while his passengers waited on the bus; others required us to leave the bus and personally present our passports. At one checkpoint, a soldier hopped on the bus and demanded that the passports be passed up to the front. At another, a soldier only asked how many people were aboard then signaled the bus to pass.

Approaching one Kyrgyzstani checkpoint, soldiers instructed the bus drivers to back their vehicles into a parking area off the main road. At the border gate leading toward China, a long line of trucks and buses waited for the signal to continue on their journey. Vladi's group sat for twenty-five minutes in the parking lot watching the line clear.

Mark, troubled by the checkpoint's operation, asked Vladi, "I can't believe their hours of operation. Could you explain this to me? Did I hear you right? If a truck arrives at the border on Saturday morning, it must wait until nine o'clock Monday morning when border control opens up again, and both Chinese and Kyrgyzstani officials only work weekdays until five o'clock and take weekends off."

Vladi replied, "Yes, that's right. I know it doesn't make sense, but that's the way it is."

Eventually a soldier with an automatic rifle slung over his shoulder boarded the bus, staring icily at us. He started to walk back through the bus, carefully reviewing each one's passport. When he reached Mark and me sitting across the aisle from each another, he motioned for my passport, which I gave silently. He told Vladi that he thought my passport had expired. I smiled at the soldier, but muttered under my breath. "Not another 'official' thinking it's expired. Can't they do math?"

The soldier reviewed Mark's passport while speaking to Vladi about both passports. Satisfied, he handed them back to Mark and me but moved no farther down the aisle. He frowned at each remaining passenger as he deliberately opened a passport and slowly examined it. Each time he reached for one of the twelve or so passports, his rifle's muzzle swung around to point directly at my face; its butt banged against the metal seat in front of Mark. I hoped my nervousness didn't show. Mark caught my eye. We both knew what was happening. My eyes widened staring down the dark barrel, and I could only hope the safety latch was on. Mark had the same worry. Neither of us moved or indicated a problem. When the soldier turned on his heels and left the bus, our sighs of relief were audible. "I don't think I could watch his stupid rifle bang around a moment longer," Mark said.

"I was looking straight down that barrel pointing between my eyes."

The bus moved on, but only a short distance down the road to another passport control office. I had had my fill. It had been a very long day, and I was ready for it to end.

34

After all the hassles of checkpoints, the bus headed towards Naryn, passing through the Torugart Pass and stopped at Chatry-Kol Lake. Vladi explained that the lake was free of ice during June, July, and August, but its water never warmed up. That day, however, it was a perfect spot for the picnic lunch prepared by him and the bus driver. A blanket thrown over the grass held a feast of bread, bologna, sliced ham, smoked cheese, chocolates, and cookies. The group was starving after the hard trip, and afterwards barely a scrap of food remained on the blanket. Vladi gave each traveler a Kyrgyz white felt hat and opened bottles of brandy and vodka for a toast. "Let's celebrate your arrival into my country," he said, "You've had a long day of terrible roads and official stops, but you are here now. I hope you enjoy Kyrgyzstan for the next few days."

A few miles down the road, Vladi signaled for the driver to stop and said, "We're going to visit the family living in the yurt over there. It's the summer home of young parents with a one-year old child. Last May they came from a village with their sheep into the mountains and plan to return at the end of September. You can see their sheep, high on the hill across the road. Shepherds on horseback tend the sheep while they graze all summer."

The friendly family invited the travelers inside. The yurt was a circular wood-latticed frame covered with thick felt and the woman had decorated its interior with colorful hand-stitched tapestries. When the family left in September, they would easily take the yurt apart before transporting it back to their village. Mark, Bill, and I had slept in yurts on past trips and found them rather comfortable and warm. I said to Bill, "I can't imagine spending winter in a yurt, can you? With a baby? In this climate? No thank you."

The smiling baby, round of face with full cheeks, sat on its mother's knee while the young woman answered the travelers' questions. I used my Polaroid to present a photograph to the family. The woman offered fermented mare's milk to her visitors, but Bill, Mark, and I, who had tasted it on our Mongolia trip, politely declined. Mark whispered to me that it ranked down there with Tibetan yak butter tea. I was becoming restless, but concealed my anxiety from the others. At the higher altitude, I had started to feel minimal effects of altitude sickness: headache, disorientation, and loss of coordination.

When we reached Naryn, our gracious hosts explained, through Vladi's translation, that there was no electricity in the town until tomorrow when it was to be restored. They assured their guests that plenty of candles were available, and dinner awaited us in the dining room. Four women in aprons served the food by candlelight. After dinner with no lights for reading or hot water for a shower, we had to turn in. I summed up the day, "Our twelve-hour drive today took thirteen hours and now this."

In the morning when the group left for the resort area of Issyk-Kul Lake and Cholpon-Ata, there was still no electricity in Naryn, which means "sunny" in Mongolian. I decided that it might be named sunny, but its nickname, the Siberia of Kyrgyzstan, was enough to make me leave. "Hey, Mark, remember our trip to Russia's Siberia and the Old Believer's Village."

"I sure do; the temperature was already freezing in August," Mark replied.

On top of Naryn's reputation for extreme cold and a short growing season, it had the distinction of being the poorest area in Kyrgyzstan. Vladi explained that the United States State Department was providing financial resources and business consultants to advise on establishing small businesses. Cynically I had to wonder if the United States support was tied to that air base deal.

Driving at over 10,000 feet through the Dolon Pass under sunny skies and warm weather was a dream compared to a few months later when winter rain and snow would rule. As we traveled, the roads, recently scraped by large commercial graders to smooth out the bumps, billowed up clouds of dust so fine it filtered into our tightly closed bus. We literally ate dust, drinking water to stop coughing. Mark wondered out loud, "How rough were the roads prior to the grader's work? We're *still* bouncing around."

After navigating through the roughest sections, the driver stopped at a scenic overlook to ventilate the bus. Vladi recommended that those who wanted some exercise could walk down the hill through the countryside to the road below where the bus would pick them up. The chance to exercise and get out of the dust-choked bus set Mark, Bill, and me on go. The last words we heard as we walked away were Alex's warning to be careful. Suddenly I stopped and looked down at my feet. Mark and Bill's eyes followed. We groaned together, "Not again."

I was wearing my black-sequined flip-flops, but I refused to give up and followed the men. Walking down the steep hill through grass, around large horse apples, away from barking dogs, and jumping over small streams, I endured all the comments from my two friends. I barely shrugged when Mark kidded, "Okay, Twinkle Toes, why didn't you wear your hiking boots today?"

"You can't keep up with us?" Bill chimed in, "You saw how fast the Sherpas in the Himalayas could walk wearing only flip-flops."

I called the guys a couple of jackrabbits and said, "I'm taking my time, just go; I'll catch up, no big deal. Meet you down at the road." I reached the road in time to board the bus, with feet not too filthy to be disgusting and a stomach ready for lunch. I couldn't resist telling the two waiting men, "You guys are real gentlemen."

At the lunch stop in Kochkor, a local women's collective impressed me. Normally we'd be told to eat first, then shop. This time, Alex instructed the group to shop first. "That's a different twist, isn't it? We don't hear that too often, right, Mark?" I added.

We entered a building filled with fur-collared coats, a damsel hat with white gauze hanging from its point, animal pelts, fur caps, cloth coats, and hand-sewn tapestries. Walking into an adjacent gift shop, a selection of handcrafted items lined the shelves: slippers, wall hangings, dolls, purses. Several tapestries featured an antique centerpiece, hand-stitched a hundred years ago and incorporated into the new tapestry quilt. Surrounding the centerpiece, blue designs indicated water, orange meant the sun and its rays, green designs signified the grass of Kyrgyzstan, and triangular pieces scattered throughout the quilt meant protection and supernatural powers.

The proprietor wore a tan babushka and a green crushed-velour top with a black vest. She demonstrated stitching to the group using a round hand-held stretcher. I admired her vest with hand-stitched decoration on the front panels. Once a quilter myself and appreciating the amount of work it took to sew by hand, I bought a medium-sized wall hanging for myself. Bill thoughtfully purchased one for his wife who also liked handcrafted items. Mark bought small purses for several relatives. Our fellow travelers bought items, too. I thought, "The seamstresses in this village co-op added to their bottom line today."

After my purchase was completed, I watched the older woman, record the sale in a ledger with columns denoting every item, its list price, its sales price, and the seamstress's name. The woman crossed out the asking price and wrote the actual sales price in both columns. I speculated that, perhaps this late in the season with fewer tourists, it was more important to make a sale in order to buy more fabric to sew during the winter months. I thought, "If the winters are as brutal as our guide has indicated, a seamstress would surely want a project to keep her busy inside."

Walking down a path to a yurt behind the handicraft shop, I passed a young man carrying a water bucket. Suddenly I realized that during the entire time spent in this village, I had not seen any men. I pulled Mark and Bill aside to pass along my observation and commented, "What a huge difference between the cultures in Kyrgyzstan and Pakistan. Where are all the men here?"

We had also noticed the importance of women in the economy, and Bill added, "Can you imagine what Pakistan could achieve if they only applied some of these same principles there?"

After lunch, we passed Orto-Tokoy Reservoir, and Vladi explained that area farmers depended on water from this huge manmade lake to sustain their crops during the summer. Its current low level was due to Kyrgyzstan's hot, dry summer.

As the bus drove along the shore of another body of water, Vladi continued, "This is Lake Issyk-Kul which means 'warm lake.' Because it's very deep with a high salt content and geothermal properties, it never freezes in the winter. The lake's fed by eighty rivers flowing into it, but not one flows out. During the era of Russian government, Lake Issyk-Kul was a military test site for torpedoes, but today it's protected by UNESCO. The lake is roughly 105 miles by 43 miles and 2,300 feet deep, the second largest alpine lake in the world. Only Lake Titicaca in South America is larger."

Bill was in heaven—more geology, and he loved hearing statistics. I, who had lived near a beach and realized the value of waterfront property, was interested to hear Vladi say that it had become a valuable commercial commodity. "Construction is regulated, but there are several new resorts on the shores, and Russian investors have built a new international airport north of the lake."

Mark, Bill, and I agreed that it would only be a matter of time before Lake Issyk-Kul's coast was lined with resorts, as older landowners sold their now-valuable property for large profits.

Aurora Hotel at the Cholpon-Ata resort area of the lake was our lodging for the next couple of nights. It bordered on seedy, not yet quite there but soon would be, if renovations weren't done shortly. I kindly called it "dated," adding, "Past Russian presidents might have stayed here, but it's resting on laurels from years gone by and locked in time. With popularity of the area increasing, newer resorts will attract tourists wanting to stay in more modern properties, and the Aurora will decline even faster."

Nevertheless the hotel's grounds full of roses, fountains, trees, and grass were meticulously maintained with an attractive strollway to the lake. Most of the group changed into swimsuits and crossed a reddish-brown pebbled beach for a dip in Lake Issyk-Kul. I tested the temperature with my toe and found the water surprisingly warm. Against a backdrop of snow-capped mountains across the lake, Harriet and I submerged up to our necks. Bill and Mark didn't want to get wet above their waists, and I taunted, "Now, who's chicken, afraid of a little water?"

I *accidentally* slapped a small splash of water toward Mark and Bill; then another, a larger one, got their attention. They started yelling threats at me, and in an instant, arms flailed everywhere. Massive walls of water were directed at everyone as a full-blown water battle developed with no dry survivors. Like children, we quickly tired of the wet war, especially upon sighting a ship turned restaurant farther down the beach. I called a truce. We toweled off, except for dripping hair, and sought the comfort of a beer in the beached ship's bar. "Life, to me," I told my traveling companions, "doesn't get much better than this."

The next day Vladi repeated the fact that Russia had used Lake Issyk-Kul as a test site for Russian navy torpedoes, adding that Moscow received the go-ahead signal if the test of a new torpedo was successful. He also said, "The only thing that remains of the test program is Pristan Prahevalsk, the torpedo research center. It still stands at the end of the lake, but we are not allowed to go there."

It seemed strange to me that a tour guide had dwelt on that information with a group who had shown more interest in the lake's geology, recreation, and development prospects and that he had mentioned a research center we couldn't even tour. I wondered if past resentments and sensitivities still prevailed here. I could see how natives might not like weapons tested in their most important lake, and I could understand why Russia would choose a landlocked, self-contained site for secret tests. "All the same," I thought, "it's an odd subject to bring up again."

The first stop on the day's itinerary was the memorial museum of Nicholas Przewalski, a famous Russian explorer of Central Asia and Asia between 1870 and 1885. Vladi's group was met at the museum door by our guide, a delightful elderly woman, slight in stature with snowy white hair. She was dressed in a blue plaid skirt, orange blouse, light gray tweed jacket with a black velvet collar, and striped socks with white sandals. I immediately thought that, though her demeanor was reserved, she probably knew her stuff. Did she ever. Wooden pointer in hand, she led us through all five of Przewalski's expeditions. As she finished her lengthy presentation, Mark leaned over and whispered to me, "That nearly took as long as his expeditions did."

I, finding it impossible to keep a straight face, cracked up laughing. Our fellow travelers stared at us. I whispered to him, "Who knew? I'd only thought that a small horse Przewalski discovered on some expedition was named after him."

Curiosity overwhelmed me as the group left the museum. I wanted to know about the guide, a woman who obviously loved her job and did it so well. I asked Vladi if he knew her story. He reported that she was eighty-three years old and had been a guide at the museum for twenty-one years; that is, after her first career teaching Russian literature for forty years.

The Suitcase Wife

I observed to Mark, "No wonder, she handled that wooden pointer so well."

Bill suggested, "Let's head down that walkway over there and check out that old Soviet torpedo area Vladi told us about. I'm sure we won't get anywhere close to it."

The group, at our own pace, strolled down paths bordered by yellow daisies and multicolored zinnias to the Przewalski Memorial, a massive stone with his likeness chiseled in relief and topped with an eagle and cross. Farther down the path, Vladi pointed out some rocks a few hundred feet away, "Those rocks indicate Lake Issyk-Kul's original depth, a hundred feet higher than today's level. Do you see those old buildings over there? That was the former torpedo research complex."

Back on the bus, we headed to the Chinese Mosque which the group was not allowed to enter. Vladi said: "It was designed in a pagoda style around 1910 by a Chinese architect, and twenty Chinese craftsmen who, using no nails, finished building it in three years. The five clocks high on the outside wall show the times the faithful are called to prayer each day: 5:45 am, 1:30 pm, 5:20 pm, 7:20 pm, and, 8:45 pm."

Vladi explained,

> For Muslims, it's important, a month after the end of Ramadan and its fasts, to make a pilgrimage to Mecca at least once in their lives. A few years ago, a group of Kyrgyz Muslims on Hadj, were stranded in Iran for a month because Turkmenistan would not let them pass through their country. Ever since, pilgrims must receive a visa from the Kyrgyzstan government, then travel to Mecca by air, no more overland travel. Now the cost for a one-week pilgrimage is two thousand dollars.

I thought to myself, "How stupid and controlling was that whole event involving innocent people, especially since they were Muslims traveling through Muslim countries."

After lunch we visited a second religious site, the Russian Orthodox Holy Trinity Church, built in 1895 and made entirely of wood. The windows, eaves, columns, doors, and walls had beautiful carving around them. Once a nightclub in the 1930s, it underwent major renovations, including five new onion-domes, and became a church again in the 1960s.

I had had enough of religious buildings. Bill and I jumped at the chance to join Alex for a walk back to the Aurora Hotel. The route, however, turned out to be indirect. When we noticed the new Karven Resort, Alex suggested that we check it out, tour its four-story hotel, and have a beer on the terrace. As a travel professional, he was interested in new properties. On a promontory above Lake Issyk-Kul, the resort's site was attractive. The tour involved climbing several flights of stairs, causing the three of us to look at each other and wonder if the hotel didn't have an elevator. The manager said it did not. Thanking him for the tour, we invited him to join us for the beer.

As soon as we sat down, Alex remarked, "All those steps for tour groups with heavy luggage must be a real problem for your staff."

The hotel manager mumbled a noncommittal, "Could be," and turned his attention to the menu, which, of course, he knew by heart.

From the terrace looking down towards the lake, new modern cottages with green tile roofs were visible scattered along the slope. To change the subject, Bill asked the manager, "Who's living in those cottages?"

"Those are expensive vacation cottages bought by Russians, Kazakhs, and one person from the Netherlands," he replied.

The Suitcase Wife

Later that evening, when Bill asked Vladi about the resort, he learned that the hotel had been financed by the Russian Mafia and a former Kyrgyzstan finance minister who had fled the country several years ago. Bill shrugged and said to me and Mark, "Borders might change, but that doesn't stop business as usual. Wouldn't it be interesting to return in a few years and see how the Lake Issyk-Kul area has changed?"

I objected, "You guys know we don't repeat trips. There's too much to see in the world."

35

Vladi set an early start time for our trip into Bishkek, the capital of Kyrgyzstan, with an overnight stay. Tomorrow was Mark's birthday *and* the start of Ramadan, a thirty-day period of fasting from dawn to sunset for Muslims. Bishkek, beware! Mark had no intention of fasting, especially on his birthday.

The bus stopped first at the Issyk-Kul Historical State Museum, just a short distance from our hotel to see petroglyphs, some dating from 1,500 BC. Vladi said, "You'll see scratched into stone boulders, centuries-old drawings of ibex, wolves, mountain goats, reindeer, men hunting with snow leopards, and a goat posing with a sun. Look for a boulder with large ibex hunted by small hunters which illustrates how important animals were during famines."

The still-drowsy travelers stumbled through an open field trying to find the faint etchings on boulders protected by UNESCO. We immediately noticed that there were no fences around the site. Anyone could park a vehicle alongside the field and walk in. Not only were they unprotected, but even Bill, the rockhound, soon lost interest in making out the weatherworn drawings. We agreed that it wouldn't be long before all the petroglyphs, threatened by vandals and weather, disappeared.

Back on the bus, conversation turned to ownership of valuable waterfront property around Lake Issyk-Kul. Vladi had already mentioned that people who had lakeside property were selling it to wealthy investors planning to build hotels for tourists. He confirmed that prices of land once devoted to farming were increasing because of the real estate boom:

"Wait, let me figure; a parcel of land measuring one fifth of an acre now costs between $10,000 and $25,000 U.S. dollars."

He said that new building codes for the lake were in place, and nothing could be built closer than two hundred feet from the water. "People planning guesthouses install two pipes: one to bring in water from hot-water springs and a second to bring cold water from Lake Issyk-Kul. No wastewater can be recycled back into the lake, however—six resorts were recently closed because they kept dumping wastewater back into Lake Issyk-Kul."

We were driving parallel to the Chuy River on the left, known for whitewater rafting. Bill, Mark, and I, wishing we had extra time to do some rafting, noticed the increase in traffic. Vladi pointed out the different colored license plates on the cars, "The yellow license plate means a joint-venture car, like Ford teaming up with a Kyrgyzstan company; red represents diplomatic or charitable organizations like United Nations or the Red Cross, and blue is our government."

"I just saw a license plate starting with KGB. What does that mean?" Bill asked Vladi.

"It's just another plate, no meaning."

Only sixty miles from Bishkek, our bus began to shake violently. The driver pulled over to check and found bad news—no more bus travel until repairs were made. Four bolts had broken off the rear right wheel leaving only six to hold the wheel in place. Mark remarked, "That doesn't surprise me. Rough roads take quite a toll on these vehicles."

When alternate transportation was soon arranged by Vladi, I said, "Thank goodness, there's cell phone service around here."

We waited an hour and a half for two vans to come to take us into Bishkek, and Vladi said that the tour would proceed on schedule. I commented that I was tired of sitting on buses and ready for some adventure.

The next stop, however, offered little adventure and another archeological site. The Burana Tower was a squat minaret in the middle of nowhere, or so we thought, until we saw the view from its top, a breathtaking vista of the entire valley. A short distance away, a cemetery full of grave markers similar to Easter Island's famous statues stood with their hands holding cups and delightful expressions on their faces. They lined the field like small soldiers, ranging from two feet to five feet tall, each one different. Vladi said that the totem-like markers were thought to look like the person buried there. We had lunch at a lake about an hour's drive from the city.

Once in Bishkek we headed towards our Ak Keme Hotel, an upscale property with a swimming pool. Owning a BMW convertible myself, I remarked that people here must also love German cars, judging from the number of BMWs and Mercedes on the streets. As the vans approached stoplights, white rectangular signs with CTON lettered in black were always visible. Alex asked, if anyone could guess its meaning. With no apparent linguists, Alex told us the letters meant STOP in Cyrillic.

Since Russians comprised half of Bishkek's population, dinner was at a Russian restaurant. Mark, Bill, and I sat down, remembering last night and thinking, "Not another Russian restaurant! How bad is the food going to be tonight?"

After tasting a beet salad, I decided it wasn't bad, much better than the night before. When the next course arrived, and the waiter poured everyone a small glass of vodka, Mark's interest perked up, "Anything to do with vodka can't be all that bad!"

A thick soup in a small pot covered by bread was set in front of everyone. Vladi explained, "The tradition for eating this course is to remove the bread, pour the vodka into the pot, and stir it into the beef, potatoes, and onions. After eating the meat and vegetables, tear the bread into pieces to sop up the remaining liquid."

The Suitcase Wife

Bill, Mark, and I couldn't believe how good it was and wondered if other courses could top it. They didn't, but after the so-so dessert blini, we celebrated Mark's birthday with a splendid chocolate-frosted cake, more vodka, and wine. Overall, this Russian restaurant was better than those we had experienced in Karakol.

Everyone sang "Happy Birthday" giving Mark an opportunity to tease Bill and me about our ability to carry a tune. I shot back, "Singing isn't our strong suit, Mark; it's having fun! Besides, we know you can't sing either."

Before leaving the restaurant, Alex relayed good news that the driver had fixed the wheel as soon as replacement bolts were delivered and has arrived in Bishkek. Everyone cheered to hear that he hadn't been stranded for the night.

Alex reminded the group to pack light for our next day's flight to Tashkent. He had arranged for our Tashkent hotel to pick up our large suitcases at the airport before we went on to Khiva. They would hold them until our return to Tashkent. "Remember that the airline is strict about weight limits. Any questions? If not, goodnight, and I'll see you tomorrow morning."

With time for sightseeing before our flight, the bus traveled down a wide avenue and stopped for the sight of Kyrgyzstan's "White House"—their seat of government, not the presidential residence, which was three miles away. The six-story building with a pool and fountains, surrounded by a black and gold fence, stood out against the cloudless blue sky. On the ceremonial avenue itself, however, there was no traffic. Mark asked why. With the words barely out of his mouth, a police car with siren blaring and lights flashing led a line of official-looking cars down the avenue. For some reason, Vladi's group had been allowed, or blundered, into the blockaded avenue. As soon as the government caravan reached its destination, traffic resumed. I noted, "That was a rare opportunity to take photos without cars blocking the view."

The next stop was a bit comical to me. "In 1991," Vladi explained, "the Lenin Square had its name changed to Ala-Too Square, and in 2003 Lenin's statue was removed to a small, unkempt park behind that building over there."

He pointed in the general direction and continued, "His statue was replaced by Erkindik or Freedom, symbolized by an angel resting on a globe with her out-stretched arm holding a representation of the sun, a symbol also on the Kyrgyz national flag. Supposedly the angel's face resembles the face of the president's wife, who hands out favors and positions for a price. Now the pigeons sit on her head instead of Lenin's," Vladi chuckled.

"Fame is so fleeting," I said, "and aren't local stories the best to listen to, even if the information may not be completely accurate?" I asked Mark and Bill, both skeptics, who often questioned the validity of guides' statements. I had chided them about letting facts stand in the way of a good story. On occasion, I had been known to twist the facts to make a better story. Life was more fun that way.

The Kyrgyzstan flag flew in the renamed square, continually guarded by two soldiers in green uniforms with gold-buckled white belts and white gloves. They stood at attention on either side of the flagpole with their rifles at rest. From the sidewalk we watched the Kyrgyz equivalent of changing the guard at the Tomb of the Unknown Soldier in Washington. From the left of the flagpole, three soldiers marched with rifles held upright in their left hands while their right arms lifted to shoulder height in unison with their goose-stepping legs. I thought, "That must have taken practice, practice, practice."

I had lived near Arlington Cemetery and often saw the changing of the guard ceremony. I was as impressed with the precision here as I had been at the Tomb of the Unknown Soldier.

As the bus headed to the airport, we worried about the weight of our luggage once again. Bill and I no longer bothered to answer Mark's usual question. "Do you think we'll ever learn to bring less or buy less on these trips?"

First in line, I heaved my suitcase up on the scale and smiled when the electronic scale showed a whisper under the twenty-kilogram limit. Mark, busy transferring items to Bill to get one of his overweight suitcases in line, called to me for help. My answer left no leeway for accommodating some of his extra weight: "Sorry, but mine only passed because I jettisoned some clothes and stuffed my carryon."

The guys would have to pay for the extra weight. Feeling bad about the surcharge, I said, "You know what, I'm going to give more clothes away when we get to Uzbekistan so I'll have more room for whatever we buy. I'll see you at the gate."

Two men stopped me as I headed toward passport control asking if I were traveling to Pakistan. I sized them up quickly: moustaches, nice suits, and both wearing wedding rings. Their fluent, slightly accented English was easy to understand. I decided to answer them.

The men had noticed the map of Pakistan on the back of my Silk Road T-shirt. I said, "Our Silk Road tour has already taken us through Pakistan from Islamabad along the KKH and into China. We really enjoyed traveling in Pakistan."

When they asked about the next destination, I told them that the group would fly to Uzbekistan, tour Khiva, and end in Samarkand. The men both wished me a safe journey; and I proceeded on to passport control. Mark and Bill wanted to know who those two guys were as soon as they met me in the passport line. I said that I only knew they were from Pakistan and had asked me about my T-shirt.

When we saw the men again in the gate area, I could tell they were curious about our relationship. Bill and Mark walked over and learned that both worked for the Pakistani Department of Agriculture and were returning from a conference in Kyrgyzstan.

I was still amazed at how easy it was to converse with strangers when traveling. Often the initial contact came through me with Bill and Mark joining in, sometimes, with topics I wasn't always interested in—many times, the guys just took over. "I like people and their stories," I thought. "Everyone has a story to tell, if given an opportunity."

The flight to Tashkent was uneventful, but after landing, we discovered the flight to Khiva had been pushed up three hours. Standing in a long line at passport control and customs, Alex realized we had only forty-five minutes to catch our next plane, and took charge: "I'm getting some porters to help with the luggage and see if there is any way we can get through this line quicker. All of us have to hurry, and we have to get on that plane. Here are your tickets."

Officials cooperated, and with porters carrying our luggage, we raced from the international to the domestic terminal and hurried through security. Four women had tickets that didn't match our passport names, but in the frenzy, the discrepancies weren't noticed. Out of breath, but arriving at the gate in time, we got the tickets to the right passengers just as our plane was boarding.

36

We landed at the Ugrench airport used by tourists going to Khiva, an important city on the old Silk Road. Driving there, we passed cotton field after cotton field on both sides of the road. Pickers, many of them women, were busy harvesting. Mark asked Yamin, our new Uzbek national guide, if he would tell us about Uzbekistan's economy, specifically cotton since we were passing so much.

Yamin, a husky six-footer with dark brown eyes and stylish hair was in his mid thirties. He stood in the front of the bus with a microphone and started, "When Uzbekistan was under Soviet government, cotton was produced by collectives. They reported five million tons of cotton grown and picked every year. Since Uzbekistan's freedom in 1991, our farms are privately owned. They grow, pick, and sell the cotton themselves. They discovered that the farmers couldn't produce five million tons, and that the Soviet government had inflated production figures. Three-and-a-half million tons is a more realistic number."

"Somehow, that doesn't surprise me," Mark whispered.

Yamin continued, "Uzbekistan's main customer in the past was the Soviet government which distributed cotton throughout the Soviet Union. Since 1991, we have struggled to find new customers and have reduced the acreage given to cotton production. The entire Uzbek cotton crop is picked three times. The first picking is done by hand and yields the best cotton, but it must be completed by the end of October, before the rains begin. The second picking, after the rains, is done by hand, but produces a lower quality. The third and last picking is done by machines and is the lowest grade."

The Suitcase Wife

By the time Yamin had touched on other subjects, sketched a brief history of the country, and answered questions from his new tour group, the bus had reached Khiva. Our hotel was conveniently located, directly facing the South Gate, also called the Stone Gate. It was one of four gates in the two-and-a-half kilometers of a high mud-brick wall built surrounding the ancient city, Ichon-Qala, now contained within Khiva. The Persians rebuilt the wall in the eighteenth century after most of the old structure was decayed or destroyed. Ichon-Qala is less than sixty-four acres in size and easily covered on foot.

As soon as Bill, Mark, and I checked in, we went to our rooms and threw our belongings on the beds. We wanted to explore the old city before sundown. Approaching the gate, we saw mounded graves lined up against the mud wall. Yamin had said on the bus that those graves had two purposes: poorer people who lived outside the wall wanted to be closer to the wealthier people living within the wall, and graves close to the wall made it harder for an enemy to attack, because of the general fear of stepping on graves.

"I guess we're the poor folks, since our hotel is outside the city wall," I joked, "but I feel so-o-o rich having friends like you guys."

The "guys" pretended to gag. "Let's stop at the gate for photos before we head into the old city, but we have to hurry so we can get inside in time to enjoy the sunset," Bill suggested.

Narrow streets twisted and turned through the old city. We made mental notes on how to retrace our steps. The streets were dusty but swept clean of any debris. We saw several women with handmade straw brooms sweeping in front of their houses, then flinging a cupped handful of water from a bucket over the dust to keep it down. "Good luck with that, a hopeless, never ending job," I commented.

Young children rode bicycles or played, while young men carved wood, and older men sat outside relaxing after the day's work. Doors standing open revealed women at work inside. We agreed that walking at dusk after the hordes of tourists had left felt somewhat unreal, as if we were intruding on the privacy of families at home. The normal sounds of activity were muted in the narrow streets. A hush had dropped over the area. The three visitors popped into a few open shops, but came away empty-handed. "That might be a first for you, Mark," I teased.

The sun dropped, and we headed back to our hotel. A bar with cold beer just outside the gate attracted us. Raising my beer bottle, I proposed a toast to another good trip and to the poor people who once lived here. Bill offered, "Here's to more fun times together."

The following morning, Alex introduced Nila, our knowl-edgeable local guide, who would lead the group for a half day. She was a middle-aged woman, wearing a beige blouse and long skirt, with a scarf draped around her neck. She meant business.

"We don't have much time, and we have much to see. Please keep up. Our tour begins at the West Gate, also known as Father Gate, where guests entered. The South Gate, facing your hotel, was used by caravans from the Caspian Sea; the North Gate was known as Bukhara Gate; the East Gate, known as the Strongman's Gate, was the one through which slaves were brought to be sold. At one time only wealthy people lived within the old city walls, and they built medressas for education."

Her rapid-fire information continued at the first stop, Mohammed Amin Khan Medressa, in the old city. It was built in the nineteenth century with seventy-five study rooms. Nila said the present day conversion to a hotel now offered some-what small accommodations. I wished with Mark and Bill that we could have stayed there, since three of us enjoyed unique surroundings.

As I looked around the lobby, a brochure caught my attention. "Hey, guys, did you notice the spelling of *madrassa* we saw in Pakistan and China is changed? Here, it's *medressa*."

Farther on, the group looked up fifty-three feet to the top of Kalta Minor, a chunky minaret completely covered in several shades of turquoise tiles. The ruling Khan had wanted to build it high enough so Bukhara, almost five hundred miles away across the desert, could be seen.

After he died, building was halted. Bill and Mark thought that the Khan's original plan was impossible, even if he had lived. I said, "You disagree with the Khan? Off with your heads!"

Nila said that the next stop was the Khan's harem and regaled us with a vivid description of life in the harem:

> The Khan built sequestered living quarters for each of the four wives he was entitled to have. All of the living quarters were tiled in different beautiful, blue and white geometric designs and had intricately painted ceilings. Naturally the Khan's quarters were grander than those of his wives—I'll give you time to look at them before we leave.
>
> The Khan's concubines lived across the courtyard from the wives, and they danced, sang, and whatever else they did in full view of the wives. Unlike the wives, however, the concubines didn't have a secure and stable life. If the Khan muttered *taloq* three times to a concubine, she had to leave the harem immediately, without retrieving any belongings or valuables, and return to life outside.
>
> Knowing that she could be dismissed at any moment, a concubine wore all of her jewelry day and night. She never even removed a piece she didn't like, in fear of the day she'd hear '*taloq, taloq, taloq.*'

I was fascinated by the story, although I had a bit of trouble believing it, until I remembered about "facts standing in the way . . ." Mark couldn't resist pronouncing those loaded words to me in a majestic voice. I quickly reminded him, "I'm not a concubine. I'm the suitcase wife, in case you've forgotten, and I'm exempt from such treatment."

As the group strolled toward the Juma Mosque, Nila pointed to bluish-green tiles randomly embedded in the walls we passed. She asked if anyone knew what they meant. Not waiting for an answer, she said that they were placed there to bring good luck. I laughed, telling Mark that maybe those concubines should have carried a few of those tiles with them.

Arriving at Juma, Nila lectured, "It was originally built in the tenth century, and a few of its unusual carved-wood columns still remain. Many wooden columns supporting the roof of this building date back to a restoration in the eighteenth century."

As the group was leaving, Mark spotted some women selling shawls. True to form, he said, "Let's stop and look, maybe we'll find something interesting to buy."

The women whipped out a series of scarves and shawls, hoping to catch our eyes. I pointed to a brownish-gold scarf with bright flecks of color at both ends, while Mark found a red one he liked for his wife Megan. A quick flurry of price negotiating followed. Walking out of the Juma Mosque with plastic bags in hand—not a familiar face was in sight. We had been certain the group wouldn't leave so soon. In the square with its several radiating alleyways, Mark, Bill, and I puzzled over which the group might have taken.

Several women were staring at our confusion. Finally Bill ventured to ask one of them if she had seen a group leaving the mosque—wrong woman, she didn't speak English. He tried again with "Nila?"

A stout, middle-aged woman nodded her head and motioned for us to follow her. She led us around corners and through tangled streets, and suddenly pointed to our group up ahead. Mark, Bill, and I were amazed and wondered how the woman had known where to take us. When we told Nila how we had found her, she said that this was the route that all the tour guides use; all the local people know it, and many of the women know her. The three of us decided that next time, we'd be more cautious—but knew that we probably wouldn't be.

At the East Gate, the area of Khiva's former slave market, a long, vaulted tunnel with cobblestone floors constructed in the nineteenth century provided cool respite from the hot sun. Nila pointed out that the niches in the tunnel once held slaves until they were sold in the nearby market. A constant source of interesting stories, she started another:

> A caravan headed to Khiva in 1871, found two young boys fishing by a stream, captured them, and took them into Khiva to sell as slaves. The Khan bought the two strong foreign boys and set them to work building medressas. Eventually, when a Russian caravan arrived in Khiva, one of the boys wrote a letter to the Tsar explaining their circumstance and smuggled it to someone in the caravan to deliver. Upon reading the boy's letter, the Tsar wrote the Khan asking him to release both boys.

> The Khan refused because he had paid a high price for the boys and would release them only if he were reimbursed. The Tsar, having no intention of paying the Khan, waited. The Khan, hearing no response from the Tsar, completely forgot about the incident.

> Sometime later, when the Khan left Khiva on a trip, Russian forces swooped in and took control of the town. They cleaned out the entire treasury and took over the Khan's throne. They gave the town twenty-four hours to find the Khan and bring him back to Khiva.

On returning, the Khan found the town closed and himself lacking permission to enter. He soon discovered that a document releasing the boys and requiring him to pay taxes to Russia was waiting for his signature. The Khan refused to sign it and continued his refusal until the Bolsheviks rose to power in the 1920s.

Mark and Bill did the math and figured that the boys were either old men by then or they had died. But we agreed with the group that Nila had been a terrific tour guide, adding color and liveliness to normal tour information.

37

After lunch our tour group boarded the bus for a long trip through the desert to Bukhara. Before we got out of town, the bus passed a barricaded street with a large group of men milling around. Thinking it must be a demonstration of some kind, Mark excitedly asked, "What's going on there?"

Yamin explained that men were waiting and hoping to be chosen to work in the cotton fields and earn money for the day.

"With Uzbekistan needing all their cotton to be picked before the end of October, all people—men, women, and children—have to work," Yamin concluded.

A short distance from town, the bus stopped at a cotton field where four women were picking fairly close to the road. The hot sun baked down and not a cloud was in the sky. I skidded down a small embankment and went into the field to meet the women. They wore muslin bags tied around their waists to put the cotton into as they picked. When full, the women would empty them into a large white sack strategically placed at the field's edge. I told Yamin I would like to photograph them with my Polaroid, and he translated for me.

The women were shy at first, but one of them giggled and agreed. I pulled the camera up to focus, but the woman abruptly waved me off with her dirty, dry, cracked hands. I watched as she left her assigned row and walked over to a shiny, black-handled kettle. She took off her printed cotton babushka, revealing thick dark hair pulled back into a ponytail. Bending over the kettle, she poured water on her babushka to wipe her face. Now I understood; she had to get ready.

The Suitcase Wife

No matter where we had gone in the world; women wanted to freshen up and look their best for a photo. Men only wanted their picture taken with their horse, camel, or vehicle and never cared what they looked like.

Back on the bus, Yamin said, "Those women earn only ten to fifteen dollars a day; the work is hard, but they need the money."

I was reminded of the summer when, as a college student seeking employment, I was offered a job in a twine factory. At times the temperature inside the factory reached a hundred and ten degrees while I stood in front of a winding machine, twisting twine into little balls for eight hours with a half-hour lunch and two breaks. Paid by the number of boxes I produced in a day, I had had to hustle and ignore my dry hands, often cut by the twine. Most of the older women I had worked with were single parents and breadwinners, who desperately needed the job to support their families. Right then I had sworn I'd finish my college education and not end up in a similar situation. Still thankful that the long-ago summer job was over, I could still empathize with the women in the hot cotton fields.

Yamin enlivened our trip with little-known camel facts like they were first domesticated in Russia twenty-five hundred years ago. Later, a Russian policy mandated all the camels in Uzbekistan be rounded up and shipped to Turkmenistan. That way "all camels could be in one location."

The logic behind this move baffled most of us, but Yamin kept the information coming: Camels can withstand temperatures up to one hundred and fifty-eight degrees. Camels now cost fifteen hundred dollars, but years ago, the price of five to ten slaves equaled that of one camel. The next time you are stranded in the desert, you can cut the neck of your camel, drink its blood for nourishment, and survive for another two days; the camel can replace the blood in only one week.

Mark and Bill, both turned to me to see if I were paying attention, so I would know what to do the next time I was in the desert with a camel. "You guys really think you're funny, don't you?" I said, feigning disgust.

Yamin had one last bit of camel information: Scorpions and snakes don't like the camel's hair; so people slept in the desert at night surrounded by a circle of camels for protection.

"Don't even try to think up a smart comment about that," I told Mark and Bill. "I hate snakes and scorpions and dislike prickly camel hair, so I guess you won't be seeing me spend a night in the desert anytime soon."

When we arrived in Bukhara, we went exploring. Three teenage girls speaking fluent English accosted us and walked alongside: "Hello, how are you? What's your name? Where do you live?"

The girls sold glazed clay cups and bowls lined up in neat rows near a mosque. They presented a "small gift" to each of us, asking that we come back tomorrow and buy from them. We declined the "small gift," to no avail. The insistent girls kept saying, "See you tomorrow", but we figured that somehow we'd have to give them the slip and avoid their relentless badgering.

The following morning began with a walking tour through the old city to Nadir Divanbegi Medressa. The school building was decorated in tiles featuring doves and had been turned into the equivalent of a one-level shopping mall. Shops were tucked into alcoves. Blankets and carpets thrown on the arcade floors doubled as shops. All were open for business and offering sparkly merchandise when our group arrived—except for three blanket-covered young men still asleep on carpets. I told Bill that I wasn't in a mood to shop and wanted to see the sights of Bukhara, knowing that he would probably agree.

We drifted toward *Lyabi-Hauz* where the group was to meet after shopping. The plaza surrounding a pool was built in 1620 with mulberry trees lining its perimeter. I felt serenity in the whole area, the calming effect of water combined with the trees' cool shade. Restaurants, where men were relaxing with friends, lined the pool, a center of hospitality. I thought that this was a true oasis within Bukhara's 'old city', a refreshing change from the dry, hot, and dusty days in Khiva.

Aziz, our city guide, arrived along with the rest of the group. He was in his late twenties, had orthodontically perfect white teeth—although I felt he was probably naturally blessed. Standing by the pool in his short sleeved blue and white plaid shirt, he entertained the group with a story: The Khan wanted the property of a wealthy woman where this pool is now, but she was unwilling to sell it to him. The Khan was unhappy not to get what he wanted, so he had an underground water channel diverted to her property and flooded her house. She had to move.

I whispered to Bill, "Whatever the Khan wants, the Khan gets: poor concubines, young boys, and wealthy women. Wonder what he would do today, if he could see his medressa filled with shops instead of students. No telling what might happen."

Next on the tour came a walk to a converted caravansary with two levels of shops. Caravansaries were the equivalent of roadside inns providing rest from a day's journey, and they were numerous along the original Silk Road thousands of years ago. Bill, Mark, and I had already seen the ruins of several caravansaries scattered along the Karakorum Highway in Pakistan and China.

Aziz explained that they were important commercial and communication centers along the route. If a traveler and his camels weren't inside the walled structure by eight o'clock in the evening, too bad; the doors were locked until morning. Inside, water and fodder were available for the animals, and shops offered a place for the merchants to buy and sell their wares.

At a shop offering handmade silk, a burly, slightly balding artisan astounded our group as he worked barefooted on an old loom to weave delicate silk, creating beautiful pieces of material. The man, translated by Aziz, proudly said that he had been to Santa Fe, New Mexico, several times to share his craft and sell his work. I purchased an intricately stitched silk jacket to help support his skill.

At the Maghoki-Attar Mosque, Central Asia's oldest one, Aziz said,

> This mosque is Bukhara's holiest site. Notice that the mosque stands twenty feet below the city's present-day level. For years, it was almost obscured by shifting sands, surviving destruction by Genghis Khan, who leveled almost everything else in his path.

As soon as the group stepped back outside, however, the hot sun brought us back to present reality. We sought a quick lunch in a cool place.

Resuming our tour at the Kalon Mosque and Minaret, Aziz said, "the minaret stands on a thirty-three-foot foundation built with reeds and straw, which had reduced the chance of earthquake damage and prevented any major damage for hundreds of years. The exterior bands of tiles are some of the first glazed blue tiles that one now see all over Central Asia. I'm sorry, but we're short on time so you can't climb its one hundred and five steps. The view of Bukhara at the top is great."

Kalon Mosque's interior beauty, with the grace and symmetry of its arches and pillars, was unequaled. Aziz showed Mark and me where to stand for the best photo. "There's where you get the proper angle. Hurry up before other tourists come."

Leaving the mosque, Mark warned me, "Wouldn't you know it? There are those three girls from last night, the ones we tried to ditch."

It was too late. The teenagers made a beeline for us. "Sahara, remember you promised to buy from me."

"I didn't promise you anything. As a matter-of-fact, you lied by saying you worked to save money for school."

Unconcerned, the teenager replied, "Well, that's my story."

When I'd asked Aziz about the girls, he told me that all they did was sell pottery to tourists, but that they were very smart and knew many languages.

I refused to buy into their lies. Mark, being a softy, felt sorry for them, "Okay I'll buy something from you."

After the small transaction was over, he turned to me, "You are such a meanie."

"I'm not mean, and I hope you never find out how mean I could be if provoked too much."

As we left the area, the girls were already pouncing on their next target. We rejoined our group at the Ark or Citadel, Bukhara's oldest structure, built in the fifth century. A few areas in the fortress, like its jail and torture chamber, its dungeons, and the bug pit, were now museums. "Imagine being down in the dark bug pit with rats, lice, and scorpions crawling all over you," Bill said to me.

"I can't, and I don't want to. It ranks up there with sleeping beside a smelly camel."

Aziz broke in with a story:

> That dungeon held two British officers. The first officer Stoddart was sent to tell the emir about Britain's invasion of Afghanistan in the 1830s, but ignored protocol. He arrived without a letter or gifts from Queen Victoria and was imprisoned. Conolly came to rescue him, and he was thrown into the same dungeon. They were marched to the plaza in front where the emir required them to dig their own graves and then beheaded them.

I kidded Mark and Bill, "Forget it, if you think I'll come to your rescue after that story. You guys better behave in Bukhara, because you're on your own."

The dungeon now served as a literal money pit. Tourists seemed eager to throw coins and bills down to a kneeling mannequin depicting captivity. Nonetheless, the sun was a welcome sight as we left.

"Another minute in Bukhara means another mosque," I told Mark as we walked to the bus. "I am *mosqued-out*, they're bleeding into each other. How do you feel?"

"The same. Isn't there something else to see, like whatever that vendor up the street is selling?" Mark answered.

Bill, who had not paused to shop, met us at the bus door, "Well, no more mosques. We're getting our wish and heading to two other places."

Fortunately, tour stops shortened considerably as day's end drew near.

Chasma-Ayub, meaning Spring of Job, was built over a spring in the twelfth century. And according to Aziz, "Job was said to have tapped his staff on the ground here, and a spring appeared. Many people still drink its fabled water."

We passed on the offer to drink from the spring, never to learn its true powers. Mark whispered to me as we left, "Maybe we missed a chance to drink from the fountain of youth, but more likely, we saved ourselves from a bout of Bukhara's revenge."

Exhausted, we followed Aziz through a labyrinth of narrow alleyways to an area off the beaten path to *Char Minar*, a structure with a tower on each corner. Aziz said, "A father wanting to find eligible mates for his four daughters, built this pleasing structure to attract potential husbands. This little building is now designated as a UNESCO World Heritage site."

Immediately impressed by the building and its story, I remarked to Bill, "What a cute little building, but I could have gone back to the hotel instead. It's been a long day."

The Suitcase Wife

After dinner, though dog-tired, we found an internet café to check our emails. Just as we were ready to leave, Mark nudged Bill and me, "Look who just came in the door, our teenage peddlers."

We couldn't believe it—would we never escape them? Apparently, the three girls were through working for the day and only nodded and passed by.

I believed that if a connection is made three times between people, a message was waiting to be heard. In this case, I thought it probably was that the girls should be more truthful. Then, suddenly the message became clear: the girl was right that it's her story, and I should just let it go.

38

Boarding the bus the next morning, I whispered to Mark and Bill, "Samarkand, I love to say that word: Samarkand, Samarkand, and I can't wait until we get there. It sounds so exotic and mystical. I hope I'm not disappointed."

Mark concurred, "We're looking forward to seeing it as much as you are. From Flecker's poem, *The Golden Journey to Samarkand* pretty much sums it up: 'For lust of knowing what should not be known/ We take the Golden Road to Samarkand.'"

Once again cotton fields flanked the road, some with pickers; others, empty. Our guide, Yamin, was asked how all the picking would get done before the rains came if some of the fields had no workers. He assured us that there would be enough pickers, and the first harvest would get done. Bill, Mark, and I looked skeptical, thinking there was no way all that cotton could be hand-picked in a month and a half.

As if on cue, a policeman directed our bus to the side of the road, and everyone watched in amazement as a convoy of about one hundred small buses passed by. All were packed with school-aged children, some standing, others waving their arms out the windows. Police cars with flashing lights escorted the buses as they raced toward the cotton fields. Large open lorries followed with the children's gear, food, and equipment.

Now it was clear how all the cotton would be picked by the end of October. Schoolchildren would soon be working in the rows of cotton.

Yamin said that each child's quota of cotton per day is thirty kilos, or sixty-six pounds, and each cotton boll weighs around three grams. Bill made a quick calculation that each child had to pick ten thousand cotton bolls a day to fill his quota. According to Yamin, the children leave school and their families for one and a half months. They work seven days a week for a half day, either morning or afternoon; and get three meals daily.

Reminiscing about his own childhood, he said, "When I was taken out of school to work the fields, the smart kids pushed to work in the early morning hours. That's when the cotton bolls are still wet from the dew, weigh more and require fewer to make quota. By afternoon, the bolls are dry and weigh less."

The children's ingenuity delighted me, "Yep, that's human nature to try to find an easier way to reach the objective."

Bill, Mark, and I all remembered before child-labor laws when American children left school to help with the family harvest. "With two pickings by hand and only one by machine, lots of manual labor is required," I thought looking over the cotton fields.

I said to Bill and Mark, "You know I lived in the deep South for years, and I've seen machines in Alabama clean the cotton fields in a few days. Maybe the Uzbek farmers can't afford those expensive machines."

Yamin added, "Pesticides, sprayed by planes, were once a concern. Neighboring property owners complained, and chemicals sickened workers and caused diseases. Aerial spraying is now prohibited."

Again, I harkened back to Alabama, "I remember when I first moved there, crop dusters diving down over the cotton fields were standard procedure."

When the bus reached Samarkand, a sign proclaimed the city's 2,750 years of existence. Yamin explained that Samarkand had celebrated its 2,500th anniversary several months ago, but a recent carbon-dating test had revealed that it was 250 years older than originally thought. He added that the city's name meant *fat* or *rich city*, "Samarkand is a city where merchants gather, and it's a rich city because many tourists visit and spend their money here."

Quickly dropping off our luggage at the hotel, the group met outside to explore the fabled city with Gav, who was to be our city guide. He was as tall as Mark with dark hair and eyes. He had majored in tourism in college and been a tour guide for ten years. I could always spot the tourism majors, who spouted dates, distances, and sizes as if they were reading out of a book, but I admitted that they had some great stories, too.

We followed Gav to the nearby Guri Amir Mausoleum built by the ruler Timur for his family and friends. The mausoleum shone in the afternoon sun. Its large fluted dome was intricately tiled in blue, turquoise, and gold geometric designs, and equally spectacular tiles capped the minarets. My mind drifted along the tile designs, returning abruptly when Gav began a story,

> The word 'minaret' means 'lighthouse.' At one time, fires burned atop all four minarets to signal the Silk Road caravans that Samarkand, their hub for commerce, was near. Men who climbed the steps inside the minarets to stoke the fires had an excellent vantage point to observe all the city's activities. To prevent spying, a change required the stokers be replaced by blind men.

Inside, the mausoleum's beauty was beyond description. Gold leaf glittered everywhere. Every tiny indentation in the papier-mâché dome and upper walls was covered in gold, according to Gav, but the lower walls of the mausoleum were made of stucco. I felt that the coldness of the marble floor and crypts were softened by the dome's warmth and huge glass chandelier.

"How could I ever describe this beauty to anyone?" I remarked to Harriet standing next to me. "Or the talent of the artisans who created it?"

The Suitcase Wife

Gav pointed to an alcove where a tree branch stood with a yak's tail hanging near the top. "The yak's tail is a sign of a buried saint," he said.

Back outside, Gav said that in 1999 Islamic militants staged uprisings in Fergana and Tashkent and were forcibly stopped by the Uzbek military. To prevent future disturbances and control Islamic radicalism, the government issued mandates forbidding mosques to broadcast calls to prayer and to teach young men in medressas. Worship, as well as religion instruction, must take place in the home. I recalled similar mandates in China.

Our next stop was Ulughbek Observatory, named for Timur's grandson who earned a great reputation as an accomplished astronomer in the 1420s. Ulughbek had determined that the earth wasn't flat, and that it revolved around the sun. He identified a thousand and eight stars and eight planets. His calculations for the calendar were off by only fifty-eight seconds.

Bill shook his head, "Imagine what might have been accomplished if there had been less warfare and destruction."

"I can't. I'm fried and ready to call it a day," I said.

Bill and Mark agreed. Alex and Gav reminded us that tomorrow's highlight was the magnificent Registan, and "the key to seeing it, is to get there early."

In fact, our group was among the first to arrive. The azure tile work and the vast courtyard were breathtaking. Gav said that some of the restoration work had been done by the Soviets in recognition of the site's unique beauty.

Standing in the middle of the courtyard, we were dwarfed by its three medressas, Gav began, "The oldest, Ulughbek Medressa, was built in three years and completed in 1420. Remember Ulughbek from yesterday? He invited area artisans to construct and decorate this building, asking that they cleverly insert stars into the mosaics."

I commented to Bill, "Well, that makes sense for a ruler who was an astronomer."

Gav turned and led us to the Sher Dor Medressa, finished by 1636. "*Dor* means lion," he said. He pointed to the mosaic above the door.

> It's full of worldly images. Notice the two tigers; they are supposed to be lions with mouths open, chasing a small deer. Do they seem out of place in the traditional geometric designs? At the time, Islamic religion didn't allow the depiction of animals or any representation of nature in art. These two medressas were guilty of refusing to obey.

He told us to step into the medressa "on your right foot, and when you exit you must step out backwards, as if bowing. The pointed arch over the entrance here symbolizes stepping through the door of the way to heaven."

Mark teased, "You better remember which foot to use. We want to go to heaven, don't we?"

I rolled my eyes at him, "I've got you covered, Mark. You need all the help you can get."

Stepping backwards out of the Sher Dor, we fell in step with Gav to go to the Tilla-Kari Medressa, the last one completed. He explained, "*Kari* means 'gold-covered' and when you see the interior you'll understand its name."

"Oh, my," was all I could say as I stepped inside.

Gold leaf dominated its interior. The walls, alcoves, and dome all sparkled. This medressa literally outshone the other two by far. A Japanese film crew was filming a documentary on the Tilla-Kari for a television show. Their light boom created an opportunity for Mark and Bill to get great interior photographs.

The Suitcase Wife

I just stood with my mouth agape, saying, "Gold leaf, gold leaf, and more gold leaf. This space is cavernous, and even though the ceiling soars up, all this gold actually adds warmth and helps bring it down to earth. I couldn't have believed it, if I hadn't seen it."

As Bill, Mark, and I walked outside and stood in the middle of the courtyard for one last look, we all agreed, "No wonder the Registan is considered one of the most beautiful attractions in Central Asia. How can we ever describe it to friends and family? It has to be seen."

Reluctantly the group left for the next destination, the tombs of *Shahr-i-Zindah*, meaning Tomb of the Living King. Gav told us that it was the burial site of a close friend of Mohammed, who had brought the Islamic religion to Central Asia.

Walking down narrow, stone corridors worn by centuries of use, we entered a room just as a mullah began chanting from the Koran. We looked at each other, but respectfully listened during the spontaneous reading—at least I hoped it was spontaneous and not a contrived tourist happening.

When he finished chanting, the mullah spoke briefly to the group. Gav translated, "The mullah asked Allah to provide protection for the tourists on their journey."

I was sure that I had seen Alex discretely hand him money, so I, too, gave him a bill as I thanked him for the blessing. Outside, someone asked Gav about the religious leader's training. Gav said, "After the mullah completed four years of study, he was sent to the College of Islam in Tashkent for six more years, then assigned to Samarkand."

We left the mausoleum and continued up an avenue of graves. Near the end a recently deceased young man had been buried in a modern section with his image chiseled on a large marker, also etched with a motorcycle and a racecar. Another marker with a simple white towel carved from stone draped over the top signified that the deceased had been to Mecca before she died.

It was hot, and everyone was more than ready to return to the bus.

"The next stop," said Gav, "is the enormous Bibi-Khanyn Mosque, Timur's last project before his premature death."

When Gav began his speech "According to folklore....my ears perked up. Gav continued,

> Timur's wife was originally married to one of his friends killed in war. Afterwards, Timur was given his friend's land and wife. While Timur was away, she wanted to have a mosque built, and its architect fell head over heels in love with her. He wanted a kiss, otherwise threatening not to finish the job. She let him kiss her but it left a blemish on her face. When Timur returned and saw the mark, he ordered the execution of the architect. However, the architect flew away from the top of the minaret.

Mark and I agreed that the mosque was in dire need of major renovations, but Bill was more direct, "Let's get out of here. It could collapse any second."

At the exit, a massive marble Koran lay open on a stand. A sign curiously written in English stated, "Crawl under this stand and you will have many children." Although somewhat past childbearing age, I didn't want to push my luck by crawling through on a lark.

I had had enough of mosques, mausoleums, and graves, and I was ready to interact with human beings—and not the ones in my group, including Bill and Mark. The three of us had been traveling together for nearly four weeks and needed some time to ourselves. We still enjoyed each other's company, but at this point, only a day or two before flying back to the United States, the scheduled aspect of trip itinerary had started to wear on us.

The Suitcase Wife

The Samarkand market, a short walk from the Bibi-Khanyn Mosque, attacked the senses as we approached the vegetable, fish, meat, lentil, and bread sellers. Although not as extensive or wild as the Kashgar Market, this one still bordered on crazy and colorful. Bill, Mark, and I immediately went in different directions. I called over my shoulder, "Meet you back here."

I got my wish to meet local people, some of whom turned out to be real characters. We communicated with smiles, pointing, pantomime, and laughs. Though I considered myself adventurous in meeting and interacting with people who didn't know English, I finally realized that local people were just as adventurous and good-spirited in trying to communicate with me. "A smile, along with a genuine appreciation for another, opens up a new experience for both," I concluded.

One area of the market had long, permanent concrete tables where merchants had meticulously arranged cones of apricots in orange plastic bowls. I devilishly wondered if I pulled out one of the apricots, might the whole cone come tumbling down, but I didn't act on my impulse. Orderly mounds of raisins, walnuts, pistachios, and dates filled baskets and bowls systematically arranged in rows on green cloths. Compared to the Kashgar in China, this one offered more organization and far less dust. Walking the aisles; I thought I might actually buy food here.

Other tables covered in pale yellow plastic offered piles of red peppers, pale green peppers, string beans, and other vegetables I didn't recognize. Herbs, candies, sweets, potatoes, eggs were displayed. Pumpkin seeds, hulled or whole, filled huge chest-high sacks. Garlic and onion tables screened from sight seven women, in bright floral-print dresses, sitting on the floor and sorting onions into sacks while catching up on the latest gossip.

A young woman, selling nine-inch round loaves of bread, urged me to buy. I shook my head, but mimed taking a photo.

The woman welcomed a break in her usual routine, especially after seeing herself in the digital camera. Other women wanted to join the fun, giggling while waiting a turn to pose. A woman in a blue print dress and purple head-scarf gestured that she'd like a photo with her friend over there. I nodded. The friend, wearing a white head-covering trimmed in beautiful lace, approached with a hesitant smile.

A woman in a black dress and yellow apron with her hair pulled back into a bun, pointed at me and then to herself, meaning that she wanted her photo taken with me. After I showed the woman's coworker which button to push, she snapped a picture of the woman and me, each holding a bread loaf, arms across each other's shoulders, smiling like old friends. The woman grabbed a pencil and wrote an address on a piece of paper, indicating that she wanted the photo sent to her. I promised to do so, but looking at the address, doubted that it would ever find its way to "Main Bazaar - Samarkand."

I grinned as I thought, "Collectively, these women have enough gold in their teeth to rival Tilla-Kari's gold leaf at the Registan, and their smiles are just as sparkling."

I bumped into Gav who wanted to be sure I was all right after leaving so abruptly. I asked him if this market attracted enough buyers to purchase all of the similar items being offered by different merchants. He explained, "One purpose of any market is to buy or sell, but it also offers a chance to socialize and exchange information."

I found Mark and Bill and boarded the bus back to the hotel to pack for Tashkent. Samarkand had lived up to every expectation for us and would remain special in our memory.

39

Early the following morning, we started to Tashkent, our final stop before flying home. While riding on the bus, one of the group asked Yamin to explain how courtship and marriage were conducted in Uzbekistan. According to Yamin, if I heard him correctly,

> Sweeping your gateway means that you are interested in making a match. A matchmaker helps about half the time, checking back seven generations for any problems and also visits the prospective mate's household, even looking under the carpets, to see if everything is clean. The matchmaker should include the aunt and the grandmother in the process. A recent change is that fathers now meet before the engagement.
>
> A wedding costs about five thousand dollars, and both families are expected to provide the new couple's household necessities for the first five years, until they can stand on their own.
>
> At the wedding when the vows are made, the Mullah asks the girl, whose face is covered, if she agrees three times, but she answers the first and second time only by nodding her head; the third time she says "yes." The boy is asked if he agrees, and he answers "yes." An exchange of rings follows, and the man and wife go to a restaurant in separate cars, but will leave the restaurant together in one car. Later, they are accompanied

to the wedding suite by relatives, who eventually leave. The bride and groom eat, drink, and talk all night long; no touching on the first night.

The next day a ceremony is held to show that the girl remains pure. Only on the second night can there be touching. If the man discovers that his wife isn't a virgin, he can immediately say, "You are divorced." If a boy and girl have sex before the wedding, they must tell the parents.

Most of the group laughed when Bill remarked, "The whole marital structure back in the States would collapse under those rules."

Yamin continued with other tidbits,

One in eight marriages ends in divorce, and it's okay for the man to cheat, but not the wife. If a husband finds that his wife has cheated, he could beat and kick her. After marriage, women in the cities can return to work, but rural wives must stay at home. The youngest age that a girl can marry is seventeen, eighteen for a boy.

I had enjoyed hearing Yamin's account but thought, "Even though I listened with interest, I can't truly imagine living in this culture, having been raised in one so entirely different."

When we checked into our hotel in Tashkent, Mark was jubilant, "Hurray, an internet connection."

I said, "I'll meet you downstairs shortly. I want to wash up before going to the ballet."

In thirty minutes, we conveniently walked across the street to the Alisher Navoi Opera and Ballet Theatre. The usher escorted us to good seats in the twelfth row with a commanding view of the stage and backdrop depicting a domed palace. We couldn't understand the ballet's storyline, since we couldn't read the program, but the dancing was good and the costumes were exotic and colorful.

Afterwards the whole group of travelers gathered in an elegant room of the building for our farewell dinner to cap our three-week Silk Road trip.

The next morning, with only half a day remaining for sightseeing, the three of us left the hotel, map in hand, to explore Tashkent on our own.

"Well, there's the Chorsu Market, supposed to be famous. Let's head in that direction and maybe we'll see other sights along the way," Mark suggested.

"Sounds like a plan," Bill and I seconded.

We all liked impromptu exploring.

"There's a grocery store, let's go in and see what they're selling." Mark said.

We bounded up the steps and into the store, pausing at a freezer chest. Suddenly, "Oh, my God!" came out of our mouths simultaneously.

"They have Magnum Bars," confirmed Mark. "This is our lucky day. We haven't seen Magnums since Dubai."

"Are we happy or what? There are only three kinds, but that should work for us." Bill gloated.

Bill, Mark, and I had developed a Magnum addiction eight years ago in Thailand. Bill recalled how we discovered them in a small freezer at "that funky-looking temple in the middle of nowhere."

Since then, the quest for the ice cream bars had had the three friends dodging in and out of grocery stores on trips to many parts of the world, sometimes succeeding in the most unusual places. I remembered when I was on a gullet anchored in a cove in Turkey. A motorboat had putt-putted up to the side of the boat with an ice chest full of Magnum bars. That one had cost me five dollars, but it was worth every penny.

The Suitcase Wife

The Magnum bars didn't last past the grocery store entrance. One could say that they were wolfed down, or more kindly, that the hot day in Tashkent would melt the bars too quickly for leisurely consumption. To the trio, finding and eating the glorious ice cream before noon was a sign of a good day.

After looking at a map we decided to ride the Metro to the Chorsu Market in Tashkent's "old town." The problem was that we didn't know where to catch the Metro from here. I asked three passersby if they spoke English before stopping a young woman who answered, "Yes, I do."

Elated, I said that we were looking for the Metro stop to get to the market. The woman gave directions, started to leave, then apparently changed her mind and personally escorted us to the closest Metro station, told us what line to use, and which direction to take. We thanked her profusely for her help, thinking how lucky we were to have found her.

As soon as we purchased subway tokens and boarded the train, we realized that we were the only Westerners in sight and objects of curiosity. Our every move and every English word spoken seemed to attract interest. Feeling increasingly uncomfortable, we studied a subway map on the wall of our car, hoping we were going in the right direction for the market stop. I glanced at the people who seemed most interested in our conversation and chose one young woman to ask, "Excuse me, do you speak English?"

She shrugged her shoulders. I took this as an indication she knew some English and proceeded with another question, "Is this the stop for the Chorsu Market?"

The woman nodded affirmatively and pointed to the map—so she did understand. At least, the three of us now knew we were headed in the right direction and knew the right stop. "We'll have to figure the rest out later," I said.

The young woman got out at the same station and motioned for us to follow her, never speaking a word. Of course we wondered what we were in for, but we followed. "No telling where is this little adventure is taking us."

It took us directly to the Chorsu Market, and four flights of concrete steps took us directly under a huge dome covering two floors of shops, the top one ringing the outside perimeter like a circular balcony open to the first floor. Walking around the market pavilion, our silent guide stopped for Mark, Bill, and me to sample an apricot from a merchant.

We finally learned that the young woman's name was Dasona and she planned to show us the entire market outside the dome, too. Dragging us up one narrow lane and down another, in and out of buildings, covering acres of territory we stopped only once for me to purchase a beautiful orange silk scarf. Mark attempted to converse with Dasona who clearly understood more English than she could speak. He did learn that she went to college, and she nodded her head when he asked, "Are you studying tourism? Business?"

Relentless at finding out more details, Mark asked, "Business Management?"

"Yes," she nodded again.

Finally, Mark said, "Let's stop for a soft drink and water."

Dasona had worn us out as an impromptu tour guide. Unbelievably, Mark, the indefatigable shopper, had bought nothing except cold drinks. When I pointed that out, he said that he couldn't add to his overweight suitcase. Bill mentioned that we had roamed through the entire market and had not seen another Westerner.

Dasona escorted us back to the subway, where Mark showed her a business card from our hotel and asked the name of our stop. She shook her head and motioned for us to follow. She came with us, getting on the subway and off at our stop. We began saying our goodbyes and thanking her for spending time with us, but Dasona was not satisfied until she had escorted us to the door of our hotel. There, we thanked her again and asked if we might give her a goodbye hug.

Watching her walk back towards the subway, I marveled at the girl's kindness in literally leading us around for the morning.

Mark concluded, "With the market spanning such a huge area, we would never have known where to go without her—our dependence even started on the subway."

Bill commented, "If you hadn't connected with Dasona on the subway, Sahara, we'd still be bumbling around trying to find the right stop, not to mention the market. For some reason this happens all the time with you. I wonder where she was going when she decided to change her plans—to college, home?"

We would never know; it was simply another unexpected encounter.

That night before leaving, I lay in my bed, reminiscing over the past four weeks and thinking about my life since meeting Mark and Bill on my very first venture in Nepal. It wasn't just that trip that changed me, but rather the accumulation of all my journeys over the years. I felt happy—and pleased with the direction my life had taken.

Traveling the world, meeting its inhabitants, experiencing their cultures and history had affected me more than all the seminars I had attended and spiritual paths I had explored. Keeping an open mind, following my instincts, and living life rather than listening to lecturers for guidance had caused my contentment to grow. I knew that there would still be times when I wouldn't make the best decision, but, I no longer fretted about that. I fell asleep, smiling at my good fortune.

Our flight left for Moscow early the following morning to connect with separate flights to the United States. In Moscow, I hugged both men. Bill said, "We still love these trips with our suitcase wife, so let's start planning the next one. Remember that next year is the tenth anniversary of our meeting in the Himalayas."

"We've been thinking that deserves special recognition, don't you?" added Mark. "Remember when we were first together in Nepal and the Himalayas, how excited we were about trekking near Mt. Everest base camp? How about if we actually trek to base camp next year to celebrate? Wouldn't that be special and something to look forward to?"

I nodded, "My only reservation is getting altitude sickness again, but I'm willing to try. Goodbye, guys, it was a blast. See you next year, wherever it might be. Keep in touch!"

I turned and walked toward my flight as tears welled up in my eyes. I would never let Mark or Bill see the tears, for fear I'd hear that familiar, "Oh, you're such a *girl!*"

It had been another memorable trip. Now, the suitcase wife, tucked away again in another state, knew that she would emerge the following year for their big anniversary trip.

5679917R00176

Made in the USA
San Bernardino, CA
17 November 2013